FAITH IN RE\
PHILOSOPHICAL E

GH00838384

Series Editors:
Laurence Paul Hemming and Susan Frank Parsons

Inspired by the challenge to consider anew the relation of faith and reason that has been posed by the papal encyclical letter of 1998, *Fides et ratio*, this series is dedicated to paying generous heed to the questions that lie within its scope. The series comprises monographs by a wide range of international and ecumenical authors, edited collections, and translations of significant texts, with appeal both to an academic community and broadly to all those on whom the apologetic task impinges. The studies it encompasses are informed by desire for the mutual engagement of the disciplines of theology and philosophy in the problematic areas of current debate at the highest and most serious level of scholarship. These may serve to illuminate the foundations of faith in the contemporary cultural context and will thus constitute an ecumenical renewal of the work of philosophical theology. The series is promoted by the work of the Society of St Catherine of Siena, in the spirit of its commitment to the renewal of the intellectual apostolate of the Catholic Church.

http://www.caterinati.org.uk

PUBLISHED

Restoring Faith in Reason
A new translation of the Encyclical Letter *Faith and Reason*
of Pope John Paul II together with a commentary and discussion
Laurence Paul Hemming and Susan Frank Parsons (editors)

Contemplating Aquinas
On the Varieties of Interpretation
Fergus Kerr OP (editor)

The Politics of Human Frailty
A Theological Defence of Political Liberalism
Christopher J. Insole

Postmodernity's Transcending
Devaluing God
Laurence Paul Hemming

Corpus Mysticum
The Eucharist and the Church in the Middle Ages
– Historical study
Henri Cardinal de Lubac SJ

FORTHCOMING

The Liturgical Subject
Subject, Subjectivity and the Human Person
in Contemporary Liturgical Discussion and Critique
James Leachman OSB (editor)

Redeeming Truth

Considering Faith in Reason

Edited by
Laurence Paul Hemming and
Susan Frank Parsons

scm press

Cover Illustration: *Discovery and Proof of the True Cross*, by
Piero della Francesca, forms part of the decoration of the choir of the
Basilica di San Francesco in Arezzo, Italy, begun in 1452, whose twelve
panels illustrate the various episodes in The Legend of the True Cross.

British Library Cataloguing in Publication data

A catalogue record for this book is available
from the British Library

978 0 334 04125 2

First published in 2007 by SCM Press
13–17 Long Lane,
London EC1A 9PN

www.scm-canterburypress.co.uk

SCM Press is a division of
SCM-Canterbury Press Ltd

Typeset by Regent Typesetting, London
Printed and bound in Great Britain by
Biddles Ltd, King's Lynn, Norfolk

Contents

Acknowledgements   vii

Contributors   ix

Editors' Preface   xi

1 Revelation as a Form of Knowledge: Notes concerning
   the Concept of Revelation in *Fides et ratio*   1
   Rino Fisichella

2 Faith, Reason and the Eucharist: Music as a Model for
   their Harmony   15
   Denys Turner

3 Redeeming Personal Truth   34
   Laurence Paul Hemming

4 Redeeming Truth: A Response to Laurence Paul Hemming   44
   Stephen Mulhall

5 Redeeming Truth, Restoring Faith in Reason: A Feminist
   Response to the Postmodern Condition of Nihilism   60
   Pamela Sue Anderson

6 Giving Way to Nihilism: A Response to
   Pamela Sue Anderson   85
   Susan Frank Parsons

7 Truth and Identity: The Thomistic Telescope   94
   John Milbank

8 Is There a Thomist Hermeneutic?   125
   Olivier-Thomas Venard OP

9 Phenomenology and Theology: The Contemporary
 Episode of a New Essay and of an 'Escape' from
 Metaphysics   154
   Vincent Holzer

10 The Ethics of Doing Theology: Towards the Recovery
 of a Withering Practice   167
   Bernd Wannenwetsch

11 On Valuing Truth in Practice: Rome's Postmodern
 Challenge   184
   Paul D. Murray

Acknowledgements

The papers with which this volume began to take shape arose from a one-day conference under the same title, co-sponsored by the Society of St Catherine of Siena and Heythrop College, University of London, in May 2003. The conference was constructed around three dialogues: on philosophy, with Fr James McEvoy and Denys Turner, chaired by Fr John McDade SJ; on truth, with Laurence Paul Hemming and Stephen Mulhall, chaired by Chris Insole, now of the University of Durham; on nihilism, with Pamela Sue Anderson and Susan Frank Parsons, chaired by Martin Stone of the Catholic University of Leuven; Martin Stone also gave a stirring, if brief, closing address. The editors are most grateful for the hospitality of the College on this occasion; to Fr Richard Price for celebrating the Mass with which the day began; to His Eminence the Cardinal Archbishop of Westminster for opening the conference, and to all the speakers and chairmen for their co-operation in making this a well-attended, lively and serious event.

Two of the papers in this volume originate from a conference with the title Truth, held in May 2003 at the Institut Catholique de Toulouse. We are grateful to the Editors of *Revue Thomiste* for permission to publish the two papers by John Milbank and Fr Olivier-Thomas Venard, which were originally published in the special issue entitled, *Veritas: Approches thomistes de la vérité*. John Milbank's paper 'Truth and Identity: The Thomistic Telescope' also appeared in the *American Catholic Philosophy Quarterly*, Volume 80, Number 2 (Spring 2006), pp. 193–226. The paper by Fr Venard has been translated from the French by Mr Henry Broadbent of Heythrop College, and Marie-Dominique Albiol-Ollivier, and appears here in an abridged form. In addition, they translated the conclusion of Fr Vincent Holzer's paper. We are most grateful for their assistance in this work.

Finally our thanks go: to all those who accepted the invitation to submit papers for this volume; to the external reader for valuable insights and advice; as always to the editors, Mary Matthews and Roger Ruston; and to our publishers, Barbara Laing at SCM-Canterbury Press and

Chuck van Hof at the University of Notre Dame Press, for their help in its production.

Contributors

His Excellency Monsignor Rino Fisichella is Rector of the Pontificia Università Lateranense in Rome. In addition to his book on Hans Urs von Balthasar (Città Nuova, 1981), he is the author of an *Introduction to Fundamental Theology* (Casale Monferrato, 1996) and co-editor of the *Dictionary of Fundamental Theology* (St Pauls, 1994).

Denys Turner is the Horace Tracy Pitkin Professor of Historical Theology in the Department of Religious Studies of Yale University. He is the author of *Faith, Reason and the Existence of God* (Cambridge University Press, 2004), *Faith Seeking* (SCM Press, 2002) and *The Darkness of God* (Cambridge University Press, 1995).

Laurence Paul Hemming is co-founder of the Society of St Catherine of Siena and the author of *Postmodernity's Transcending: Devaluing God* (SCM Press/University of Notre Dame Press, 2005), *Benedict XVI: Fellow Labourer for Truth* (Burns & Oates, 2005) and *Heidegger's Atheism: The Refusal of a Theological Voice* (University of Notre Dame Press, 2002).

Stephen Mulhall is Fellow and Tutor in Philosophy at New College, Oxford. He is the author of *Philosophical Myths of the Fall* (Princeton University Press, 2005), *On Film* (Routledge, 2002) and *Inheritance and Originality: Wittgenstein, Heidegger, Kierkegaard* (Clarendon Press, 2001).

Pamela Sue Anderson is Reader in Philosophy of Religion and Fellow of Regent's Park College, Oxford. She is the author of *A Feminist Philosophy of Religion: The Rationality and Myths of Religious Belief* (Blackwell, 1998) and co-editor of *Feminist Philosophy of Religion: Critical Readings* (Routledge, 2004).

Susan Frank Parsons is co-founder of the Society of St Catherine of Siena and President of the Society for the Study of Christian Ethics. She is the author of *The Ethics of Gender* (Blackwell, 2002), editor of *The Cambridge Companion to Feminist Theology* (Cambridge University Press, 2002) and editor of the journal, *Studies in Christian Ethics*.

John Milbank is Professor of Religion, Politics and Ethics in the Department of Theology and Religious Studies of the University of Nottingham. He is the author of *The Suspended Middle: Henri de Lubac and the Debate Concerning the Supernatural* (SCM Press, 2005), *Being Reconciled: Ontology and Pardon* (Routledge, 2003) and co-editor of *Theological Perspectives on God and Beauty* (Trinity, 2003).

Olivier-Thomas Venard OP belongs to the Studium de theologie des Frères precheurs de la Province de Toulouse, and is a member of the École Biblique et Archéologique française de Jérusalem. The first volume of his series, *Littérature et Théologie: une saison en enfer*, is entitled *Thomas d'Aquin, poète-theologién* (Ad solem, 2003), and the second is *Une interprétation théologique d'Une saison en enfer d'Arthur Rimbaud* (Ad solem, 2005).

Vincent Holzer is a Professor in the Faculté de Théologie et de Sciences Religieuses, Institute Catholique de Paris. He is the author of *Le Dieu Trinité dans l'histoire: Le Différend Théologique Balthasar-Rahner* (Cerf, 1995).

Bernd Wannenwetsch is University Lecturer in Ethics in the Faculty of Theology, University of Oxford, and Fellow of Harris Manchester College. He is the author of *Political Worship: Ethics for Christian Citizens* (Oxford University Press, 2004) and co-editor of the international book series, *Ethik in theologischen Diskurs* (LIT Verlag).

Paul D. Murray is Lecturer in Systematic Theology in the Department of Theology and Religion of the University of Durham. He is the author of *Reason, Truth and Theology in Pragmatist Perspective* (Peeters, 2004).

Editors' Preface

What does it mean to suggest that truth is redemptive? Does truth come from beyond us, or do we already know it – can we draw it out of ourselves, by clever means, by calculation and self-contemplation, as if it were a blueprint on which we are already stood and which sets out in advance what can and cannot be true (and this means 'be' at all)? If we want to understand truth, must we not be open to the way in which truth arises, and must we not ponder the truth of what we do not yet know, and what we are only coming to know, in the light of what we already know for certain? And if we want to say that truth is of God, and that all that is true is confirmed by its being in God, must we not know how the true God creates, sustains, and makes possible the true in itself? Who or what brings the truth to us?

Did not the sons and daughters of Israel await the truth by waiting for Moses by a burning mountain, these to whose eyes the glory of the Lord seemed liked a devouring fire on the mountain top?[1] Here truth appeared in the midst of the fearful, the dangerous, the sacred – a place of admonishment and prohibition: a place where it was not possible to go (because of sin) – the *Shekinah*, the holy of holies. When the worship of Israel took form in the Temple, the holiest place (the place of the Presence) was indicated as the innermost absence, as the forbidden, empty place at the heart of the very structure of the building. Here only the high priest could enter, on the day of atonement, once a year. This place of truth was a place denied to mortal men. Were the Israelites on the mountain not warned that even so much as to come into the bounds of the mountain would demand forfeiture of their (or their animals') lives? Neither should one who dared touch this place be touched thereafter. This trespasser must be executed by a means where there is no touch between culprit and one who executed the prohibitive command of God. Any living thing that trespassed on the mountain was to be killed by means of things thrown – stones and arrows.[2] To

---

1 Cf. Exodus 24.4.
2 Cf. Exodus 19.12, 16–24.

dare to touch the place wherein God appears, the place of truth, is to render oneself untouchable, to make oneself also deadly to the touch. Who can hear this now, or who would believe it?

And so the sons and daughters of Israel were told to wait. And in their waiting, did these living beings not turn to produce a dead *thing*, something fashioned and of their hands, rather than endure at the mountain-side for the return of the prophet of the One who drew them there? (And should we not recall that it was the prophet who was called to receive the truth of God, not the priest, who remained behind?) Was it, as has so often been claimed, that they forgot the reason they were next the mountain, adjacent to the presence of the God who called them forth for an encounter, and so turned to the making of idols? Yet who could have lived in forgetfulness in such a place, a furious theophany of God enfurnacing a mountain in its entirety, whose precincts were marked by the fear of death and whose character was the darkness of a permanently overhanging thunder-cloud? These men and women of Israel did not merely slip into forgetfulness: they sought out to forget through another, a god at their hands, a god whose truth they could decide for themselves. And as God wrote the tablets of the law with his own finger, so at the very same time, Aaron, the priest of the people, fashioned a calf, not with a metal-working tool but with what the Septuagint calls a *graphis*, or in Hebrew *heret*, a 'graving-tool' or stylus – not for gold, but for making a written plan for how the gold was to be laid out.[3] Aaron made a plan of the idol, which means decided in advance the form, for the calf to be wrought, the calf which would be the object for the forgetting of Israel and its evasion of God. The parallel acts of writing, the one of God's finger, the other of a scribe's tool, illustrate the way in which writing itself differentiates the two events. The first, of God's self-disclosure in writing not as God, but in the law of being towards him and for the sake of him; the second of describing and delimiting who the god(s) of the Israelites should be, in advance of its appearing.

It is not that Aaron *writes* that is at issue: rather, it is what is *given in the writing*, a plan of manufacture for the calf, that distinguishes this act of writing from that of God. The plan determines the future for what is written. In contrast, the giving of the law is not the giving of a plan or 'blueprint' for something – rather it puts those who receive it into question. They must inscribe their lives into what is written. The inscription is not sacred because it bears the commands of God, rather it is sacred because through this writing the distance between God and Israel is overcome: the law opens a path to the untrodden presence of

---

3 Exodus 32.4. γραφίς / חֶרֶט

God. It puts Israel at a sacred risk, that it must keep the command-
ments to know and love God: the risk here is in Israel's future, in its
resolve to keep the law.

Even before the law is given, and as it is written, Israel apostatized.
Faced with an intangible, occluded, God, a God whose very presence
occurs in separation and the preservation of distance – who appears as
darkness and through absence – Israel seeks to *make* a god for itself, a
thing of gold, a thing of permanent presence (is this not the role of gold,
even in the *Timaeus*, that it functions as the permanent, the incorrupt-
ible, the ever-present?). Gold is, in the *Timaeus*, analogous to what can
receive all things while remaining itself in underlying form unchanged.[4]
Just as the holy things of Israel, the altars of holocaust and incense, the
furnishings, and all the sacred objects of Israel's peregrinatory worship
were adorned, by divine command, with rings so that they could be
borne around and at the same time as they were moved, they were also
set aside as things untouched, not to be touched, and so sacred, so too
were the sacred vessels for the receipt of the law, the ears of the men
and women of Israel, pierced with rings. And these earrings were what
Aaron took for the producing of the divine calf, destroying the symmetry of ears to the vessels and furniture of worship and consecrating
sight over hearing for the presence and truth of the sacred.

Forgetting of this kind, the flight from terror, is not amnesia, but
has a practice, proposes a method. Forgetting is not in the passing of
time, though time's passing can afford the place for forgetting – but
actively to forget means *in the very face of what is to be forgotten and
forcibly erased* consuming the time that otherwise would lend itself to
memories. Consuming the time through distractions – cheating time by
wrapping up its longing and lengthening in folds that ruche and pleat
its extension into densities that can enter the hands. The distractions
of forgetting are manufactures, objects for focusing the mind, they dis-
tract from the truth of enduring what it is to be. Even an emptiness
can be made object for this kind of focus. This practice of forgetting,
because anodyne, because it subtracts pain from us, becomes too easily
a habit which becomes something we expect to be practised on us. We
rejoice to be distracted, and so make ourselves vulnerable to forgetfulness. Our implication in the processes around commodities and their
consumption are based on this forgetting. These wounds are rarely felt
in terror, but are hallmarked in the retreat of their effects with melancholy, anxiety, and disease. Forgetfulness, the flight from terror, is our
staying in the present and retaining it through the distraction of *things*
– commandeering the immediate and securing it awhile, against the past

---

4 Plato, *Timaeus*, 50 B–C. δέχεται ἀεὶ τὰ πάντα

which unsettles us, and the future which, unknown, we shrink from. To remain always in the present as time passes, to mask the passing of time in the present, is to remain always with the familiar, or to recycle a present marked only by euphoria into constant presents – staving off the future with the enduring presence alone of what we already know. Cheating time cheats nothing, because time is nothing that can be cheated – or rather, it is our own self-deceiving, our flight from the dread and splendour of the true.

Israel's resistance to God is to become engrossed with a thing of its making. From the outset, for Israel, the question of God is posed not in the question of who God is – the endlessly troubling word of God to Moses[5] – but in the flight from God into things, and so installing divinity in objects (before the calf, Aaron does not say 'this is your god, O Israel', but '*these* are your gods'), so transporting their meaning into exchangeable values, and reducing God to thinghood.[6] This concern with things contains within it a danger. If to be concerned with things is to be distracted, to be drawn in a direction away from God, or from the question, then *that* question which lies at the basis of all Western thought – τί τὸ ὄν; – 'what is the thing?', may itself prove to be a formula, not for an enquiry into being and truth, but the very mark of its distraction. The desire to discover God as the basis of all things drives us into the embrace of things themselves, so that we attempt to make the question, 'what is a thing' a question about God and God's having caused that thing. Yet the question concerning the meaning of God, our presence before him and in relation to him, does not arise on the basis of things that stand before us: we learn that God caused the thing only after the fact, only in the light of faith. Indeed it should hardly surprise us that when things in their thinghood have overtaken us, and when their presence seems easy to construe by the very brute fact of their being here before us – at this precise moment the absence of God and the questions that absence poses have befallen us. How when we are overcome by things in the absence of God can we go on claiming to be working out who God is from out of what things are?[7]

Upon Moses' return from the mountain with the tables of the law he finds Israel dancing before the calf. The dancing signifies the movement of the cosmos before the unmovable figure of the golden calf – the ecstasy of those not put into awe – and the very claim of every idolatry, that the realm of human being is a 'moving image of eternity'. And Moses breaks the tables of the law at the foot of the mountain. The law

---

5 Cf. Exodus 3.14. 'God said to Moses, "I am who I am." And he said, "Say this to the people of Israel: I am has sent me to you."'

6 Exodus 32.4.

7 Cf. as Aquinas implies in *De Veritate*, Q. 1, art. 2, resp. *et passim*.

here stands in judgement on Israel, and enacts truth as a judgement of God, and for the punishment of men. It is to free men from this punishment – that the truth of man is death, unable to impart motion to idols – that Christ is given by the Father to die and rise again. Moses returns to Israel a second time with the tablets of the law, and this time with his face shining in consequence of his encounter with God.

The punishing proclamation that no one shall see the face of God and live is not an utterance based on God's desire not to be seen.[8] This utterance is not the Jewish counterpart to the Greek myth of Semele, lover of Zeus, and mother to Dionysus, to whom (in one version of the myth) Zeus makes a vow that she can have anything she desires. Semele, tricked by Zeus's consort Hera, demands to see the god in all his glory. No mortal can gaze upon the glory of Zeus, or any god, but Semele will not relent, and Zeus in fulfilment of his vow unmasks himself, consuming Semele to death in the ensuing intensity of the fire-filled vision she is granted.

But this is not the threat to those addressed by the God of Israel: rather is it that so alive is God, and so much life, that none can capture an image of God, for to do so would itself be death – all images, being stable and without motion, are dead. Eternity, if that is also God's name, is not without motion and not at rest. So vital is God that death is the fate of those who have reduced him to a stable image, a matter of something to be known, and thus an *object* of knowledge. Death is their fate because to desire such a thing is already to be dead to God. St Gregory of Nyssa dwells on this utterance of God and comments 'how would the face of life ever be the cause of death?' And concludes 'he who thinks God is something to be known does not have life' and so is already one dead before God.[9] God is by nature 'life-producing' (ζωοποιὸς).

This vitality of God is at the same time the vitality of truth – only this can make sense of the Cappadocian's assertion in his *Life of Moses* that 'truth is what ensures understanding concerning being'.[10] It is customary to read Gregory of Nyssa's *Life of Moses* as an example of Christian Neoplatonism, therefore in accordance with the view that all actual beings are illusory falsifications of being itself; being, which is at the same time divine and 'over there' (ἐπίκεινα).

---

8 Cf. Exodus 33.20.

9 St Gregory of Nyssa, *De vita Moysis*, in Migne, *Patrologia Graeca*, Vol. 64, 404 A–B. πῶς γὰρ τὸ τῆς ζωῆς πρόσωπον, αἴτιον θανάτου τοῖς ἐμπελάσασι γένοιτ' ἄν ποτε; . . . ὁ τῶν γινωσκομένων τι τὸν θεὸν εἶναι οἰόμενος . . . ζωὴν οὐκ ἔχει.

10 St Gregory of Nyssa, *De vita Moysis*, 333 A. ἀλήθεια δὲ, ἡ τοῦ ὄντοσ ἀσφαλὴς κατανόησις.

This would be to misunderstand entirely the essentially Christological meaning that St Gregory finds in the Exodus account, and to misunderstand from the outset how the Fathers as exegetes of Scripture, and particularly the Old Testament, understood themselves to be revealing the true, Christological meaning of the sacred texts. It would be to reverse the transport of light from God to Moses, both at Sinai and in the event of the transfiguration described in the Gospels, when Jesus encounters Moses and Elijah on the mountain. Here Jesus' face 'shone like the sun',[11] but Jesus is the Christ, the divine Son, whose shining face conferred light upon Moses both here *and* on Sinai (as indeed before the burning bush, itself a prefiguration of the Virgin Mother of God).[12] Inasmuch as God is the divine ever-living, vital fount of truth, his truth can only be revealed in the vitality of the living person of the Son, at first in the signs and portents of his life, and then above all in that moment when death is revealed to be dead, in the resurrection of the Christ, the ever-living Son of the eternal Father. At the heart of this is the truth of the cross, which means the true cross is the crux of Truth. When we discover the meaning of the cross, that the accursed tree unbinds the curse of death, then we discover that Truth himself is ever-living, ever-vital, ever-rising, that he transcends and exceeds every claim of philosophy, everything we already know, for the sake of his ever-ascending in the mystery that is God, which we follow.

For this is how St Gregory describes the encounter of Moses with Divine Truth. On Sinai Moses sees only God's back through the cleft in the rock. The mind, beginning in light, enters into the darkness of God. Here again is the *reversal* of Plato, of the allegory of the cave and the ascent into the light from the realm of shadows. In receiving the meaning of truth from God – as the mind progresses and receives the ever-moving, ever-deepening truth that God *is* and who the living God is – the mind leaves behind what it already knows for what God has yet to give it. The spoliation of Egypt which Moses commands to the departing Israelites is precisely this – the wealth of learning, likened to a gold offering to the Church from those entering into faith[13] – is only a beginning, which culminates in a mystical descent into divine Truth which is a kind of seeing of God, a seeing by not seeing: a proceeding into darkness, not up into dazzling light.[14] It is this that the Cappadocian intends, when he suggests that Moses is summoned out of the cleft and sees only the 'back' of the one summoning him, a back

---

11 Matthew 17.1.

12 Cf. Exodus 3.1–4; St Gregory of Nyssa, *De vita Moysis*, 332 D.

13 St Gregory of Nyssa, *De vita Moysis*, 359 C. Πολλοὶ τὴν ἔξω παίδευσιν τῇ θεοῦ Ἐκκλεσία καθάπερ τι δῶρον προσάγουσιν.

14 St Gregory of Nyssa, *De vita Moysis*, 377 A. τὸ ἰδεῖν, εν τῷ μὴ ἰδεῖν.

that is ever-receding and moving away while at the same time drawing Moses onward and into where it leads. What is offered to all of us who seek the truth and so seek to follow Truth, is that following the divine summons becomes an eternal following (and so is beyond death), by means of the cross, into ever-deepening truth.

The cover of this book depicts St Helena's discovery of the cross of Christ in Jerusalem. St Helena, mother to Constantine, discovered not one, but three crosses in the place where it was promised the true cross had been hidden. But how was she to know which was the cross of Christ? The legend of the discovery – or invention – of the true cross tells that a dying woman was summoned to the site and each of the crosses was placed before her for her to touch. Only one – the true cross – revived her from sickness and gave her life. The true cross is the cross that gives life, for life and truth are one.

Our Lady of Sorrows in Passiontide, 2007

Editors' note: Use of the word 'man' and of masculine pronouns is understood to be inclusive wherever it appears in these chapters.

1. Revelation as a Form of Knowledge: Notes Concerning the Concept of Revelation in *Fides et ratio*

RINO FISICHELLA

Revelation has set within history a point of reference which cannot be ignored if the mystery of human life is to be known. Yet this knowledge refers back constantly to the mystery of God which the human mind cannot exhaust but can only receive and embrace in faith. Between these two poles, reason has its own specific field in which it can enquire and understand, restricted only by its finiteness before the infinite mystery of God (*Fides et ratio*, §14)

Background

This text can provide a meaningful background to an analysis of the thirteenth encyclical of John Paul II concerning the relationship between faith and reason. The context shows that the quotation comes before an initial conclusion regarding a synthesis of the teaching about revelation offered by Vatican Councils I and II. An attentive reading of this passage allows one to understand some fundamental considerations expressed by the encyclical which deal not only with the reception of the novelty springing from Vatican II in terms of the theme of revelation, but also with the implications of this concept for the relationship between faith and reason.

First, let us examine the reference to 'history'. This dimension is not merely secondary but implies a series of specifications regarding the very concept of truth which qualify the Judeo-Christian perspective in relation to a philosophical-Greek one.[1] With this mention of history, a

---

1 In terms of this perspective, cf. J. Ladrière, 'Historicité et vérité: Approche philosophique', *Le Supplément* 118–19 (1994), pp. 11–41; R. Fisichella, *Introduzione alla Teologia fondamentale* (Casale Monferrato: Piemme, 1985), pp. 97–9. [ET: *Introduction to Fundamental Theology* (Casale Monferrato: Piemme, 1996).]

'reference point' is revealed in history itself which cannot be ignored in trying to discover the answer to the question concerning the meaning of existence. With a simple term, *Fides et ratio* brings to mind fundamentally important theological content; initially, that of the central role that Christ occupies in the history of salvation. He is truly at the centre of history, just as the narration about the disciples of Emmaus bears out. All that had occurred prior to him was in reference to him: 'Then beginning with Moses and all the prophets, he interpreted to them what referred to him in all the scriptures' (Luke 24.27). All that happens next is accompanied by his sacramental presence which allows his disciples to feel a longing for him, while they recognized him always present in their midst during 'the breaking of bread' (Luke 24.35).

In this introductory text, we should not undervalue the reference to the dimension of 'mystery'. This qualifies both the horizon in which we should place the novelty of revelation which opens up to the knowledge of divine life, as well as the existential horizon of every person in which the perennial questions that characterize personal existence arise. The highlighting of the reality of 'mystery' returns often throughout the encyclical, which allows one to understand the cognitive value it possesses, and at the same time, opens up the possibility of a reinterpretation of the revelatory function.

An examination of the biblical meaning shows how the concept of 'mystery' is united to the theme of the salvific plan of God, which is developed progressively throughout history. Above all, it is the Apostle Paul who expresses this dimension in his epistles: the mystery is bound to God's revelation and makes it known. At the beginning, this process is explained, in the First Letter to the Corinthians, as the generic presence of a 'Divine, mysterious wisdom, hidden, which God predetermined before the ages for our glory' (1 Cor. 2.6–9). Therefore, we see a project born from the very Trinitarian life of love and originally expressed in the order of creation. In the Letter to the Romans, the Apostle takes a further step and better focuses the issue, perceiving in the ancient Scriptures a progressive manifestation of the mystery: 'The revelation of the mystery kept secret for long ages, but now manifested through the prophetic writings' (Rom. 16.25–26). And yet, those prophetic words look ahead towards the fulfilment of a promise that will come about in the human form of the Son of God. The Letter to the Colossians states: 'The mystery hidden from ages and from generations past. But now it has been manifested to his holy ones; it is Christ in you, the hope for glory' (Col. 1.26–27). The intimate presence of the mystery of Christ in people's lives, however, must progress towards the full manifestation of the mystery. This is what emerges from the Letter to the Ephesians which places the full knowledge of the mystery in the eschatological fulfilment: 'He has made known to us the mystery of his will in accord with his favour that he set forth in him as a plan for the fullness of times, to sum up all things in Christ, in heaven and on earth' (Eph. 1.8–10).

As can be seen by these brief observations, the *mystérion* is presented as the sacramental moment of the salvific work of the Father in history throughout time, until its complete fulfilment in the eschatological event. Each believer, indeed, every human being, is placed before the progressive disclosure of a mystery which arises in the knowledge of the plan of salvation. It is always a 'mystery which becomes manifest'; it does not remain in the sphere of that which is arbitrary or incomprehensible, but rather as the form of revelation which is offered to man. With the reference to 'mystery', therefore, *Fides et ratio* recalls something that is not extraneous to man, who perceives it as a reality which envelops his own personal existence. Man's knowledge demands a reflection on his cognitive modality which cannot be reduced to the mere sphere of rationality.

The mention of 'reason' brings us to consider the peculiar space that critical thought possesses regarding the 'mystery' and the proper role that it should take on.[2] Here, it is not possible to analyse further the different types of knowledge that are common to human intelligence.[3] It is worth observing, however, that John Paul II strongly emphasizes throughout the encyclical that reason must not renounce being itself. Reason has a role to develop that implies not fixing goals that are too modest, but to occupy itself with the understanding of being and truth:

> I cannot but encourage philosophers – be they Christian or not – to trust in the power of human reason and not to set themselves goals that are too modest in their philosophizing. The lesson of history in this millennium now drawing to a close shows that this is the path to follow: it is necessary not to abandon the passion for ultimate truth, the eagerness to search for it or the audacity to forge new paths in the search. It is faith which stirs reason to move beyond all isolation and willingly to run risks so that it may attain whatever is beautiful, good and true. Faith thus becomes the convinced and convincing advocate of reason. (§56)

As can be appreciated by these initial remarks, revelation is the central theme which creates a determining relationship between faith

---

2 Cf. the meaningful sub-title of these numbers: 'Reason before the mystery'.
3 See R. Fisichella, 'Oportet philosophari in theologia' (III), *Gregorianum* 76 (1995), pp. 701–15.

and reason once they become related to the mystery, whether concerning the life of God or personal existence and the perennial questions that demonstrate its elusiveness.

The keystone

An encyclical such as *Fides et ratio* cannot be read in a hurried manner, as many precious intuitions, wise comments and profound analyses would be missed. From this perspective, a rushed reading could easily lead to deception, ignoring the underlying originality. *Fides et ratio*, in fact, requires that the two notions which characterize the entire document be placed up front. Faith and reason are like two poles between which John Paul II develops his teaching; and yet, a close reading immediately shows that the true centre lies elsewhere. The heart of this encyclical is *revelation*. Faith and reason look to revelation, although with different motivations and finalities. Revelation is the focal centre referred to and without which the entire content remains suspended in emptiness.

Fides et ratio makes abundant use of the term 'revelation', which appears at least 68 times from the Introduction to the Conclusion, cutting across the seven chapters of the encyclical. Along with the terms 'faith', 'reason', 'philosophy' and 'theology', also quoted frequently in the apostolic exhortation, 'revelation' is certainly an essential hermeneutical key in order to interpret coherently the teaching of the document.

The first reference to the theme of revelation appears in the Introduction, where there is an indication which deserves to be remembered for the entire reading of the text: 'Sure of her competence as the bearer of the Revelation of Jesus Christ, the Church reaffirms the need to reflect' upon truth' (§6). The truth that *Fides et ratio* probes takes its starting point in the revelation of God in Jesus Christ, that is, the truth that is considered primarily is neither the conclusion of a speculative process nor a mere theory, fruit of critical analysis. Truth is investigated from God's free decision which makes him visible in an historical event. Here, God reveals the definitive truth about himself, about man, about the world and draws a path that must be travelled to allow humanity to reach the truth in a complete and total way.

It is therefore necessary to deal with the theme of revelation in order to understand the sense and value that the Church applies to the nature of truth and the different ways of investigating it. To take a short cut and immediately analyse the contents of 'faith' and 'reason' would lead down a blind alley, making it impossible to understand the originality of *Fides et ratio*: there would not be sufficient explanation of the two poles 'faith' and 'reason' nor of the uniqueness that characterize the contents of each.[4]

Thus, we must go to Chapter I of the text in order to understand the link between revelation and truth. John Paul II offers in §§7–15 an authentic synthesis of the theology of revelation, as it emerges in its novelty from Vatican Council II. The meaningful sub-title, 'Jesus, revealer of the Father', seems to constitute the entry point for 'Revelation of the Wisdom of God', the title of the whole Chapter. This perspective is simply the re-stating of the teaching of *Dei Verbum*, quoted several times in these numbers. Some characteristics proper of the conciliar constitution emerge in a clear way: the Trinitarian connotation of revelation, the centrality of Jesus Christ, the gratuity of the self-manifestation of God and the calling to the participation in the divine life offered to humanity. The first four numbers of *Dei Verbum* are here explicitly recalled with the primary goal of understanding the profound connection between the revelation of God and man's search for meaning.

The framework that is offered allows us to take one step further. No one doubts the real progress in the exposition of revelation that John Paul II initiates in this encyclical. The document makes explicit that which *Dei Verbum* had only highlighted and allows us to understand the constant development that began with Vatican I. A brief look at this dimension will help us understand better the novelty of the encyclical.

As is known, the theme of revelation has been treated in both Vatican Councils. One cannot assert that at the origin of the two council documents there was the primary intention of dealing with revelation. It is certainly not the principal argument of *Dei Filius*, which instead speaks about faith, and only later does it become the main theme for *Dei Verbum*. In Vatican Council I, the council fathers dealt with the theme of the supernatural aspect of revelation in terms of faith. At a time when any possibility of supernatural knowledge was denied, limiting to reason alone the space for the knowledge of truth, the Magisterium was obligated to intervene in order to defend the nature of Christian faith and its non-contradictoriness with truth belonging to reason.[5] In Chapter V of *Fides et ratio*, it is explained why that Council 'for the first time' felt the need to intervene in such matters:

---

4 The lack of due attention to this consideration has led some to misinterpret the encyclical, as will be seen shortly.

5 For a complete examination of this theme, see H. J. Pottmeyer, *Der Glaube vor dem Anspruch der Wissenschaft* (Freiburg: Herder, 1968); Idem, 'La costituzione *Dei Filius*', in R. Fisichella (ed.), *La Teologia Fondamentale. Convergenze per il terzo millennio* (Casale Monferrato: Piemme, 1997), pp. 19–39.

If the Magisterium has spoken out more frequently since the middle of the last century, it is because in that period not a few Catholics felt it their duty to counter various streams of modern thought with a philosophy of their own. At this point, the Magisterium of the Church was obliged to be vigilant lest these philosophies developed in ways which were themselves erroneous and negative. The censures were delivered even-handedly: on the one hand, *fideism* and *radical traditionalism*, for their distrust of reason's natural capacities, and, on the other, *rationalism* and *ontologism* because they attributed to natural reason a knowledge which only the light of faith could confer. The positive elements of this debate were assembled in the Dogmatic Constitution *Dei Filius*, in which for the first time an Ecumenical Council – in this case, the First Vatican Council – pronounced solemnly on the relationship between reason and faith. The teaching contained in this document strongly and positively marked the philosophical research of many believers and remains today a standard reference-point for correct and coherent Christian thinking in this regard. (§52)

The conclusion reached by the council fathers is synthesized by the encyclical in these words: 'The First Vatican Council teaches, then, that the truth attained by philosophy and the truth of Revelation are neither identical nor mutually exclusive' (§9).

At its beginnings, Vatican Council II also did not take the theme of revelation as its primary objective. The document, *De fontibus revelationis* clearly shows that the goal of the Council was that of resolving the *vexata quaestio* left open by the Council of Trent, concerning the relationship between Scripture and Tradition in terms of the transmission of the contents of revealed truth.[6] Between the level of man and the level of the Holy Spirit, however, there is often a difference and at the end that which prevails amidst numerous and unimaginable mediations is always God's action. The *De fontibus revelationis* was held up after the first conciliar session while the commission began its work with its first significant agreement precisely concerning a new title to be given to the document: *De divina Revelatione*.[7]

---

6 Cf. U. Betti, 'Storia della costituzione dogmatica Dei Verbum', in *La Costituzione dogmatica sulla divina rivelazione* (Turin: Leumann, 1967), pp. 13–68.

7 Cf. the various draft changes of the document in F. Gil Hellin, *Constitutio Dogmatica de Divina Revelatione 'Dei Verbum'. Concilii Vaticani II synopsis in ordinem redigens schemata cum relationibus necnon Patrum orationes atque animadversiones* (Vatican City, 1993).

The proposed changes dealt not only with the title: what the fathers elaborated was authentic progress and development in doctrine. Revelation, centred on Christ 'mediator and fullness' (*Dei Verbum* §2), recuperated the category of 'economy' proper of the thought of the fathers of the Church. Just how much this dimension was charged with meaning and further development which would significantly modify the successive theology of revelation becomes clear in light of the past 30 years that have witnessed a change regarding revelation.[8]

In this context, it is appropriate to recall at least two passages which, although from different sources, allow us to understand the evolution that was occurring. The first one refers to the speech given by the Melchite Bishop Georges Hakim during the debate about the first draft of the text. The Bishop explained his *non placet* concerning the draft with these words:

> The outlines certainly contain the richness and values of Latin theology, and we would like to render a fervent homage to this magnificent '*intellectus fidei*' which this theology has given to the Church; yet we are disappointed that completely ignoring Eastern catechism and theology, like that of Cyril of Jerusalem, of Gregory Nazianzus and Gregory of Nyssa, of Maximus, of John Damascenus and of many other Fathers of the East, the drafters have monopolized the universal faith to profit their own theology, so much so that it seems that they wish to establish as a conciliar, exclusive truth that which is a valid, yet local and partial, expression of the revelation of God. In Eastern theology – where the liturgy is the efficacious place of the transmission of the faith, where initiation takes place within the sacramental mystery, and not in an abstract instruction without symbolic connections – the mystery of Christ is proposed directly as an 'economy' which unfolds in history, prepared by the ancient Covenant, fulfilled in Christ and completed in the time of the Church. The theoretical explanations, however legitimate and necessary they may be, must never be separated from the Scriptures and the witness of the Fathers.[9]

---

8 For a concise look at this perspective, see D. Valentini (ed.), *La teologia della Rivelazione* (Padova: Edizioni Messaggero, 1996); H. Waldenfels, 'La comprensione della rivelazione nel XX secolo', in M. Seybold and H. Waldenfels (eds), *La Rivelazione* (Bologna: Edizioni Dehoniane, 1992), pp. 493–534; M. Seckler, 'Der Begriff der Offenbarung', in Walter Kern, Hermann J. Pottmeyer and Max Seckler (eds), *Handbuch der Fundamentaltheologie 2, Traktat Offenbarung* (Freiburg im Breisgau: Herder, 1986), pp. 60–83.

9 Text given in Hellin, *Constitutio Dogmatica*, p. 276.

It would not be farfetched to think that precisely on the base of this contribution, in spite of its apparent naïveté, a new meaning to the ancient term (so dear to the fathers), 'economy', began taking shape within the halls of the Basilica of St Peter's. This term was charged with meaning for the history of theology, and was becoming an essential aspect of the presentation of revelation. With this concept, it was now possible to recuperate biblical understanding of history and its placement in the divine salvific plan which finds its actuation and fulfilment in the Incarnation of the Son of God.

The second passage, of a different ilk, refers to a brief comment of Fr S. Tromp, at the time professor of Apologetics at the Gregorian University and member of the Theological Commission which supervised the first submitted draft. Precisely during the debate concerning the terminology to be used to express the reality of revelation, Tromp jotted down these words in his *Observanda ad Prooemium Constitutionis*: 'It appears that if this new definition of revelation is accepted, necessarily it would also be required to change the concept of the Catholic faith, which indeed would be in no small way a cause of great confusion.'[10] The change in question went from the use of '*locutio Dei*' to that of '*Verbum Dei*'; as is known, this provoked revolutionary effects: not only due to the terminological shift away from a more philosophical reading of revelation (in the shadow of which theology had been developed up until that point), but above all, due to the implications brought about by the biblical foundation and due to the consequences that will become evident in post-conciliar theology.

It is in this sense that we must recognize the great theological courage of John Paul II and the originality of *Fides et ratio*, which can be summarized thus: while *Dei Filius* defends the theme of knowledge through faith, *Fides et ratio* presents the road of knowledge through revelation. This, we believe, is a true element of innovation which deserves to be considered. Revelation is presented as a form of knowledge and as a vehicle for an always deeper knowledge of the 'mystery' and of being.

Of course, the privileged way of knowing the contents of revelation is still the faith in that very revelation. This is truly the most adequate and coherent way that allows revelation to be expressed in that depth

---

10 '*Accedit quod si nova definitio illa revelationis admittitur, necessario quoque mutari debet conceptus catholicus fidei, quod etiam reapse a nonnullis fit et causa est magnae confusionis.*' These *Observanda* were prepared by Fr S. Tromp, Secretary of the Theological Commission regarding the session of the Mixed Commission of 4 December 1962. Let us recall that the very same Tromp had written also in the *Observanda*: '*Loquendum est de revelatione in ordine ad fontes revelationis*', cf. the text in H. Sauer, *Erfahrung und Glaube* (Frankfurt am Main: Lang, 1993), p. 676.

which is enveloped in the mystery. The Holy Father clearly emphasizes this: 'Faith alone makes it possible to penetrate the mystery in a way that allows us to understand it coherently' (§13). Revelation remains, however, as the permanent novelty offered to reason to be able to expand her knowledge and progress in the search for truth. Revelation, in this way, allows us to capture the presence of a content that can only be given as gift and grace within God's free plan of salvation. From the time in which the truth of God about himself becomes revealed within history and in an historical event, then in that event of revelation we discover the key to unlock and interpret the truth about man and about the world. This truth, *Fides et ratio* recalls, is 'given to man and not demanded by him' (§13). We are thus placed before a true recognition both of divine liberty and of a content offered to reason so that she can ever more fathom the newness of being.

Revelation produces thought

The harmony between faith and reason that ancient and medieval thought had experienced due to revelation's unquestioned primacy was destroyed 'as a result of the exaggerated rationalism of certain thinkers' (§45). The result was the emergence 'of a philosophy which was separate from and absolutely independent of the contents of faith' (§45). One of the consequences of this breaking down of harmony, clearly visible even today, was a certain scepticism concerning that knowledge which came from revelation and from faith in revelation. The step towards this scepticism and general lack of confidence in terms of both faith and reason was quick and brought painful consequences.

John Paul II often returns in *Fides et ratio* to the danger of subjectivism and of reason's closing in on itself. Feeling strong under the illusion of being the only source of knowledge of the truth and under the weight of the conquests of its knowledge, reason 'little by little has lost the capacity to lift its gaze to the heights, not daring to rise to the truth of being' (§5).[11]

---

11 Cf. the other meaningful expressions of *Fides et ratio* concerning the instrumental use of reason: 'In the field of scientific research, a positivistic mentality took hold which not only abandoned the Christian vision of the world, but more especially rejected every appeal to a metaphysical or moral vision. It follows that certain scientists, lacking any ethical point of reference, are in danger of putting at the centre of their concerns something other than the human person and the entirety of the person's life. Further still, some of these, sensing the opportunities of technological progress, seem to succumb not only to a market-based logic, but also to the temptation of a quasi-divine power over nature and even over the human being' (§ 46); 'It should also be borne in mind that the role of philosophy itself has changed in modern culture. From universal wisdom and learning, it has been gradually reduced to one of the many fields of human knowing; indeed in

It is precisely by recalling revelation that reason can retrace its steps and regain a speculative focus.

It would be mistaken to think that revealed content is relevant only to faith; *Fides et ratio* correctly emphasizes the universal character of this content and the profound meaning that it offers to philosophical reflection: 'Revelation has set within history a point of reference which cannot be ignored if the mystery of human life is to be known. Yet this knowledge refers back constantly to the mystery of God which the human mind cannot exhaust but can only receive and embrace in faith' (§14). Revelation, the Popes insists, 'produces thought' (§15), because it allows thought to become enveloped in the 'mystery'.

The value of the preceding observations concerning the meaning of the 'mystery' can now be fully appreciated. Revelation is placed against the background of the mystery and can be seen itself as mystery. Such highlighting is not accomplished in order to limit reason's range of investigation, yet rather to insist on its autonomy even when faced with the extreme challenge posed by the 'mystery'. Often accustomed to surrendering in front of that which cannot be understood, we commonly identify the 'mystery' with that which is impossible to know for man. *Fides et ratio*, however, treads a different path. The mystery is presented as the space offered to reason in order to proceed always beyond itself in the search for truth that can only and always be given as gift. In other words, it is precisely through the reality of the 'mystery' that it is possible to recover the abandoned equilibrium between the subjectivity of personal knowledge and the objectivity of the offered knowledge. The reading in perspective of the subject must recognize that the object of its knowledge is always greater than that which it is able to embrace. This is precisely the condition of the strength of reason, which it cannot renounce without irremediably weakening itself.

With the bringing to mind of the 'sacramental horizon' of revelation, John Paul II touches upon a point of great demonstrative power: he places reason in front of the mystery, provoking it to disclose the intelligence that it holds. Reason, precisely because it investigates the mystery autonomously, encounters the signs which express it and from them it is moved to go continually further in its attempt to reach the meaning that the signs contain. In a context in which various analyses of language highlight the value of signs without, however, grasping the

---

some ways it has been consigned to a wholly marginal role. Other forms of rationality have acquired an ever higher profile, making philosophical learning appear all the more peripheral. These forms of rationality are directed not towards the contemplation of truth and the search for the ultimate goal and meaning of life; but instead, as 'instrumental reason', they are directed – actually or potentially – towards the promotion of utilitarian ends, towards enjoyment or power' (§47).

profound value of the link to the underlying meaning, this dimension opens an ulterior space of dialogue and research with philosophical thought.

The guiding star

The primacy that the encyclical had confided to revelation from the very beginning was not lost during the course of the treatise; just the opposite. From the moment in which John Paul II reveals the proper 'demands' and 'inescapable' exigencies towards philosophy, these become assumed and mediated by the Word of God. The three fundamental demands that *Fides et ratio* presents are situated at the very heart of revelation: the first one deals with the 'question of meaning' (§80), the second consists in the spurring on of 'man's capacity to grasp the knowledge of truth' (§82), while the third opens up towards the 'metaphysical horizon' (§82). From beginning to end, therefore, the encyclical conserves the original scheme without variation and brings together the entirety of its teaching around the centre of God's revelation.

A keen Jewish scholar, F. Rosenzweig, wrote in his *Star of Redemption* that 'it is the concept of theology's revelation that builds a bridge between the extremely subjective and the extremely objective'. This text comes to mind while continuing to read *Fides et ratio*. John Paul II has truly built a bridge between philosophy and theology so that both can once again speak and dialogue together concerning the theme of truth: the truth that revelation carries within itself and expresses in itself; a truth which enters into the history of humanity, not to impose itself extrinsically, but to invite every human being to enter into his or her most intimate reality and discover where that truth resides. In this sense, the Holy Father's suggestion is very relevant:

> Christian Revelation is the true lodestar of men and women as they strive to make their way amid the pressures of an immanentist habit of mind and the constrictions of a technocratic logic. It is the ultimate possibility offered by God for the human being to know in all its fullness the seminal plan of love which began with creation. To those wishing to know the truth, if they can look beyond themselves and their own concerns, there is given the possibility of taking full and harmonious possession of their lives, precisely by following the path of truth. (§15)

God's revelation, therefore, becomes the synthesis and point of encounter of the road that both faith and reason travel in their investigation and search for truth. In a time such as ours, characterized by a profound 'crisis of meaning' (§81), *Fides et ratio* allows us to recuperate one of the essential traits of the common patrimony of theology and philosophy: the universality of truth and its salvific value. This has been a conquest in which Christians have been authentic pioneers and always on the front line in its defence. Throughout this process, Christian thought can be accused of neither arrogance nor intolerance, for a prejudice-free analysis will clearly show that Christianity has given rise to a decisive contribution in this area.[12]

The unbreakable link between truth and salvation has rendered the Christian message always and inevitably one of the truth about man and his condition. It is not by deceiving man that we will be able to free him from his condition and from his fears; he must discover that his freedom is truly such only when he encounters the truth about himself. His call to transcendence and communion of life with God, the supreme form of personal freedom, is only possible if he becomes aware of his own sin and opts for the road of conversion. A simple phrase of *Fides et ratio* opens up a very meaningful avenue of reflection: 'Once the truth is denied to human beings, it is pure illusion to try to set them free. Truth and freedom either go together hand in hand or together they perish in misery' (§90).

Apologia of a concept

It is unfortunate to recognize how over the past couple of years some commentators have not grasped the innovative dimension that *Fides et ratio* presents. Given that it seems to us that the text of the encyclical is quite clear in this regard, one can only deduce that such a failure on their part is due either to a superficial reading, or the continued resistance of unjustified prejudices towards Magisterial teaching. Like it or not, *Fides et ratio* represents an authentic challenge that faith poses to contemporary culture. Some have complained that not only does the document contain nothing new, but also that it advances, as always,

---

12 The relevant text in this sense is quite appropriate: 'That seems still more evident today, if we think of Christianity's contribution to the affirmation of the right of everyone to have access to the truth. In dismantling barriers of race, social status and gender, Christianity proclaimed from the first the equality of all men and women before God. One prime implication of this touched the theme of truth. The elitism which had characterized the ancients' search for truth was clearly abandoned. Since access to the truth enables access to God, it must be denied to none. There are many paths which lead to truth, but since Christian truth has a salvific value, any one of these paths may be taken, as long as it leads to the final goal, that is to the Revelation of Jesus Christ' (§38).

the Church's presumption of possessing the truth and of limiting other people's truth and freedom. How singularly appropriate to call to mind a text of the encyclical:

> To believe it possible to know a universally valid truth is in no way to encourage intolerance; on the contrary, it is the essential condition for sincere and authentic dialogue between persons. On this basis alone is it possible to overcome divisions and to journey together towards full truth, walking those paths known only to the Spirit of the Risen Lord. (§92)

As we can see, that which makes us strong is not the presumption of guarding a truth produced by man. On this level, that would be a source of intolerance because it would bring with it the typical hubris of the arrogance of one subject over another. The truth of the faith is of another kind; it is universal, because it is revealed and offered as gift to all of humanity. Of course, as long as one remains stubbornly attached to the view that only man can produce truth, then the temptation of intolerance will also remain; yet such a temptation does not belong to us and no one has the right to foster such a suspicion, equivocating the meaning of the contents in which we believe.

One writer has even observed that because Adam disobeyed God's commandment, he finally became 'man': 'He would never have become man if he had remained in the Eden of innocence.'[13] Here we might raise the inevitable rhetorical question: why punish Adam in the moment in which he acquires knowledge? If that is how things were, everything would be much easier. And yet, those who think along these lines are forgetting the most important thing with which to construct their intellectual edifice: disobeying the commandment meant placing man as the criteria of good and evil! This, however, cannot be granted to any creature without falling into the delirium of omnipotence and power over others. The ancient words of the *Letter to Diognetus* are a powerful reminder: 'but it is not the tree of knowledge that destroys – it is disobedience that proves destructive' (XII, 2).

In order to approach the content of *Fides et ratio* with greater objectivity, it may prove useful to return to the beginning where the Pope asserts the special character of the truth dealt with throughout the encyclical:

> The Church is no stranger to this journey of discovery, nor could she ever be. From the moment when, through the Paschal Mystery,

---

13 E. Scalari, 'La fede del papa e quella dei laici', *La Repubblica*, 18 October 1998.

she received the gift of the ultimate truth about human life, the Church has made her pilgrim way along the paths of the world to proclaim that Jesus Christ is 'the way, and the truth, and the life' (John 14.6). It is her duty to serve humanity in different ways, but one way in particular imposes a responsibility of a quite special kind: the *diakonia of the truth*. This mission on the one hand makes the believing community a partner in humanity's shared struggle to arrive at truth; and on the other hand it obliges the believing community to proclaim the certitudes arrived at, albeit with a sense that every truth attained is but a step towards that fullness of truth which will appear with the final Revelation of God: 'For now we see in a mirror dimly, but then face to face. Now I know in part; then I shall understand fully' (1 Cor. 13.12). (§2)

The '*diakonia of the truth*', therefore, is the true goal of *Fides et ratio*. In this way, we can see in a complete way the service that the Church and the Magisterium renders to revelation. We should always be subordinate to this truth, never thinking that we are its masters. Only in this way can the truth of revelation remain within the bounds of authentic freedom and a source of meaning for one's personal life. This also entails the existence of a true path in the search of truth, making every human being truly human, yet only if placed within the horizon of truth. Outside of this light, one's existence would be constantly subjected to doubt, to uncertainty, and therefore incapable of providing meaning for the future.

We hope that *Fides et ratio* continues to provoke discussion; in any event, the document will represent always a milestone in the history of Christian doctrine. Philosophy, for its part, if it desires to have a future, must leave the tunnel of scepticism in which it has placed reason, and look towards the horizon indicated by the radical novelty coming from the incarnation of the Son of God. Faith and reason placed under the ray of light coming from revelation can thus coherently express two sciences – theology and philosophy – which while remaining autonomous, are able to dialogue and investigate the one truth that gives meaning to personal existence. Reason, therefore, discovers in revelation the possibility of truly being itself: free to search for truth, capable of investigating it once it is found and audacious in abandoning itself to her, recognizing its own limits.

2. Faith, Reason and the Eucharist: Music as a Model for their Harmony

DENYS TURNER

Introduction: the faith of rational beings

A short while ago I wrote a book called *Faith, Reason and the Existence of God*.[1] I would be quite pleased to know that none of you have read this book, for what I propose here is a sort of paraphrase of its main lines of argument, and in putting it together I have pretty shamelessly self-plagiarized. This, I suppose, won't matter if you don't know the source. On the other hand, if you have read the book you might find it easier to see in this paraphrase, in which I have ruthlessly pruned away the flesh, what is deficient about the skeletal remains. That would be a good thing, since for my part as its author I was happier that there were some bits of solid red meat in the book than I was with its anatomical structure as argument. In any case, if much of what follows seems old hat and repetitive of what I have written elsewhere, I apologise.

In that book, as in this chapter, I thought it would be a good idea to begin with a deliberate provocation. I will put the case,[2] if only in a pro-grammatic way, for the defence of a decree of the First Vatican Council of 1870–72. As I read it – though I acknowledge that not everyone reads it that way – this decree expressed unqualified confidence in the power of human reason to know God. It declares – rather drastically you will think – a person to be anathematized who denies 'that the one true God, our creator and lord, can . . . be known with certainty from the things that have been made, by the natural light of reason'.[3] Reason,

---

1 Cambridge: Cambridge University Press, 2004. This paper was first given at the Heythrop conference in May 2003, and revised for presentation to the Divinity School of Duke University in January 2005, which version is published here.

2 I am grateful in particular to four graduate students in the Faculty of Divinity in Cambridge for their careful, perceptive, and helpful comments on earlier versions of this paper: Férdia Stone-Davis, Vittorio Montemaggi, Donna Lazenby and Ed Morgan.

3 *Dogmatic Constitution on the Catholic Faith*, in Norman Tanner SJ (ed.),

the decree says, can by its own unaided power know God to exist, that same God we address when we pray, the same God who was incarnate through his Word in Jesus, the same God who forgives us through the Church's power of reconciliation. When you put it this way the claim seems as startling as it is implausible. Therefore, for the most part what I have to say in this chapter is by way of explaining an account of 'reason' such that the Council's proposition can be seen to be more defensible than many today find it; for especially among those who, as I do, interpret the decree in this its strongest sense, few think it defensible, whether they are committed or loosely Christian theologians and philosophers, or more neutrally academic students of religion – and, of course, no atheists do. What is more, I propose to argue the case for the equally contentious proposition that the Council's decree, on this strong interpretation of it, expresses the mind of Thomas Aquinas on the matter. But before taking the plunge into so deep, cold and turbulent a pool of contention, a preliminary word or two seems in order with a view to removing some obvious sources of misunderstanding of what my main proposition entails.

First, I want to get something out of the way concerning that *obiter* of Anselm's about *fides quaerens intellectum* proposed as a way of paraphrasing Thomas's view of the relationship between faith and reason. The *quaerens* bit of it seems to me to be fine, though I do feel that not enough is made of Thomas's conception of faith as a kind of *eros*, as an unsatisfiably passionate drive for understanding, for there continue to lurk within readings of Thomas on faith – even of those who profess to find in him a 'dynamic' conception of it – the implied assumption that for Thomas the 'understanding' faith seeks at least *ends* in *question-stopping* answers. Thomas, however, as we will see, seems to think of the whole *dynamis*, whether of faith or of reason, as culminating rather in *answer-stopping* questions, in a deepened apophaticism. He seems to think that only that could satisfy the erotically unlimited demands of human reason lying beyond all that faith could of its nature provide.

Which brings me to this word *intellectus*, often enough translated, misleadingly I wager, as 'understanding' within the following sort of rather pat formula, crudely put: faith plus reason equals theology and *that's* 'understanding'. But that cannot be right. What faith seeks, but falls short of, is nothing achievable in this life: the beatific vision. And as for theology, that just *is* 'faith seeking'. But for want of getting this sort of very elementary and obvious point right, all too many read Thomas as thinking that you can get your account of faith off the ground first,

The Decrees of the Ecumenical Councils, 2, *Trent to Vatican II* (Washington DC: Georgetown University Press, 1990), pp. 804–11.

and then work out from that how faith may, or perhaps more strongly must, make use of reason in the conduct of its seeking 'understanding', as if, making use of reason as a tool, faith can pick up or leave reason down according as it sees need or fit. I find no such conception of faith and of its relation to reason anywhere in Thomas's theology.

What is more to the purpose of my argument, however, is that neither do I find in Thomas any such conception of reason as is implied by this crude formula. To suppose that you can work up an account of faith and *then* derive from it some account of its relation to reason seems almost exactly to reverse Thomas's conceptual priorities. In general the mistake here would, for Thomas, be rather like that of supposing that rational agents use their hands or feet or eyes or brains, or whatever, as tools at the disposal of their rational powers, roughly as Plato sometimes says, when in fact, as Thomas sees it, you could not even begin to work out what you meant by 'rationality' independently of the conception of bodies as possessing hands with opposed thumbs, or as standing vertically on two feet, or as possessed of binocular vision. It is only agents that have the sort of bodies that are thus physically equipped which could be described as 'rational' in the first place. Just so, as I understand Thomas, with 'faith' and 'reason': there isn't a conception of faith available to us otherwise than that in terms of rational agents discovering that nothing will satisfy their rational tendency otherwise than the immediate vision of God. Of course, that they do come to know of this goal of all their desire is something given to them as a purely gratuitous gift of the divine condescension and mercy. But equally, it could not be otherwise than to rational agents that the gift of faith could be given in the first place. So faith just is the gift by which reason has learned to desire an understanding it couldn't know it could seek; as gifts are with us, so with grace; as among ourselves the perfectly judged gift meets a desire we didn't know we had. So, as I see it, says Thomas about faith.

It is this sense of rationality simply and generally as characterizing the only sort of being that could be the recipient of grace, which is what I think of as being Thomas's broadest sense of 'reason' – the 'maximal' sense of it, as I shall say. In the meantime there is in Thomas a more restricted sense of reason which is the matter of the first half of this chapter. And I propose in the first half to get at that 'minimal' sense by way of appeal to a medieval philosophical truism. The truism is one which you find Thomas Aquinas sometimes appealing to, though in fact he and others got it from their Latin translation of Aristotle's *Peri hermeneias*. *Eadem est scientia oppositorum*, Thomas says, paraphrasing Aristotle – 'one and the same is the knowledge of opposites'. One sort of implication of this truism is that you can get worthwhile disagreements going only where there is agreed common ground to contest. Where you don't agree, or can't, as to what you are disagreeing about, where there is no *eadem scientia*, you have but heterogeneity, or as the medievals called it, a *diversitas*, you get cross-purposes, not genuine disagreement. Thus we can disagree about whether this object is red or green, but we don't exactly *disagree* over whether it is green or 6 ft long; or, to take a more medieval example, I suppose medieval theologians thought of heretics, whether of the Christian variety, or Muslim or Jewish, as belonging to a common family of disagreement, since with them you knew what you were disagreeing about – the falling-out was within the family, as it were – whereas they would mostly have been simply puzzled by Buddhists, hardly knowing where to start with them.

That said, let me put in very blunt terms the first of two propositions, subsidiary to the defence of the Vatican decree, that I have it in mind to explain: and this first proposition is about 'reason' in what I shall call its 'minimal' sense. My purpose – and I do confess the tactics are a bit manipulative – is to provoke you *all* into disagreeing with me about reason – though here hiding behind the ample figure of Thomas Aquinas – and thereby trap you all into agreeing with me and with each other about where lies the common territory of our disagreement. And then I shall tell you that I have won the argument one way or the other. For either you won't disagree with me and Thomas about reason, in which case there is nothing to contest; or else we will have found some territory common between us all, a shared territory of disagreement, and I shall say: in doing *just that* we show that we agree with Thomas Aquinas about what reason is, and about its place within our common enterprise: for *eadem est scientia oppositorum*. How about that, then – I mean, that reason is, for us all, a common currency of the exchange of disagreements? Agreed? No? Then tell me, *how* do you propose to disagree with me? Only answer that, and we will, after all, have agreed in two moves rather than one.

Rational demonstration as a matter of faith

So much for the hovering at the edge of the icy pool. Let me put a first tentative toe into it with a provocation to some theologians, who might want to disagree with me in the following way. The decree of the First Vatican Council tells us that it is a matter of *faith* that the existence of God is demonstrable by reason alone. I think that this amounts in practice to the negative proposition that if your account of faith is such as to entail the rational indemonstrability of God, then you must have got something wrong either about the nature of faith or about the nature of reason. And I think Thomas agrees with that minimal claim. But even though theologians today are much better disposed towards Thomas than they used to be, there is hardly one among them, of whatever theological tradition, who thinks he is right on that score, preferring on the whole the proposition that, on the contrary, it is essential to the defence of faith that the existence of God is shown to be rationally *in*demonstrable. There are all sorts of grounds offered, Kantian and non-Kantian, for the theologians' scepticism of Thomas's optimism about what Kant called 'speculative' reason, but one of the most commonly put, and as casually as commonly, is neo-Pascalian. You still hear it said that even if it were philosophically possible it's simply no use a theologian's trying to prove the existence of God on rational grounds, because any God you could prove the existence of by purely rational means would be, as Pascal so famously put it, a 'God of the philosophers'; and a God of the philosophers could not be the same God as the 'God of Abraham, Isaac and Jacob', the 'God of faith'. Hearing this from a good Barthian theologian would not be surprising. More so is to get a reading of Thomas himself, such as that of Fergus Kerr, according to which even if a rational proof that God exists could be had – and he implies that Thomas isn't really serious in supposing that it can be – the 'God exists' of the philosopher could not *mean the same as* the 'God exists' of Christian faith.[4] From which Kerr seems to think it follows that rational proof of God, even if successful, wouldn't get you to the *same God* as the God of Christian faith. But this appears to be a non-sequitur.

For I cannot see Thomas Aquinas being much disconcerted by what Kerr puts to him by way of the non-equivalence of the divine names, since Thomas knows perfectly well that the descriptions under which he thinks God's existence is proved – 'prime mover', 'first cause', 'necessary being' and so forth – do not *mean* the same as 'Father, Son and Holy Spirit'. After all, he knows that 'prime mover', 'first cause', 'necessary being' don't mean the same even as each other. But he would have been upset to know of this being considered an objection. Just because two descriptions do not mean the same it doesn't follow that they are not descriptions of the same identical thing, just as 'the square of 1' and 'the square root of 1' do not mean the same, though the value both formulae yield is in either case 1; or, as John Haldane has put it, just because 'blockage in the system' and 'a small piece of masonry' do not mean the same, it does not follow that what's blocking the system isn't

---

4 Fergus Kerr, *After Aquinas: Versions of Thomism* (Oxford: Blackwell, 2002), p. 67.

a small piece of masonry.[5] Just so here: you would of course have to *show* that the 'necessary being' known by reason is the same God as the cause and object of Trinitarian faith, but then Thomas puts in some 149 articles of close argument between the famous 'five ways' and the opening of his discussion of the Trinity, purporting to show just that. When Thomas says at the end of each of his 'proofs' *et hoc omnes dicunt Deum*, this should be translated not as 'and this is *how* all people talk about God', because manifestly they don't commonly talk about God as 'prime mover', or 'necessary being', and you shouldn't imagine Thomas not knowing that; nor even as: 'and this is what all people *mean* when they talk about God' because they don't do that either, and Thomas knows that too. The phrase is more properly translated as: 'and this is the [same] God [as the one] all people speak of', for example, when they pray, or make the sign of the cross, or whatever; and though of course that is a proposition which itself needs some argument which you could dispute, there is no good reason for the theologians to take offence in principle, at any rate not on Pascal's grounds.

More telling, however, is the objection that the bishops' case about faith is simultaneously both outrageously over-bearing in its claims to dictate to the philosophers' rational autonomy and, at the same time, riskily self-undermining. It is a provocation to the philosophers by appearing to tell them what they can and can't do, and on non-philosophical grounds. But the theologians also will have cause to worry about the decree, because it would appear to place faith in thrall to what must in principle be a contestable philosophical proposition – for a proposition's being philosophical would seem to guarantee its contestability. For were the philosophers to succeed in showing that reason could not in principle demonstrate the existence of God then any account of faith that entailed that it could do so would fall with the success of the philosophers' counter-arguments, since if what a proposition entails is refutable, then the proposition which entails it is thereby refutable. But I do not think either fear is justified, and as to the latter anxiety, I confess that I have never fully understood the grounds of this fear of faith's refutability, which causes so many theologians today to retreat into the apparently safe-haven of fideism in one form or another. I cannot see why, that is to say, theologians do not simply accept that what faith claims is certainly true: after all, we believe what faith reveals on divine authority, and shouldn't that do by way of warrant for them? The price you pay for construing those claims as *logically* invulnerable to any *possible* counter-evidence is the

---

5 J. J. C. Smart and John J. Haldane, *Atheism and Theism* (Oxford: Blackwell, 1996), p. 143.

price logic always entails for analyticity – the more necessarily true the more vacuous your claims must be.

As Thomas says, no claims of faith are necessary truths. Anyone can deny them without contradiction. Moreover, one wonders sometimes whether theologians who wish to shore up the certainty of their faith behind a barrier of invulnerability to counter-evidence ever recite the Nicene Creed: for every time we do so we declare what we know to be certainly true. And among the truths the Creed declares to be of faith are some obviously plain historical facts, namely that Jesus was 'crucified, died and was buried'. If those contingent historical assertions were not true Christian faith would be in vain. So says the Creed. I therefore cannot see why theologians should want to box themselves into so conceptually tight a corner as they do if they insist that were your faith to *entail* factual consequences it would be *reduced* to those consequences, as some do who suppose that, for that reason, resurrection faith could not depend on the tomb's being empty on the third day. Nothing of the sort follows. You can with perfect consistency say first, that resurrection faith *depends* upon a certain historical fact's being the case, namely that the tomb was empty, and, second, that faith in the resurrection could not *consist* in that fact's being the case. For the hypothetical proposition '*if* belief in the resurrection of Jesus is true then the tomb was empty' is not of course convertible to the proposition, 'if the tomb was empty then belief in the resurrection is true'.[6] Of course, then, resurrection faith consists in more than belief in a 'mere' historical fact. But for sure its truth entails one.

So I concede that these matters merely of logic say nothing at all of interest about that resurrection faith itself. But then I did not intend to be interesting about the resurrection, but only to illustrate a parallel point, and equally one in 'mere' logic, about faith's authority and reason's autonomy. Just as to say that belief in the resurrection of Jesus entails a certain empirical fact's being true without robbing that 'fact' of its empirical, contingent, character, so to say that faith's authority dictates that a certain philosophical proposition is true, is neither to rob faith of its certainty by virtue of thus linking it into a contestable truth-claim, nor is that linkage to reduce faith to that proposition. So the Vatican decree does nothing to rob reason of its autonomy. On the contrary, faith's certainty *concedes* that autonomy to reason. For if by faith we know that reason is capable of knowing God, then it would seem to follow that reason can by itself know that it is capable of knowing God. And that of course would remain to be shown philosophically. So

---

6 I am grateful to Donna Lazenby for pointing this out.

all the work of reason remains to be done by reason itself of its own resources. None of it is done for it by faith's.

Neither does it follow, just because faith entails that reason is capable of knowing of its own power to know God, that this leaves faith vulnerable to refutation by mere philosophers' arguments, such as Kant's: to the contrary. For if you know with the certainty of faith that Kant is wrong to deny that speculative reason can know God, then you know that Kant is wrong *simpliciter*. And this, of course, means that, as Thomas says, no faith depends subjectively on actually producing a knock-down proof of God's existence. It certainly does not depend upon his own 'five ways' having to be counted on as valid proofs of God. It just requires that you do not so construe faith objectively as to entail the impossibility of rational proof in principle. Even more surely, you do not yourself have to be a philosopher, able to refute Kant philosophically, to be certain of your faith. In fact, quite obviously, you can have the firmest faith possible without having the least notion that Kant denied one of its entailments. Better still than that, there is a blessed majority of faithful believers who haven't the faintest idea even that there ever was anyone named Kant at all, such is the happy life for some. So it would seem that you *can* eat your cake and have it, and that the merit of Thomas's position is that it allows consistently *both* for reason's autonomy *and* for faith's authority over it. And, prima facie, that would seem to be a motive for taking Thomas's position and the Council's decree a bit more seriously than theologians commonly do.

A minimal sense of reason and the possibility of argument

Except that the postmodernists won't let them. Let us just for a moment recapitulate. My case is that either all is heterogeneity and there is no argument to be had about God's existence, or else there are some arguments to be had; but that, if there are arguments to be had, then this can only be across a common territory of dispute. Now what I propose by way of this 'minimal' account of reason – and note, I do *not* say that there is nothing more to be said about it – is that it consists in the territory occupied in common by opposed beliefs such that they contest with one another over it. But the postmodernists will tell alike the theologians and the students of 'comparative religion' that there is no such territory for reason to occupy, that 'reason', as offering any overarching narrative, whether of contestation or of comparison, is a myth of the 'Enlightenment' and of 'modernity'. And a good number of theologians and students of religion of my acquaintance have bought into this story, maintaining that it is indeed true that all is heterogeneity, or as the medievals say, *diversitas*, or, as one of the postmodernists says, 'every otherness is absolute otherness', *tout autre*, and they propose to conduct their respective businesses on those terms of plurality, rather than on any of a pretentiously 'universalistic' kind. Nothing 'overarches', least of all 'reason'. Of course the nose twitches in suspicion at a critique of 'grand narratives' which is itself rooted in as grand a narrative of intellectual history as one could imagine, consisting as it does in an historically unsatisfying 'epochization' of that history into the pre- and the postmodern, with a sort of mythological 'modernity' set in the middle as a point of contrast with both. But what is crucial to this critique of 'modernity' is the critique of its 'rationalism', as a 'totalizing' and hegemony-claiming, plurality-denying, and no doubt phallocentric and neo-colonialist, conspiracy. Fair enough: for all I know 'modernist rationality' is all of these things, and for sure no theologian is going to want a petty godlet who is the idolatrous product of a reason so conceived – not Thomas, not I.

In view of this may I make my meaning plain: the case for revisiting Thomas's quite drastically minimalist account of reason owes nothing much to what theologians or cultural theorists defend as 'modernist' when they do, or reject as today more do in the name of the 'postmodern'. It owes little to either the so-called 'metaphysical' God of Enlightenment theodicies, or to the post-metaphysical God of a John Caputo or a Jean-Luc Marion. Hence it neither stakes claims to a pretentiously 'universalistic', over-arching and *given* normativity of reason in respect of religious belief-claims, nor does it make concessions to its mirror-image, deregulated pluralisms. Rather, it tells you of a plague to be visited upon both houses of the a priori: it tells you to *explore* how differences themselves differ, neither in order to collapse them into some higher, universal, 'modernist' rationality, nor to dissolve them into some 'postmodern' ultimacy of the penultimate, but in order to discover the common ground you differ over, the *eadem scientia* you are drawn into precisely by the *oppositio*. To give but one kind of example: you can't know a priori whether a Christian's saying God is a trinity of persons, and a Jew or a Muslim's saying God is one, is like saying God is red, not blue, a true *oppositio*; or whether it is more like saying God is red, not 6 ft long, a *diversitas*. How, otherwise than within the debate between them, could you know whether what Jews and Muslims affirm by way of divine oneness is that which is denied by the Christian's trinity? Don't you need to explore that? And then, when you explore it, do you not discover all sort of problems all share equally about what goes for counting things up in God one way or the other, one way *or* three? And why does counting become problematic in God for all three theologies? Because in all three theologies we are caught in the same tension: if we have to say, with Jacques Derrida, that God is the *tout autre*, the 'absolute other', do we not also have to say, with Nicholas of Cusa, that God is *ly non aliud*, 'the one-and-only-*not*-other'; and so conclude that any decent theology ends with the defeat of *all* our categories of otherness and difference, that 'otherness' as such collapses before God: and so counting too – which depends upon the identifications of 'this' rather than 'that'. So Christians and Muslims just have to work it out whether they do or they don't disagree, whether what is at stake is an *oppositio* or a *diversitas*. And what they are exercising in that working out gives us a sort of minimal, but still normative, conception of reason, an *eadem scientia*. Well, I say, when Thomas maintains that theology is *argumentativa*,[7] he means that it is in this way exploratory of the *sic et non* of faith. And this 'minimalist' account of reason is just that which is discovered in the course of exploring the possibilities of theological argument, and, so far as that minimalism goes, is not much more than that. Does not faith have to concede at least that much to reason? It is hard to see how any articulated faith could concede less than that to reason, to reason*ing* in this minimal sense.

So, sketchy enough as it is, that is as much as I will say in defence of the first of those two subsidiary propositions about reason, and pass on to the second. For there is, of course, more to reason on Thomas's account than that 'minimal' conception – a richer, more complex, conception of it than any which has been available to us among the theologians and philosophers since his time; but it is also one without which it is impossible to understand his case for the possibility of a rational proof of God. And I want now to suggest that if we are to recapture something of what he has to offer here we could do well to start elsewhere than among the theologians and cultural theorists of our times, and would do better to look specifically among the arts, but especially to poetry and music.

A fuller sense of reason

But you will have to forgive me if, in doing so, I give you little more than heads of an argument, an outline for an 'argument-strategy' as it were, for *ars longa et vita brevis*. First, let us dispose of an instinctive, though often unarticulated, prejudice about 'reason' which can get in the way of our reading Thomas properly. There are theologians who just don't seem to *like* reason very much. It seems so unfriendly to feeling for a start, and to the rich complexity of life more generally.

7 *Summa Theologiae* Ia, Q. 1, art. 8.

24

And one has to concede that reason reduced to the 'minimal' sense, as formal ratiocination, is a dull, flat, and thus far not very profitable thing. And you might correspondingly be uninspired, as many are, by how far Thomas's 'essential definition' of a human being as 'rational animal' limps so laggardly behind the living, complex, vibrant, carnal reality of any actual human being. And while it is true that Thomas is no enemy of reason in that narrow sense of 'reason*ing*' he is equally clear that you cannot get the role of reason in theology right, even in that limited employment of it which is ratiocination, until you place it within a far wider understanding of what it is for a human being to be a 'rational animal' than any which might be deduced exclusively from a 'rationality' so minimally conceived.

Now though Thomas doesn't quite put it this way himself, I want to suggest that you get the hang of the full-blooded thing that he means by 'rational animal' if you can see how it is that of all the activities in which human beings engage, it is music-making which best exemplifies how animals can be rational, that is to say, 'human'; and I will first say a few things by way of explanation of that. Then I will say that you can see why this should be so in his theology of the Eucharist. There you can grasp a sort of ideal-type of what 'rationality' means to Thomas Aquinas, and that 'reason', in that sense in which music is typically 'rational', has a sort of eucharistic, or perhaps more broadly a sacramental, 'shape', epistemologically speaking. And then I shall say that a proof of the existence of God is just a case of reason in its minimal expression as 'ratiocination' fulfilling itself in the same sort of epistemological shape that music and the Eucharist have. But *all* of them, poetry, music and proof, belong with what Thomas means by 'reason' in its most general, and fundamental, sense, the 'maximal' sense, as I shall call it.

The bodily basis of meaning

To understand this maximal sense the first step is to begin where Thomas does, placing us humans where we belong in the big scheme of things, that is to say, with the proposition that we humans are generically animals. Therefore, whatever we humans do we do as animals do it.[8] If we love, we love as animals do, and if my cat cannot reciprocate

---

8 Thomas does not suppose that our being animals is *part* of what we humans are. It is the *whole* of what we humans are, our difference from the brute animals being included 'indeterminately' in our generic animality. We are, therefore, wholly animals of a certain kind . . . *quidquid est in specie, est etiam in genere ut non determinatum. Si enim animal non esset totum quod est homo, sed pars eius,*

on equal terms the affection I bestow upon it this is not because she is an animal and I am not, it is because I am, and she is not, a *rational* animal. If we suffer, we suffer as animals do; if I know and love God, then I know and love God as only an animal can, and if my cat cannot know and love God this again is not because my cat is an animal and I am not but because the cat is a different sort of animal from me. So, from one point of view my animality contrasts with a brute animal's in that mine is rational and the brute's is not. But for Thomas my rationality places my nature in another point of contrast, namely with angels. For it is only an animal that can be rational. Angels know many more things than humans do, but are not rational, God knows everything knowable, but not as humans do, not rationally. When it comes to how to know things, animals, and only animals, do it by the rational means of 'thinking': angels do not know by 'thinking', neither does God. Only animals think. And only animals speak, and that, as one of Thomas's earliest followers, Dante Alighieri, says, is what it is to be human, or, as he puts it, all forms of failure to be human are in some way, or show up in, failures of language.[9]

Another way of 'placing' human beings is to say that only rational animals have meaningful bodies,[10] bodies which bear and transact meanings, bodies which 'speak'. If you have a problem with my saying this, think about how a smile speaks,[11] and since I happen to have mentioned Dante already, think of how Beatrice's smile in *Paradiso* speaks to him. Or just consider how 'a man may smile, and smile, and be a villain', his smile saying one thing, his villainy another. Or think of the complexity of communication contained in that other famously ironic act which speaks, the kiss of Judas, that greeting of friends whereby he betrays Jesus: 'do you betray the Son of Man with a kiss?' says Jesus, protesting at a cruel irony. If you have a *problem* with how a smile or a kiss or a laugh can speak, thinking them to be somehow more *material* than formal language, do not be misled: for you will not find it

---

non praedicaretur de eo, cum nulla pars integralis de suo toto praedicetur. De Ente et Essentia, cap. II.

9 *De Vulgari Eloquentia*, I.ii, ed. and trans. Steven Botterill (Cambridge: Cambridge University Press, 1999), pp. 5–7.

10 Thomas does not suppose either that our being rational is part of what we humans are. It is the whole of what we are as being just that kind of animal. Hence, insofar as our being animals implies that we have bodies, our being rational implies that we have bodies which are included within our natures as rational ... *Sic ergo genus significant indeterminate totum id quod est in specie, non enim significant tantum materiam; similiter etiam differentia significant totum et non significant tantum formam. De Ente et Essentia*, cap. II.

11 I am much indebted in what follows to Vittorio Montemaggi for many informative conversations on the subject of Dante, meaning and the body.

any easier to explain how formal speech speaks, conveys meaning. For how less material than gestures are written squiggles bearing meaning? How are the vibrations of the larynx any less material than the *rictus* of the lips, either being expressive, sometimes, of the most profound thoughts? You may have a general problem about how meanings get into matter at all, but if that is so your problem about meaning and formal language is no more nor less difficult of solution than how it is that a smile, or a kiss, or a laugh can be the bearer of ironies. All are bits of body which *say* things. Explain the one if you can: but only by such means as explain both.

Such, at any rate, is the view of Thomas Aquinas: a rational animal is a meaning-bearing, a sign-conveying, lump of organized sensuous matter, and we call those human bits of matter 'bodies' because they are matter alive with that sort of life which consists in the transactions of meaning – they are alive precisely as communicating, and their quality of life is in the quality of their communicatings. A rational animal is speaking matter, it is a body in its character *as language*. So back to language, and to help us out there, back to Judas's kiss. You can grasp the terrible irony of that kiss because you grasp how its twofold meanings contradict one another: what Judas's kiss says as conventional sign – the greeting of friends – is subverted by what is said by his doing it – betraying his saviour and lord. It's not of course a unique case: think of the performatively contradictory behaviour of the parent who smacks their child in order to teach it not to solve problems by means of violence. I smack to correct a misbehaviour: but the same smack itself unsays the correction. So that is step one: utterances perform something, we say, or, as we might add, signs 'effect', as to say the words 'I promise' *is* to promise. But also performances utter, that is to say, the very materiality of the signifier itself can bear its own meaning. That is part of what is meant by saying that humans are rational – in Thomas's sense – namely that human bodies signify, or rather, some matter is a *human* body precisely if it signifies. You might say that brute animal bodies signal things, but don't signify. Angels don't have bodies *and so* as Dante says, if they transact meanings, it is not by means of language that they do so, which is the same as to say that they are not rational. And that is step two.

To take step three, consider poetry. Herbert McCabe once said that 'poetry is language trying to be bodily experience',[12] and that seems right, except for the 'trying to be'. Poetic meanings work through a

---

12 'The Eucharist as Language' in Sarah Beckwith (ed.), *Catholicism and Catholicity: Eucharistic Communities in Historical and Contemporary Perspectives* (Oxford: Blackwell, 1999), p. 26.

complex set of transactions between what is conveyed by the meaning
of the words considered as formal speech, and what is conveyed by
the signifier in its material, physical character as shape on the page,
or as sound uttered. Think of the difference inflection makes between
saying 'Emma Kirkby is not just a pretty *voice*' and 'Emma Kirkby is
not just a *pretty* voice' – here it is the words' music, inflection, which
delivers the difference of meaning, not the words as verbal signs, for
they are in either case identical. Poetry is the meal made of such material tonal devices in a sort of contrapuntal interweaving of verbal and
tonal meanings. As Oliver Davies puts it, in poetry the signifier itself
is 'foregrounded'[13] so that the work of meaning is carried not alone by
the formal meanings of the words but also by that meaning which is
conveyed by the material, aural, qualities of the speech-acts themselves,
the rhythmic speech-patterns, assonance, inflection, and so forth, these
two in their contrapuntal interplay. That is poetry *being* bodily experience. It doesn't have to 'try' to be one – in fact it might have been better
if Herbert had said that it is *music* that poetry is 'trying to be'.

Which is to the point. For then McCabe added: 'and music is bodily
experience trying to be language',[14] which again seems right, except for
the 'trying to be'. For if in poetry there is a contrapuntal weaving of the
verbally signified with the signifier itself, in whose materiality of being
uttered there is also an utterance, in music the signifier in its materiality
is so absolutely 'foregrounded' that all is reduced to it, with nothing left
to it in the character of verbal language at all,[15] for music is all rhythm,
pitch, melody, harmony and dissonance. To see the difference between
the verbal and the musical, therefore, think of this: when I say 'The cat
is on the mat' you can attend to the meaning exclusively, so that the
sounds disappear, absorbed entirely into the meaning – you hear the

13 *Meister Eckhart, Mystical Theologian* (London: SPCK, 1991), p. 180.
14 'The Eucharist as Language', p. 26. Dale Martin, of the Department of
Religious Studies at Yale, objected when I read this paper there that what I say
hereafter about 'music' is too 'essentialist', as if to say that was just some one set of
characteristics possessed of all music in all times and cultures, which he doubted.
It is true that what I say about music here is based upon reflection on a certain
classical paradigm in the Western tradition, perhaps, say, the late string quartets
of Beethoven or Schubert, and possibly my account of music would not be true
of other times, cultures and traditions. I do not for my part know. In any case I
am happy to allow a mental reservation on the part of any reader who doubts the
universal applicability of what I say about music here: it will make no difference at
all to my argument if anyone chooses to do so.
15 Though she should not be held responsible for what I have drawn from
them here, the following remarks about music and language owe much to discussions with Férdia Stone-Davis as also to her unpublished paper, 'Plato, Kant and
the Reduction of Music' delivered to the Music Research Group conference on
'The Intellectual Frontiers of Music' at the University of Aberdeen, June 2002.

sounds as something said, as *words*; or you can, if you try hard enough, attend to the mere noise of the utterance, the meaning disappearing into it – you hear the words simply as sounds. But either way there is a distinction between the formal meaning of the words as words, and the performance of the words as sounds, there is a 'surplus' physicality of sound which you can identify separately from the verbal meaning. And even in poetry, the most nearly musical of all the verbal arts, the musicality of the sound can work its effect only in conjunction with that formal verbal meaning. But in music you cannot make any such distinction, nor ought you to try. Music has no *verbal* meaning at all. What you hear is what you get, meaning as sound, sound as meaning. In music there is no surplus either of physicality over and above the signifying sounds themselves or of signification over and above those sounds and their structuring in rhythm, pitch, melody and harmony. So you could say that music is, like the Cheshire cat, all smile and no cat, because the matter has disappeared into the meaning and the meaning has disappeared into the matter. Music is matter entirely alive with meaning, the most bodily, and at the same time the most formal of human communications. And that is why I suggested that if you were Thomas you might say (though of course he did not say it) that music is the most 'rational' of human activities, for in music physicality and meaning, body and language, have become perfectly identified. Music is sound and fury signifying nothing that the sound and fury themselves do not signify. Music is all body but precisely as language. It is body entirely transparent to meaning. It is animality in its most transparent form as rationality. And that was step four.

And now that I have got Thomas to take you about as far as is possible from what you thought he meant when I first used the word 'rational' in this lecture, I can begin to explain what might truly be at stake when he talks about a 'rational' knowledge of God. There is a fifth important step needed yet, but on the way could I point you in the right direction by hazarding a speculation: it is that the nearest you can get to a sort of spontaneous and demotic 'natural theology', to a sort of pre-theological anticipation of theology, is in poetry and in music, but especially in music. And if this is so, perhaps it is because of those paradoxical conjunctions of music's being closest to us in its intense physicality and yet wholly open as to its significance, so very indeterminate, so lacking in particular *reference*, so purely *formal*: and for that reason it opens up spaces of experience beyond our particularity, beyond our confined individuality. Ancients did not think, as we do now, of some music as sacred and some secular. They thought music was sacred as such, and whatever the reasons of the ancients I think we moderns too intuitively experience in music a natural capacity for the transcendent, we can see it as a sort of 'natural' theurgy. And if that is so, it would appear to have to do with the fact that music's very impersonality and 'otherness' is what allows for such a free, spontaneous, and utterly personal response. To paraphrase Nietzsche, music is all feeling, but as subjectively and objectively 'unhooked':[16] subjectively unhooked, because it's no one's sadness or joy; and objectively unhooked, because its sadness or joy is not about anything in particular, it is feeling as *anyone's*, feeling which is absolutely self-less, so it can be absolutely yours as well as absolutely mine, but always transcending us both, moving experience into a space free of the constative.[17] And perhaps that is why music is the most commonly experienced form of what the medievals called an *excessus*, or in Greek, *ekstasis*, or in English, 'taking leave of your senses': but in music, by the most sensual, most bodily, of means.

Music, Eucharist and the sacramental quality of reason

Which brings us to step five. And this is that music is, as I put it, 'prototypically Eucharistic'. And maybe by now you have caught hold of the connective tissue of thoughts, the formal similarity of thought-structure: for on Thomas's account, in the Eucharist is brought to the absolute limit possible before our resurrection that same conjunction of absolute bodiliness and absolute transparency of meaning, for the Eucharist is a communication of the Word which is all body, and a body which is all communication, all word, all sign, an identity of message and its medium.[18] Or, and this is just another way Thomas has of putting the same, in the Eucharist there is nothing left of the bread and wine's materiality but only their character as *signs*, all smile and no cat again.

---

16 *The Birth of Tragedy*, ed. Raymond Geuss and Ronald Speirs, trans. Ronald Speirs (Cambridge: Cambridge University Press, 2000), p. 37.

17 Férdia Stone-Davis objects that the cat is not entirely absent from music, whether as 'subject' or as 'object'. There is a gap between the music as written score and the actual performance of it by the players on the one side; and there is likewise a gap between the performance and its reception by a hearer on the other side, and these gaps are filled by the individualities of the performers and listeners: at those two points the cat comes back into it. And this is true, though it is not clear to me that anything in what I say about music here entails the denial of it; for it remains the case that even if Beethoven's Eroica symphony exists only as performed, and thus as performed and heard by individuals, the Eroica retains its identity as Beethoven's E flat symphony independently of particular performances: for the E flat symphony is what those performances are performances of. And as to those performances, it is true of each of them that 'what you hear is what you get'. The players and the hearers still do not 'come into' the music in the way that Beatrice 'comes into' her smile to Dante, where its being Beatrice's smile is intrinsic to the smile's identity and meaning.

18 Once again, I am grateful to Donna Lazenby for this way of putting it.

There is, as he rather unhelpfully puts it, a 'transubstantiation' – signs that make 'real' a 'presence' of Christ's body which pushes to the very limits any force we can lay hold of for the words 'real' and 'presence'. And then we have to add, 'and beyond such limits'. For the doctrine of the 'real presence' of Christ in the Eucharist is, in Thomas, also a doctrine of the 'real absence'. We might say that it is in his teaching on the Eucharist that we find Thomas's last word on ontology, about what is most 'real'. That ontology tells us that his paradigm of 'the real' is the presence of Christ in the Eucharist, a bodily presence which is total communication, all word, but just for that the more intensely bodily, not less. So, on the one hand, no body could be more present, nor more bodily, than Christ's body as present in the Eucharist. For no body could be more purely language, Word.

But if that is so, then, on the other hand, it is a word which is also beyond all understanding: for its intrinsic transparency of meaning must remain opaquely mysterious to us because our bodies are 'opaque' receivers of the mystery, are not yet themselves totally communicative, for our bodies, like formal speech, retain a surplus of unmeaningful materiality over and above their capacities for meaning. And that is because, unlike Jesus' body, ours are not yet raised. Jesus' body is wholly present to us because his is raised. But it is experienced in our bodies as absence because in our present historical contingency ours are not. Hence, what the Eucharist makes 'real' is both the 'now' of presence and the 'not yet' of absence, and it is just that *conjunction* of presence and absence which is made 'real', for the Eucharistic presence is caught up into an 'eschatological', not a merely 'linear', temporality. Thomas's ontology, then, his account of 'the real' is essentially 'sacramental', because essentially eschatological, inscribing in the body in its present condition an openness to a future which is not yet. The Eucharist is, then, an uncompleted eschatology realized as bodily exchange: the bread and wine *become* that body, a body which is all communication, the flesh made most perfectly to be Word, *futurae gloriae nobis pignus datur*, as Thomas says in one of his Eucharistic antiphons, a 'pledge given to us of future glory'.

It is in all these respects that music both shows us what is central to 'reason' and in doing so shows how reason is 'proto-typically Eucharistic' – at any rate we could mean that much by 'reason' if we did not simply abase ourselves before the altar of that recent intellectual history which has reduced 'reason' to 'ratiocination'. If music is a kind of spontaneous natural theology, it is because it is a kind of spontaneous natural eschatology. Which is why it is, I think, that all great music, it does not matter whether in mood it is happy or sad, is in a certain way which is characteristic of it *as* music, always sad. Music is the *lachry-*

mae rerum, the world's tears, its recollection of what cannot yet be. At any rate, whether it is that weird and terrible Trio of the Schubert string quintet, or the hushed moment of reconciliation of the finale of *The Marriage of Figaro* – whichever it is at one end or the other of the emotional spectrum, or wherever between – *all* music makes you cry. And I think it does so because music is in a way a shadow cast onto human sensibility of that eschatological temporality of the Eucharist, the sadness of music is a sort of sensual nostalgia for what one has caught some glimpse of but cannot yet possess, it is as it were a premonition of a premonition, it is a shadow of the Augustinian *anamnesis*, a depth dug into memory, scoring it with a sort of hope made real, but as loss and as absent, made present, but as yet to be real, our homeland glimpsed, but as yet from a distance.

But if that is what is meant by 'reason' in its 'maximal', as also its most fundamental, sense – it is our animality as being itself the quasi-sacramental bearer of that self-transcendent significance – then we take our final step to the conclusion, namely that that too is the shape which must be possessed by that very particular exercise of reason, which I have been trying so hard till now to get you *not* to reduce reason to, that 'minimal' sense which consists in ratiocination, in inference, argument and in proof. Reason for Thomas is always bound to end up with God, so why not that minimal form of it which is ratiocination too? For reason in that sense of 'reasoning' gives names to things, it names all that which music, through its very indeterminacy, its refusal of any 'constative' character, can gesture towards but does not and cannot name, because 'naming' is precisely what music refuses to do. But if reason, in this form as reasoning, names – it has to, because that is just what *it* does – it does so also in the shadow of music's inarticulateness and indeterminacy, in the shadow of its apophaticism. For if reason ever dares name the name 'God', it may do so only as that which finally defeats its powers: naming God is reason's supreme achievement but only insofar as in doing so it knows that what it so names escapes from under the naming, dodges all the arrows of naming that reason can fire at it. And that, as Thomas says, is *quod omnes dicunt Deum*, naming stretched out to the end of its tether until its tether snaps. In God reason reaches the point of collapse, because over-weighted with significance. And now when Thomas says this '*omnes*' I think we can with greater confidence agree on that 'all': Christians, Muslims and Jews, but just as well as those atheists it would be worthwhile having around to do their denying, engaging through their *oppositio* in an *eadem scientia*.

I have no intention of taking you through, still less of defending in point of formal validity, those famous and much derided 'five ways' of Thomas Aquinas. I simply ask you to note the 'argument-strategy' by which they work, for it has, as music has, the shape of the sacramental, the form of the body's transparency to the mystery we call 'God'. It is the same ontology at work. It is only through our bodies' intimacy to the world's materiality that we achieve that glimpse of its ultimate significance which is the unknowable mystery of God. And herein is the paradox of our human rationality, of which, I say, music is the sign. When in *Prima pars*, Question 2, Article 3 of the *Summa Theologiae*, Thomas tells us that we can, by these five ploys of inference, prove the existence of God, he notes immediately afterwards in Question 3 that what proves God to exist also proves that, as of God we have finally lost our grip on the meaning of 'exists' itself, so in proving God to exist we push reason beyond the point of exhaustion. And so it is that by means of rational inference we do in a merely speculative way what the Eucharist draws us into the very life of. Reason gets you to where unnameable mystery begins but stands on this side of it, gesturing towards what it cannot know, and there it is self-emptied, 'kenotically' as we might say. It is stunned into a sort of babble at the shock of its final defeat – this reduction to babble, by the way, being what is otherwise called 'theology'. But by the Eucharist we are drawn into that same mystery as into our very, and oh so very *carnal*, life, so that we live by the mystery, we eat it; though the mystery is no more comprehensible, as Thomas says, for being eaten than it is for being thought. For he tells us that we do not resolve the mystery by faith as if it were some conundrum that reason could not solve, to which faith on the other hand held the solution; for we do not know what God is, even by the revelation of grace: by grace, he says, we are indeed truly made one with God so as to share in the divine life, but as to one who is unknown to us, *quasi ei ignoto coniungamur.*[19]

Conclusion: faith affirms reason's autonomy

So there you have it: that, I think, is how animals know God whether by reason or by faith, at any rate according to Thomas. Put at its simplest, his position is formally that of the Vatican I decree, that there are grounds of faith for affirming reason's autonomy, that it can, of its own resources, know God. Reading Thomas alerts us not to confuse his baby of reason with the bath-water of rationalism. If unalerted you do confuse them, you will have all sorts of unnecessary and theologically damaging 'zero-sum' problems, trading off faith and reason against one another – at any rate, that is what Thomas seems to say.

---

19 *Summa Theologiae* Ia Q. 12, art. 8 ad 1.

3. Redeeming Personal Truth

LAURENCE PAUL HEMMING

What does it mean that truth is located in a person? What possible connection with philosophy can the biblical verse 'I am the way, and the truth, and the life' have?[1] *Fides et ratio* has, as a major preoccupation, the dissolution of truth in postmodernity, arguing that 'more recent philosophy in its failure to interest itself in "being" has laid all its emphasis on human knowledge. Instead, therefore, of exalting the capacity given to man for recognizing the truth, it has preferred to accentuate his limits and conditions.'[2] I want to try to provide an answer as to how truth may be located in a person, and how that question may find an answer in virtue of a philosophy of *being*, in opening this debate with Stephen Mulhall.

The encyclical argues that the discovery of the truth, and the need to cleave to it, springs from the questions which confront men and women in the unfolding of the magnitudinous things of their existence. From where have I come? Where am I going? What remains to me after this life? These are the questions which in disclosing us to ourselves, also bring before us our relationship to truth: 'man may be defined, therefore, as *the one who seeks the truth*'.[3]

However, the encyclical retains a strong understanding that truth is something which remains, which nags and portends for us even when reflection on it has degenerated into the relativism which John Paul II decries. Thus, says the Holy Father, 'truth disturbs existence'.[4] This moves the document continually to speak of the need for a truth that

---

1 1 John 14.6. Ἐγώ εἰμι ἡ ὁδὸς καὶ ἡ ἀλήθεια καὶ ἡ ζωη

2 John Paul II, *Fides et ratio* in L. P. Hemming (trans.) and S. F. Parsons (eds), *Restoring Faith in Reason* (London: SCM Press, 2002), §5, pp. 10–11. 'Recentior philosophia, omittens suas perquisitiones in ipsum "esse" dirigere, opus suum in cognitionibus hominum collocavit. Non ergo extulit facultatem quae homini data est veritatis cognoscendae, sed extollere eius limites maluit et condiciones.'

3 John Paul II, *Fides et ratio*, §28, pp. 48–9. 'Homo igitur definiri potest *ille qui veritatem quaeritat.*' Emphasis in original.

4 John Paul II, *Fides et ratio*, §28, pp. 48–9. '[Veritas] existentiam permovet.'

34

is certain and absolute. The search itself culminates in a truth of an absolute kind.[5]

If one thing above all has marked the transition to postmodernity it is the dissolution of truth as a foundation, as a ground. Truth has, especially since the rationalism of the Enlightenment, been understood as a *ground* or basis for the things that are true, and so therefore something like a *value* or a determination of correctness. Taking too much for granted the claims of the ancients that truth and falsity are essentially properties of what is said,[6] and therefore of propositions, much contemporary philosophy has either been preoccupied with the evaluation of language as such with respect to truth, or with deconstructing any attempt to infer truth from the meaning of what is said. With the dissolution of this understanding in postmodernity, nothing seems to have a universal ground or value, and so truth is no longer understood as *ground*. As the encyclical notes, 'as a consequence of the crisis of rationalism, something akin to *nihilism* has appeared'.[7]

It is important not to be seduced by this analysis, however. For the advent of the kind of nihilism described has resulted in a most curious state of affairs. With the appearance of this nihilism, the sky has not fallen in, the earth has not been shaken to its roots, an abyss has not, apparently, opened up before us. In postmodernity and in the context of this nihilism, truth does not disappear, but it becomes an essentially private affair. Essentially well-intentioned people in the contemporary situation can believe themselves to be living a good or moral life, while not acknowledging that goodness or morality to extend beyond the domain of their immediate, personal, or domestic arrangements. Contemporary concerns for otherness, for 'difference in the social sphere' mean that many believe that far from having a duty to proclaim a wider understanding of truth, they have no right to do so.

Rationalism itself has not collapsed, but rather been relativized to the technical sphere. If truth is no longer a value, this is to some extent because we are living under a tyranny of value as such, where value no longer has to be true, it simply has to be calculable in the favour of some particular group. How else do you explain what it is to live in a society that is at one and the same time driven by efficiency, and by the desire for margins of return on share-capital? If this all sounds very abstract, try travelling on the tube in London – the inherent conflicts of the need to move people around efficiently with the need to make a

---

5 Cf. John Paul II, *Fides et ratio*, §33, pp. 54–5.

6 Cf. Aristotle, *De anima*, III, 430 b 27ff. ἔστι δ᾽ ἡ μὲν φάσις τι κατά τινος, ὥσπερ ἡ κατάφασις, καὶ ἀληθὴς ἢ ψευδὴς πᾶσα.

7 John Paul II, *Fides et ratio*, §46. 'Veluti consequens discriminis rationalismi tandem *nihilismus* crevit.' Emphasis in original.

profit out of doing so manifests itself in an organization characterized by *in*efficiency, *under*investment and constant breakdowns.

We find ourselves in fact increasingly instrumentalized to the onslaught of a set of technical-financial processes which do not obliterate whatever deviates from them, but rather relativize and depotentiate everything whose value cannot be calculated with respect to the master processes of power itself. It is in this context that, for instance, the then Secretary of State for Education for the British Government, the parliamentarian Charles Clarke was able to tell us in a recent Government consultation paper on education that the purpose of universities is to 'to help turn ideas into successful businesses'.[8] Thus in the midst of being enjoined to live, as one supermarket advertisement recently put it, the 'Asda way of life' – which means a way of life having at its roots the economic interests and drive for profit of one of the largest global retailing conglomerates, Wal-Mart (owners of Asda), there is also room for other ways of life, but they will always be adjunct (if indeed they survive at all, and if they don't, it does not matter) to the sheer power of the onslaught itself. Power, in this sense, orders, and that means re-orders, everything to its own immediate drives and requirements.

However, even in this supposed crisis of rationalism, rationalism itself overlooked and forgot an essential feature of truth that was at one time taken for granted. Truth and the true is also that which gives order and assembles what it orders in such a way that at the same time as what is true *in particular* appears, so the *whole* is able to be understood. The original meaning of the word κόσμος is not 'universe', the whole, but *order*. The Cosmos is the *means by which* the whole, the universal, is able to appear and so be understood alongside and at the same time as the particular. It is for this reason that the moral may be said to be true – as that which in a particular person's actions and deliberations nevertheless is ordered to the whole, the whole of the social.

And already we can see something that the encyclical takes some pains to trace, something that we also are required to understand, that philosophy, and therefore the understanding of what truth itself is, has a history, a trajectory which unfolds over time. Yet the encyclical also relies on a second understanding: namely, that not only is there a history to the understanding of truth, but that very history is to some extent a history of the transformations which have resulted in – not a progress towards highest or best truth – but truth's occlusion. Thus in the face of the flight from truth in the contemporary situation, truth

---

8 Secretary of State for Education and Skills, White Paper *Higher Education Funding* (London, January 2003), http://www.dfes.gov.uk/highereducation/hestrategy/pdfs/DfES-HigherEducation.pdf, §1, p. 2.

continues to disturb. For what is at issue here is not a simple narrative, an unfolding of a story that can be told, but rather the existential consequences of our less and less being able to tell what truth is, while at the same time living with its persisting effects. This being able to 'tell what truth is' I mean in a double sense – to tell it, to speak it, to connect it with speaking or what the Greeks knew as λόγος at all, and at the same time to recognize it. Here we return to a question I cannot even consider in the short space available – how was it that truth came to be a property of propositions, of what is *said*?

And here has been the dilemma for contemporary philosophers and contemporary theologians. The question has several times been posed: why should a voice that essentially springs out of *faith*, the voice of the Pope, be a voice that calls philosophers to a reconsideration of their discipline? What can this mean – and is there not even something inappropriate here? Moreover, one philosopher above all, Martin Heidegger, has with a relentless rigour argued across almost the whole span of his vast out-giving that the present situation of decline with regard to truth is a direct result of the Christianization of philosophy.

This chapter traces precisely that Christianization in some of its most critical moments – a process that took multiple forms and two thousand years to complete. At its simplest, one could say that Christian Neoplatonism transformed the unity of being that is the central concern of Greek philosophy – of Parmenides, Heraclitus, Plato and Aristotle – and ascribed the unity of being to the *Christian*, monotheist,[9] simplicity of God. This unity is not only a cause in the Greek sense (something posited, a dependency, a 'first cause' in the sense of the 'first in being' and 'most potent' and so 'highest') but also originating, a 'first cause' which is temporally prior to every other cause and which makes all other causes possible. As a *prior* first cause it is also a purposive cause, one which decides in advance that everything it does is a 'good' in itself and so *morally* good. The Christian Neoplatonic first cause is also the best, most purposive, and so most highly moral, cause.

Greek thought held the unity of being to be divine in the abstract sense, because this implicit unity is the completedness and the fulfilment of the cosmos. 'Divine' here functions as an adjective – it is the perfection and finality to which the gods had themselves pointed and made visible. Being, and the truth of being, is at the same time (abstractly) divine. However, the Christianization of philosophy has the result that the Divine (as noun) is the unity of being, a first and originating cause that *decides* and so *wills* all that there *is*, and so *produces* everything

---

9 Here we should also understand the influences of the Islamic and Jewish metaphysicians, especially of the Baghdad schools and the Iberian Caliphate.

extant and present. This cause is the highest, culminating, and originating presence (beingfulness) of everything that *is*, that *could be*, and (above all, morally taken) *should* and *ought to* be. The Divine, as the truth of being, is at the same time (not abstractly, but personally) 'being' in the fullest, highest, most (morally) proper sense.

The effects of this Christianization are, for Heidegger especially, far-reaching. Even when the *person* of this divine unity of the truth of being is declared to be dead (after Nietzsche), it continues to exercise its effect negatively, as an absence, a melancholy, a demand that it be reproduced and reasserted. Heidegger's savage critique of political liberalism and ethics understands contemporary so-called atheistic liberalism to be *exactly* this melancholy, as the last gasp of the moral imperatives of the theistic age. As a last gasp this is no weakening exhalation of one in the throes of death, but the diabolical and infernal gasp with the strength of an all-consuming furnace, in a totalizing demand of the will to power.[10]

Contemporary theologians have increasingly fallen into the trap set them by our age, that in the face of what they have perceived to be the demise of truth in philosophical discourse there has been an urgent demand to reassert its claims, often with an only partial understanding of what that means.

It would be in this context that we would have to understand the attempt by John Milbank and Catherine Pickstock to rehabilitate the *adaequatio* understanding of truth in their recent work *Truth in Aquinas* – an attempt to drive truth back into being. We should begin therefore, by recalling that the *adaequatio* is actually a formula, not a demonstration in and of itself. St Thomas provides the formula that 'truth is the adequation of thing and intellect'.[11]

Heidegger notes that the correspondence definition does not mean in

---

10 M. Heidegger, *Beiträge zur Philosophie (vom Ereignis)* in *Gesamtausgabe*, vol. 65 (Frankfurt: Klostermann, 1989), pp. 24f. 'Diese gegenchristliche "Weltanschauung" ist nur *scheinbar* unchristlich; denn sie kommt im *Wesentlichen* dennoch überein mit jener Denkart, die den "Liberalismus" kennzeichnet.' ('This anti-Christian "worldview" is only *apparently* unchristian, for it is *essentially* in agreement with that way of thinking which is known as "Liberalism".') See also pp. 118f., §13 for the full effects of this 'flight of the gods' and 'death of the moral, Christian, God'.

11 Aquinas, *Quaestiones disputatae: De Veritate*, Q. 1, art. 1, resp. 'veritas est adaequatio rei et intellectus'. This is also how St Thomas defines it in the *Commentary on the Sentences*, where he speaks of the 'relatio adaeqautionis, in qua consistit ratio veritatis' (*In I Sent.* Disp. 19, art. 5, resp.; cf. Disp. 40, art. 3 resp. and *In IV Sent.* Disp. 46, Q. 1, resp.) and in the *Summa contra Gentiles* (Book 1, ch. 59, no. 2) as well as the *Summa Theologiae* (Ia, Q. 16, art. 1, resp.). The formula is attributed by Aquinas to Isaac, although it is more likely that its origin is in fact Avicenna.

its mediaeval form what it comes to mean in Kant, that objects conform to our knowledge, but rather 'it implies the Christian theological belief that, with respect to what it is and whether it is, a matter, as created (*ens creatum*), is only insofar as it corresponds to the idea preconceived in the *intellectus divinus*, i.e. in the mind of God, and thus measures up to the idea (is correct) and in this sense is "true"'.[12]

Heidegger argues that the full explication of the 'correspondence' definition found in Aquinas's *Quaestiones disputatae* is that the truth of created things, having been already intended and made (literally created) to correspond to the ideas in the divine intellect, thereby supplies a guarantee for the correctness of the correspondence of things to the human intellect. In this sense, truth in the human intellect becomes a kind of passive faculty, which can always rely on the correctness of what it knows because what it knows has been intended to be so known by one no less than God himself. Heidegger's point, therefore, is that Aquinas's understanding of truth has an explicitly theological resolution, and moreover, works within the understanding of being that Heidegger sees as flowing from the createdness of all things (beings) in God.

However, we can see that the *adaequatio* formula is *one* attempt to resolve the question I posed at the beginning of this chapter, in the sense that it answers the question of how truth is located in a person. This person is, however, the mind of God. This answer is achieved, therefore, by fusing together a certain kind of philosophical enquiry into truth with belief in revelation, in whom God is. It is for this reason that God as the *creator omnium*, the creator of all things, is an essential part of the adequation formula. Such a God, however, is no longer taken to be self-evident: indeed it is precisely this God, God as *ground*, whom Nietzsche observed had been declared to be dead. Every attempt to resuscitate such a god is undertaken in the teeth of the very trajectory I named earlier. But the trajectory does not begin with the *adaequatio* formula, rather this formula appears in its midst. Truth is not resolved philosophically at all with regard to the being of the Christian God until, at the earliest, Philoponus.[13] How is this done? Precisely because

---

12 M. Heidegger, *Vom Wesen der Wahrheit* in *Wegmarken* (GA9), p. 180. 'Sondern [meint] den christlich theologischen Glauben, daß die Sachen in dem, was sie sind und ob sie sind, nur sind, sofern sie als je erschaffene (ens creatum) der im intellectus divinus, d.h. in dem Geiste Gottes, vorgedachten idea entsprechen und somit idee-gerecht (richtig) und in diesem Sinne "wahr" sind.'

13 Especially in his commentaries on the works of Aristotle and against the interpretations of Proclus. Cf. esp. the translation by Wildberg, C., of Philoponus's *Against Aristotle, On The Eternity Of The World* (Ithaca: Cornell University Press, 1987). For an extended discussion of the very different ways in which Philoponus interprets φύσις, see H. Lang, 'Aristotle and Philoponus on Things That Are

of the fusing together of the divine in Greek thought as the unmoved, the ἀεί ὄν, the ever-same, with the God of Christian revelation. It is this that Heidegger means by 'ontotheology', both when he first coined the term in relation to Hegel in 1930, and later. Precisely because the Greeks assigned the working out of truth to being as the unmoved, and because Christians took for granted that God and being were the same (because God is to be understood as the origin of the being of all things) so the ground of truth is assigned to being-as-God.

The very trajectory we have identified – what became at a moment in the West a fusing together of theological and philosophical concerns, has at the same time prepared for their very prizing apart. Heidegger's valiant attempt to undertake that prizing apart in the wake of Nietzsche's proclamation of the death of God, God taken as ground, is named by Heidegger as the 'Überwindung' or fulfilment and overcoming of metaphysics. It is in this respect that we have to understand Heidegger's declaration that philosophical research is and remains atheistic. Heidegger believed that because the thought that God as the ground of all things, and so of truth, has *collapsed* and become untenable – precisely this – permits philosophy to return to the question of the origins of what truth is all over again. In this sense we are called, not to resist and decry the demands and claims of our own age, but to be acutely and humbly sensitive to what they are. Simply railing against relativism (which after all is only the cheapened and popular effects of this prizing apart coupled with the absolute ubiquity and supposed self-evidence of all the technical-economic drives that mask our understanding of it) will not do. Nor will attempts to reassert earlier formulations because they are congenial to us or supposedly repair the 'damage' of nihilism. Nihilism has something important to tell us – it is the very persisting and disturbing of that occlusion of truth and occlusion of being that John Paul II names and with which we began.

If John Paul II has urged us to develop an understanding of truth from out of a philosophy of being, and if on the other hand the contemporary situation with regard to truth represents the splitting apart of a philosophical understanding of truth from a theological understanding of God as the creator of all things, how are we to proceed? One other way to ask this question is to ask: To what being in its being should truth be assigned?

Let me first indicate what the dogmatic consequences are for not undertaking the separation of philosophy from theology. Sir Isaac Newton added to the third edition of the *Principia Mathematica* the

---

by Nature' in H. Lang, *Aristotle's Physics and Its Medieval Varieties* (New York: SUNY, 1992), pp. 97–124.

'General Scholium' where he discusses the relationship of God to the system of the universe. Newton says: 'This most elegant system of the sun, planets and comets could not have arisen without the design and dominion of an intelligent and powerful being . . . He rules all things, not as the world soul, but as the Lord of all.'[14] Newton's understanding of the workings of the universe is derived from out of, and drives, an understanding of God as the originating creator of all things. Newton believed, in other words, that it was possible to demonstrate the existence of the Christian God from the workings of the universe – indeed a little later in the same passage he cites some of the divine names as they arise and were worked out in scholasticism: 'The supreme God is an eternal, infinite, and absolutely perfect being.'[15] This perfect being however *cannot* be perfect unless this perfection finds formal expression, Newton proceeds, 'but a being, however perfect, without dominion is not the Lord God'.[16] Thus for God to be God, there has to be creation, and creation is, conversely, the *proof* that God is God. Creation is the manifest meaning of whom it is God is. In this Newton is simply developing and stressing something we have already found in Aquinas. Newton's collaborator and translator Samuel Clarke, in his Boyle Lectures of 1704, took this argument to its logical conclusion. The lectures were entitled *A Demonstration of the Being and Attributes of God*. Clarke argued in them that atheism was untenable, indeed was a sign of stupidity, of debauchment (that is of immorality) or because of a failure (in the atheist) of the proper use of speculative reasoning.[17] Clarke intended and sought to demonstrate an argument for the existence of God and the foundation of God as both first being and highest truth by the right means of reason that would be *ineluctable*. Newton was famously suspected of Arianism, as was Clarke – indeed Clarke was not given the archbishopric of Canterbury precisely because of this suspicion.

Why is this important? The being that Martin Heidegger makes the locus of truth, the very *essencing* of truth, which means the one who

---

14 I. Newton, ed. and trans. by A. Koyré and I. B. Cohen, *Philosophiae Naturalis Principia Mathematica* (Cambridge: Cambridge University Press, 1972), 2 vols, Vol. 2, pp. 759–60. 'Elegentissima haecce Solis, planetarum & cometarum compages non nisi consilio & domino entis intelligentis & potentis oriri potuit . . . Hic omnia regit non ut anima mundi, sed ut universorum dominus.'

15 Newton, *Principia Mathematica*, p. 760. 'Deus summus est ens aeternum, infinitum, absolute perfectum.'

16 Newton, *Principia Mathematica*, p. 760. 'Sed ens utcunque perfectum sine dominio non est dominus Deus.'

17 S. Clarke and E. Vailati (eds), *A Demonstration of the Being and Attributes of God and Other Writings* (Cambridge: Cambridge University Press, 1998 (1705)), p. 3.

lives in the 'between' of being 'as such' and beings 'in their particulari-
ties' – the human being, is so because this being understands truth as
a self-enquiry. There is not time for me to unfold this in great detail,
but I believe Stephen Mulhall will allude to how it is that Heidegger
unfolds this understanding in his work *Being and Time*, at least in some
of its aspects. It was Heidegger's strongly held view that a philosophy
of being could only arise out of the atheistic self-enquiry that the truth
of the being of being-human is. Only *this* being can have the truth of
its being as an issue for itself, and as a *question* for itself. In this sense
Heidegger was fascinated by the ways in which so much of Aristotle's
thinking, especially in the *Rhetoric*, worked as what he understood as
a phenomenological self-uncovering of the structures of the truth of
the being of being human. Heidegger's phenomenological enquiry into
angst precisely follows this path, as an interpretation of certain moods
of being-human that make it possible to open up the question of truth,
of being, and of time, primordially and originarily, that is without
regard to opinion, but rather as the very revealing of these structures of
being in themselves.

Heidegger's later work nuances this, in that it later became increasingly important to him to show how there is a double movement of
complexity in the disclosure of the truth of the being of being-human
– both truth as the structures of being as they manifest themselves to
us, and the historical place out of which they unfold, so that who *I* am
both in my self-manifesting and as given to be *here*, at this time and in
this place, are in play in unfolding a philosophy of being.

And yet, Heidegger claims, this enquiry into truth is an atheism – the
very thing Clarke declares to be immoral, stupid, and unreasonable.
Clarke and Newton disposed of the meaning of Christ. Christ is just an
exemplary human being – the best form of 'jolly nice chap' of English
Deism. Clarke and Newton overlook the fact that the very divine names
which they cite as exhibiting the *necessary connection* between creation
and the creator – the fulcrum of the proof that God is and is who we
say he is – were originally worked out, not with respect to God the
Father, but *with respect to the second person of the Divine Trinity, the
Christ*. It is the *incarnation* and the disclosure of the meaning of the
incarnation in the sacred three days, the death, descent into hell and
rising again of the man Jesus who is the Christ which demonstrate the
meaning of creation, which provide for the possibility of knowing *who
the Father is*. 'I am the way, and the truth, and the life', because 'no one
comes to the Father but by me' (John 14.6). Thus the divine names arise
from an encounter with Christ, *not* through an enquiry into reason.
In other words the divine names, which arise out of discovering that
Jesus the man is the Christ the Son of the Living God *in faith* cannot be

used to demonstrate an argument *in reason*. Put the other way about, it is only in understanding the truth of being-human, that is to say the ontological relation to truth of Jesus the Man can we discover that this man is the Son of God who can save us – this revealed *truth of faith* is built upon and fulfilled by knowing that Jesus' ontological relation to the truth is the same as our own.

4. Redeeming Truth: A Response to Laurence Paul Hemming

STEPHEN MULHALL

My starting point in this exchange is the same as that of Laurence Hemming; it lies in an attempt to respond to the three questions that he invokes at the beginning of his comments on *Fides et ratio*. What does it mean to claim that truth can be located in a person? What possible connection can there be between the concerns and resources of philosophy and the biblical proclamation 'I am the way, and the truth, and the life'? And how might a philosophy of being provide answers to these questions?

The underlying motivation common to the first two of these questions is, I believe, a widespread sense that the primary home for any conception of truth is that of belief or assertion. It is claims about the world – whether advanced in conversation or simply in thought – that we think of in the first instance as being the bearers of truth (and hence of falsity); whereas the biblical verse quoted above emphasizes that Christianity sees Truth as embodied in Christ – hence, as primarily an attribute of a person rather than of a proposition. Of course, it is not the case that we have a simple opposition here. The 'common sense' idea that truth belongs with propositions would allow us to understand talk of persons as truthful (insofar as they tend to advance true claims about the world, and to do so primarily because they believe them to be true), and even to grasp the idea of living in the truth (insofar as that amounts to putting into practice some range of – perhaps primarily ethical – claims that are themselves true). Similarly, the Christian understanding of Christ as the Truth does not prevent us from talking of Christ's proclamations as themselves truths, and indeed from talking of some human claims as true and others false; but it thinks of the human capacity to discover such truths as itself fundamentally dependent upon our relation to the Being whose very nature and existence constitutes the *fons et origo* of reality, and hence of any possibility of properly aligning ourselves with that reality in thought, speech and existence. The difficulty, then, might be rephrased in the following way: how should we conceive of the relation between propositional and existential truth? Is the latter conception a more or less figurative extension of talk that finds its primary sense in the context of the relationship between thought or language and reality? Or is it propositional truth that is the derivative phenomenon – one which has preoccupied philosophy to such an extent that it has lost any sense of the legitimacy and the priority that in reality attaches to the idea of truth as lived, as a mode or structure of human being?

Our third question picks up a suggestion in *Fides et ratio* that a satisfying resolution of our difficulties here might be found by utilizing the resources of a philosophy of Being. Now patently, many philosophical systems, from Plato's onward through Aquinas to Hegel and beyond, might legitimately be described as 'philosophies of being'; but I will also follow Hemming in focusing my attention on the work of Martin Heidegger – who is, among many other claims to fame, a primary influence on the intellectual formation of the encyclical's author. I will not, however, follow Hemming in approaching Heidegger's answers to these questions primarily through his interpretations of Aristotle; for while Hemming's summary of this highly controversial reading might well alert us to a new understanding of Aristotelian conceptions of language and truth, it risks obscuring the precise lineaments of Heidegger's own conception of truth. This conception – although indebted to his reading of Aristotle among others – is to an equal extent the presupposition of that reading, and is anyway possessed of distinctive complexities and obscurities of its own that might be more helpfully identified through an unmediated interpretation of Heidegger's own analyses of truth.

Accordingly, my approach to our common questions will focus on Heidegger's conception of truth as it is laid out in his first major published work, *Being and Time*.[1] In order, however, to sharpen our sense of the distinctive articulation of that conception, and to see more clearly its relevance to our primary business of grasping the relation between philosophical and religious conceptions of truth, I will begin by sketching in a proximate context for Heidegger's thinking here. That context is, I believe, justified by the series of (admittedly limited but nonetheless undeniably) complimentary remarks Heidegger makes in *Being and Time* about the stimulation his thinking received from his acquaintance with the writings of Søren Kierkegaard. Given those remarks, it seems unlikely to be entirely coincidental that one of Kierkegaard's most influential pseudonymous texts on the relationship between religion

---

1 Trans. Macquarrie and Robinson (Oxford: Blackwell, 1962), hereafter *BT*. References will be keyed to section numbers followed by page numbers.

and philosophy should not only pivot around the question of truth, but more specifically on the hypothesis that the Christian answer to that question is necessarily antithetical to its philosophical counterpart. In effect, then, I am going to suggest that Heidegger's early conception of truth is an implicit riposte to this apparent Kierkegaardian imputation of an abyss between authentically philosophical understandings of truth and truth as understood by Christianity.

Kierkegaard

Johannes Climacus, the pseudonymous author of the *Philosophical Fragments*,[2] begins his text with the following question: How can the truth be learned? Recounting the canonical treatment of this question in the Socratic dialogue the *Meno*, Climacus draws out the underlying paradox. If we don't already know the truth for which we are inquiring, how could we even begin to search for it – what would give our search any orientation? But if we do already know it, then we patently have no need to search for it. Hence, it makes no sense to think that we can ever acquire knowledge of the truth.

Climacus then outlines the Socratic response to this paradox. In its essentials, as conveyed by the way in which Socrates encourages a slave boy to arrive at a geometrical theorem, it amounts to the claim that all learning is in fact recollection. The seeker for truth always already has the truth within him, even if he doesn't know this about himself; if he does not have some particular truth consciously or explicitly to hand, then he is at the least perfectly equipped to recover it. Hence, on the Socratic model, the seeker's teacher is of vanishing significance; he is no more than a midwife to the process of acquiring or recovering truth that the seeker must undergo by himself and on the basis of his own innate capacities, and so his specific identity or personality is entirely irrelevant to the process, and hence to the seeker after truth.

Climacus then asks: is there any alternative, essentially un-Socratic, way of resolving the paradox? Suppose we assume, not that the teacher is of vanishing significance, but rather that he is of indispensable significance. This would involve assuming that in the absence of the teacher, the seeker after truth would not only lack the truth, but would also lack the capacity to discover it; for if he possessed that capacity, then the teacher's role in the process of discovering the truth that the seeker lacks would still be essentially dispensable. Hence, we must assume that the teacher brings with him not only the truth sought for but also

---

2 Trans. H. V. Hong and E. H. Hong (Princeton, NJ: Princeton University Press, 1985).

the condition for uncovering and understanding it. But if the seeker lacks this condition, then he is not just accidentally lacking a truth or a set of truths but is essentially lacking in any orientation towards the truth, any fundamental openness to and directedness towards truth as such; in short, he is existing in untruth. Hence, his encounter with the teacher amounts to a radical reorientation of his capacities, and hence his nature; it amounts to a conversion, or a rebirth, the beginning of a new existence in the truth.

For Climacus, therefore, there are two internally cogent but essentially antithetical ways of responding to the paradox of truth with which he began. The Socratic or philosophical conception of the human relation to truth and its antiSocratic or Christian counterpart amount to one another's negations; and of course, from the point of view that each constructs, the other is fundamentally flawed.

From the Socratic perspective, the Christian hypothesis is offensive to reason and to morality. For it assumes that a genuinely truthful or authentic human existence is possible only in relationship to a particular Teacher; and this means not only that human nature is essentially oriented away from the truth (essentially inauthentic, essentially incapable of flourishing or improving itself) in the absence of that relationship, but also that, since human beings can relate to the Teacher only if he enters human history, which means his being born and living at a particular time and place, those human beings born before him are condemned to existence in untruth through no fault of their own. In short, the Christian hypothesis commits itself to a repellent vision of human beings as originally sinful, standing in need of grace in order to fulfil their own humanity and achieve any genuine relation to the true and the good.

From the Christian perspective, by contrast, the Socratic hypothesis is unaware that its whole conception of human nature as essentially oriented to the truth, and hence capable of relating itself to the true and the good without the aid of any external source, is not only flawed, but is also the articulation of a mode of untruth that its proponents live out in their existence. But of course, they will necessarily lack the resources to understand themselves and their mode of existence in this way until they establish the relationship to the Teacher that will provide those resources, and also provide the means for overcoming their existence in untruth.

If, then, each rival hypothesis can explain and justify its condemnation of the other, how can we rationally determine which is superior without begging the question against one by inhabiting the perspective of its competitor? Is there a perspective other than that constructed by each hypothesis from which such an evaluation might be made? The problem is that, from a wholly external perspective, each hypothesis seems a match for the other. After all, each resolves the initial paradox, and each offers an internally consistent conception of truth in its relation to human being in so doing; hence, neither appears to have a specific weakness or a specific strength on the basis of which one might choose between them from the outside, as it were. Hence, most readers of Kierkegaard are tempted to conclude that the *Philosophical Fragments* presents philosophical and religious conceptions of human existence in relation to the truth as inverted images of one another, between which we must choose (since we cannot accept both hypotheses at the same time), but in a way that is essentially ungrounded in reason – a decision that amounts to a passionate leap.

Heidegger

What I want to argue in this section is that *Being and Time*'s account of truth can usefully be read as inverting Johannes Climacus' conception of the relationship between the Socratic and the Christian conceptions of truth. In so doing, it offers us a way of seeing a logical continuity between the philosophical conception of truth as propositional and the Christian conception of truth as primarily located in a person; more specifically, Heidegger will argue that any adequate understanding of propositional truth will turn out to presuppose a conception of truth as existential.

Truth: from the propositional to the existential

Heidegger's analysis of truth is presented in section 44 of *Being and Time*, at the end of the first division of his analysis of the distinctively human mode of existence (what Heidegger calls his 'existential analytic of Dasein'). He begins from the phenomenon that the philosophical tradition, on his view of it, takes to be central to any understanding of truth – that of truthful judgement about some aspect or other of reality. Heidegger's specific example is of someone judging that 'the picture on the wall is askew'. His first claim is that the truth of this judgement is a matter of its corresponding to the picture itself, and not to any intermediary (whether abstract or mental – perhaps the underlying Form of the object of the judgement, or the idea that the judger has of it); this is why what confirms its truth is our perceiving that the picture really is the way the judgement claims that it is. Hence it is already implicit in the conception of truth as propositional that truthful assertion is in the service of illuminating or clarifying its subject-matter, and hence not so much a matter of relating a human subject to an object, but more a matter of the subject making space for the object, releasing it into the open. And in establishing this claim, Heidegger goes on to indicate one of its consequences:

> To say that an assertion 'is true' signifies that it uncovers the entity as it is in itself. Such an assertion asserts, points out, 'lets' the entity 'be seen' in its uncoveredness. The *Being-true* of the assertion must be understood as *Being-uncovering*. Thus truth has by no means the structure of an agreement between knowing and the object in the sense of a likening of one entity (the subject) to another (the object).
>
> Being-true as Being-uncovering is in turn ontologically possible only on the basis of Being-in-the-world. This latter phenomenon . . . is the *foundation* for the primordial phenomenon of truth. (*BT*, 44: 261)

We might think of Heidegger's line of reasoning here as follows. Before it can be determined whether the picture on the wall truly is askew, we must know what the terms 'picture', 'wall' and 'askew' mean – grasp the elements from which that proposition is constructed. This means grasping what (in reality) counts as a picture and what doesn't, what distinguishes a picture hanging askew from one that hangs level, and so on. Hence the question of the truth of a proposition can only arise against the background of a certain intelligible articulation of reality – what Heidegger calls the structure of discourse. A particular entity can be uncovered as it is in itself only within a particular horizon of disclosure, one which manifests itself in the fundamental categories in terms of which we encounter entities as entities of particular kinds, and indeed as entities (existing independently of our experiences of them) at all. And we cannot intelligibly ask whether these categories are themselves true or false, on pain of an infinite regress; for to regard any such categories as true or false, we must presuppose a background horizon of categories in terms of which that truth or falsity can coherently be judged, and the very same question would arise about that categorical horizon, and so endlessly on.

Hence, any worries we might have about Heidegger's account thus far as threatening a relativized or subjectivized conception of truth and reality are misplaced; for to think of a given horizon of disclosure as merely relative or subjective presupposes not only an idea of alternative such horizons, but also the thought that we can coherently measure the degree to which any one of them corresponds to a reality that exists prior to any and all of them. But anything recognizable as reality must itself be intelligibly articulated, and hence can appear only within a horizon of disclosure; so our original anxiety depends for its appearance of substance upon an incoherent idea of a reality that is no reality in particular. And of course, if it makes no sense to think of any given horizon of disclosure as false or inaccurate to the way things are, it makes no sense either to think of any such horizon as true to the way things are. In other words, the horizon of disclosure is the point at which our concept of propositional truth meets its limits or conditions.

And what are those limits or conditions? Well, Heidegger has already argued in the earlier chapters of *BT*, Division One, that what he calls the disclosing structures of discourse must be understood as an aspect of Dasein's Being-in-the-world – that is, as an articulation of Dasein's openness to entities as entities within the context of a particular environment for practical activity. For example: to be able to apprehend a tool as a tool, Heidegger claims, it must be disclosed as one item in a family of interrelated items (what he calls an equipmental totality), and hence in terms of a network of assignments of significance that relate it to other entities, to other Dasein, and to the tool-user himself. A hammer can be grasped as such only in relation to nails, clamps and saws; that totality of equipment is in turn related to certain kinds of raw material and certain kinds of end-product (say, wood and furniture); and both the tools and the end-product are not only suitable for Dasein to use, but subservient to Dasein's particular practical goals (to have a table to write on, or a chair to sit on, or a house within which to find shelter). Hence, for Heidegger, Dasein's distinctively worldly existence is always lived out within a specific intelligible articulation of reality; it involves Dasein disclosing things and other Dasein not only as comprehensible but also as mattering (as being of value and as posing problems or setting tasks) in specific ways.

To summarize the course of Heidegger's argument thus far: propositional truth entails truth as correspondence; truth as correspondence presupposes truth as uncovering; entities can be uncovered as they are only within a particular horizon of disclosure; and any such horizon of disclosure presupposes the disclosedness of Dasein. If, however, the underlying essence or nature (what Heidegger calls the Being) of propositional truth must ultimately be understood in terms of the Being of Dasein, then the essence of truth is not propositional but existential-ontological – it lies in Dasein's Being as disclosing. In this sense, Dasein can and must be said to exist in the truth; and the traditional conception of truth as propositional must be derivative with respect to this more primordial, existential phenomenon.

Truth: from existence to inauthenticity

If, however, Heidegger can conclude that truth is primarily an aspect of Dasein's Being, then the earlier stages of his existential analytic license a further step in our argument. For according to that earlier analysis, Dasein is the kind of being whose Being can be either authentic or inauthentic; in other words, it can live out its life in ways that manifest its distinctive Being (its capacity to relate comprehendingly and questioningly to the Being of all beings) or it can fail to do so. This is what Heidegger means when he claims that Dasein is the Being for whom Being is an issue. Unlike any other kind of being, Dasein comprehends all the beings it encounters as existing (as opposed to being non-existent) and as having a distinctive nature; but the authentic mode of its understanding is that of questioning – its provisional grasp of an entity's nature only raises further unanswered questions about it, and thereby spurs it to understand it more deeply, and thence to generate further questions to answer, and so unforeseeably on. And of course, one being whose Being is an issue for Dasein is itself, its own Being. In relating to itself, Dasein understands itself in a certain way – as having certain tasks, values, commitments and responsibilities, conceptions of the good and so on – and in its authentic mode, that comprehending grasp of itself is questioning; Dasein thereby grasps that how it should live out its life (and indeed whether it should continue to live at all) is not determined by its nature but is rather a question that its own existence raises for itself, and to which the course of its existence constitutes an implicit answer, for which it is itself responsible, and that might itself be subject to further question, and so on.

But of course, any being for whom a questioning relation to Being is an essential possibility is also one who might fail to realize that possibility; only a being who can question its comprehending grasp of things can also leave its modes of comprehending its world – call this its ways of disclosing that world – entirely unquestioned. And Heidegger believes that the very worldliness of Dasein's Being ensures that, for the most part, Dasein's mode of existence is unquestioning and hence inauthentic. The forms of practical activity we engage in, the things we value, the opinions we espouse – these are aspects of our existence that we endorse and enact simply because we conceive of them as what one does, as what everyone does, as simply what is done. Heidegger calls this a *das Man* mode of existence, one in which our lives are not our own, in which we disown our individual responsibility for what we do and think, as if it were fated or determined. This uncannily impersonal, unquestioning relation to our own existence and that of other Dasein finds expression for Heidegger in a peculiarly unquestioning mode of

disclosure of the things we encounter in our world – a mode he speci-
fies as idle talk and chatter, curiosity and ambiguity. In this mode, our
understanding is uprooted from any careful uncovering of entities as
they are in themselves; instead it is carried away into an endless search
for novelty (whether new experiences and situations or new ways of
grasping old experiences and situations) purely for novelty's sake, a
desire to circulate to others what is said about things by others (rather
than to attend to the things themselves), and a fundamental inability to
distinguish the insightful from the superficial (a loss of any sense that
discourse might be weighty or penetrating, as opposed to unanchored
and empty). In other words, for the most part, Dasein lives not in truth
but in untruth, in flight from its capacity to encounter beings in their
Being.

Truth: from inauthenticity to authenticity

If, then, inauthenticity is Dasein's typical mode of existence, what is
required, on Heidegger's view, for Dasein to wrench itself away from
its own untruth, and hence to make it possible for it to wrench or
snatch entities from their veiledness?

The short answer to this question is striking, particularly in the
present context: the voice of conscience. By this, Heidegger means a
mode of internal or self-addressed discourse in which Dasein discloses
itself to itself as it is in itself. This voice addresses Dasein purely as a
being whose Being is, as Heidegger puts it, 'in each case mine' – that
is, one for whom genuine individuality is a possibility, even if one that
it can lose or repress. Hence it addresses Dasein sole and constantly
in the mode of keeping silent; it asserts nothing, gives no information
about the world and no blueprints for living. It rather holds up every
aspect of Dasein's present existence in the light of its capacity to be
itself, and recalls Dasein to the fact that any given state in which it
finds itself is never all that it is or could be, and so never something
with which it can fully identify or to which it can be reduced. Hence,
the voice of conscience disrupts the inauthentic state of *das Man*, which
might be defined as Dasein's relating to its present state as one to which
there is no alternative, to which one is fated or necessitated (as is everyone else), and hence which is incapable of giving expression to one's
individuality. One might, then, say that, for Heidegger, the voice of
conscience restores Dasein to its necessary non-self-identity, and thereby introduces into his analysis the theme of Dasein's internal relation
to negation and nullity – the theme around which the second Division
of *Being and Time* as a whole is organized.

We don't have the space in this context to explore the further ramifications of that issue; what matters for our present purposes is that, on the face of it, Heidegger's invocation of the voice of conscience as the pivot on which Dasein might effect a transition from inauthenticity to authenticity appears to overlook a fundamental problem – and indeed, a problem whose structure should be familiar from our opening invocation of Climacus' *Philosophical Fragments*. The difficulty is this: if existence in *das Man* means not just Dasein's being lost (both to its own individuality and to the being of all the other beings it encounters) but also its loss or repression of any awareness that there is an alternative to its present state, so that the lostness of that state remains concealed from it, how can any inauthentic Dasein be in a position to hear the voice of conscience? As Climacus, and the Socrates of the *Meno* might have put it: if Dasein could hear the voice of conscience, it wouldn't need to.

I have argued elsewhere that if we stick with Heidegger's official (although not always consistent) line on the location of the voice of conscience – namely, that it cannot come from outside the Dasein whose voice it is – then this problem is simply irresoluble.[3] The only solution is to elaborate upon Heidegger's occasional attempts to relocate the voice of conscience – as when he talks of the call as 'coming *from* me and yet *from beyond* me' (*BT*, 57: 320), of conscience as 'the voice of the friend whom every Dasein carries with it' (*BT*, 34: 206), and of Dasein as capable of becoming 'the conscience of Others' (*BT*, 60: 344). In short, we must suppose that the voice of conscience comes from someone else – someone who diagnoses us as lost, and has an interest in our overcoming it. If this other refrains from imposing a blueprint for our existence, he can function as an external representative of our internal, ownmost capacity for authenticity. And he can be thought of as creating the conditions for his own audibility through the sheer fact of his own authentic existence. For if we, out of our existence in *das Man*, encounter another Dasein whose selfhood is not lost in a slavish identification with others, he will refuse our desire to have our own inauthentic anonymity mirrored back to us by others, and he will prevent us from relating inauthentically to him. After all, we could mirror another who exists as separate and self-determining, and who relates to others as genuinely other, only by relating to him as other and to oneself as other to that other, that is as a separate, self-determining, internally differentiated individual. In other words, an encounter with a genuine other disrupts Dasein's inauthenticity by awakening otherness

---

3 See especially sections 38–40 in Part Two of my *Inheritance and Originality* (Oxford: Oxford University Press, 2001).

in Dasein itself; Dasein's relation to that other instantiates a mode of its possible self-relation (a relation to itself as other, as not self-identical).

Even if we rewrite Heidegger's analysis along the above lines, however, we are left with a further difficulty – or more precisely, with the anxiety that we have simply displaced our original problem rather than having resolved it. For even if such a genuine, authentic other could effect our transition from inauthenticity to authenticity, what explains his authenticity? Why is he not lost in *das Man* like every other Dasein, proximally and for the most part, as Heidegger's own analysis would have it?

At this point, I would argue that Heidegger's text holds out two possible ways of answering this question; both ways would constitute a coherent elaboration of what has been established thus far, but each line of development takes the analysis as a whole in a very different direction to the other.

The first way to answer the question would be to say, on Heidegger's behalf, that his claim that inauthenticity is pervasive – that it is, indeed, Dasein's default position, the stance from which any such worldly being is bound to commence – is not equivalent to the claim that inauthenticity is universal. On the contrary: given that it is definitive of Dasein's Being that it is the being for whom its own Being is an issue, to imagine an utter lack of authentic human otherness in the world amounts to imagining an absolute absence of beings with the Being of Dasein. It is difficult to see how Heidegger could directly countenance such a possibility; if anything, he rather suggests (in, for example, his readings of Dilthey, Count von Yorck and Nietzsche) that there will always be traces of genuine human authenticity in the margins of text, traditions and cultures to be encountered by inauthentic Dasein, and to hold open the possibility of their redemption.

There is thus some real textual support for this first response to our difficulty. But we should note that it would amount to a definitive withdrawal from the idea that Dasein always already exists in untruth – and yet this, too, is a claim to which Heidegger notoriously commits himself elsewhere in *Being and Time*, when he variously declares that *das Man* (as opposed to Being-with), and fallenness, are *existentiale* of Dasein, and thus ineliminable aspects of every possible mode of Dasein's Being rather than pervasive but not exceptionless ontic or *existentiell* modifications of its Being (to which there could be other ontic alternatives).

Accordingly, the second way of answering our question would begin from an unqualified sense of Dasein as always already inauthentic, of the kind attested to in the passages from *Being and Time* just mentioned. Then the intervention of a genuinely authentic other who might disrupt our existence in untruth, revealing it to us as such and reorienting us towards existence in the truth, will have to be seen as utterly inexplicable, as the gratuitous insertion of an exemplar of genuine humanity from somewhere beyond or other to the human realm. If we took this interpretative tack, we would run into conflict with those passages which plainly support the first reading; but we would without doubt find ourselves developing what Climacus would recognize as a variant of his non-Socratic hypothesis about truth – in short, with the Christian idea of the incarnation.

Heidegger and Kierkegaard: the love of wisdom

As I have tried to make clear, certain aspects of Heidegger's thought in *Being and Time* could legitimately generate a strong resistance to any sense of Dasein's existence as being unqualifiedly in untruth. But even if we incline towards that reading of his project, his argument about truth would still entail the conclusion that what philosophy treats as the essence of truth (the model of truth as a relation between a proposition and reality) is in fact a derivative conception whose very possibility is conditioned by the availability of a more primordial existential-ontological conception of Dasein as existing in the truth (and hence, as capable of existing outside it, in untruth); and this is at the very least a secularized variant of the Christian conception of the human relation to truth. Accordingly, insofar as we accept this strand or dimension of Heidegger's philosophy of being, we would seem to be forced to conclude that Climacus' picture of the relation between philosophical and Christian conceptions of truth is the very reverse of the truth. For if Heidegger is correct, then the two conceptions are not one another's negations or inversions; rather, the philosophical conception's passionate rejection of the Christian conception appears as a form of flight from its own conditions of possibility, from its own primordial origin and ground. And Heidegger's authentic phenomenology of truth and of human life would thereby constitute itself as at the very least the way to the way, the truth and the life.

But are matters really quite so clear-cut? Is the opposition between Kierkegaard's and Heidegger's understanding of these issues quite so stark? If we pause for a moment to look more closely at the twists and turns of Johannes Climacus' text, it could be argued that his presentation of the relation between the Socratic and the antiSocratic positions goes awry from the outset, and does so because it presents those positions as alternative responses to a distinctively Socratic question. In other words, Christianity is made to appear as if it were fundamentally one (admittedly internally consistent and powerful) answer to an intellectual puzzle – quite as if Christianity were essentially a cognitive phenomenon, the bearer of a body of doctrinal truth, and hence something that must before all be assessed before the tribunal of dispassionate reason. But this precisely contradicts Climacus' own emphasis throughout his text on the fact that, for the Christian, Christ is not the bearer of a truth or truths, but rather is the truth – as the biblical verse has it, the way, the truth and the life. If the truth of Christianity is not separable from the person of Christ, then living in the truth is not a matter of apprehending an intellectual message, but rather of living a particular kind of life – one in relation to Christ, a Christlike life, the *imitatio Christi*.

One might further argue that Climacus means his readers to detect this contradiction in his overt message, and thereby to exemplify for us the sheer difficulty of living up to his central insight, by showing us how easily even a sophisticated advocate for the view that Christianity is a matter of existential challenge rather than intellectual achievement can fall into the trap of presenting his own view as itself an intellectual insight that must be articulated, defended and evaluated before we can go on to accept or reject the existential challenge of Christian living. By enacting an error to which he thinks that his philosophical readers – even, or rather, especially the ones who are sympathetic to his concerns – will be particularly prone, but in a way that allows them to become conscious of it as an error, he is in effect trying to inoculate them against it – to make them see how easily they can fall into it, and how important it is that they avoid this trap. In short, he offers his own text as a mirror in which his readers might see an aspect of their own perversity, and thereby avoid its baleful consequences. Why else, for example, should Climacus himself precede his opening Socratic question, with which all the trouble starts, with the following epigraph or motto (he calls it a 'propositio' – a proposal or hypothesis): 'The question is asked by one who in his ignorance does not even know what provided the occasion for his questioning in this way'? I have tried to justify this reading of Climacus' intentions, and hence of Kierkegaard's, in much more detail elsewhere; but even if that reading is found unconvincing, the contradiction in the text of which it is a reading remains undeniably central to it.[4]

And what of the cogency of Heidegger's own position in this respect? As we have seen, his secularized conception of human beings as living in truth or untruth would have a good claim to have successfully accommodated Climacus' and Kierkegaard's emphasis upon truth as an

---

4 For more on this, see sections 1–13 of Part Three of *Inheritance and Originality*.

existential phenomenon. But in arguing that there is an internal relation between the traditional philosophical conception of truth and his more primordial, existential one, and thereby at least preparing the ground for the thought that the philosophical and the Christian conceptions of truth are not separated from one another by an abyss of essence, does he not undercut his own existential orientation by presenting that orientation as the solution or resolution of a certain set of traditional philosophical problems?

This anxiety might be thought to disclose a perfectly general risk run by any attempt to suggest that a religious conception of truth as located in a person might have some internal relation to philosophy. For if one argues that religious or quasi-religious conceptions are needed to resolve difficulties that are internal to any philosophical perspective on these matters, religious belief threatens to transform itself from an existential challenge to an intellectual resource – a body of doctrine rather than an address to the soul. In short, does even Heidegger's philosophy of Being threaten to transform the God of Abraham, Isaac and Jacob into the God of the philosophers?

Or does the internality of Heidegger's phenomenological trans-formation of philosophy rather show that philosophy's idea of itself as a purely intellectual enterprise is no more than a means of avoid-ing its inherent engagement with matters of existence – its ineliminable concern with the question of how to live? It is worth recalling that, for Socrates himself, the question of truth was not a purely intellectual puzzle. What, then, does it mean – what should it mean – to respond lovingly to wisdom's call?

Coda: philosophizing with Mary

It is perhaps unsurprising that this question should resonate so closely with what Pope John Paul II presents as his final thought in the encyc-lical under discussion here, a thought which is directed towards her whom the prayer of the Church invokes as *Seat of Wisdom*. Her life is a true parable which can shed light upon all that I have said here. We can perceive a close connection between the vocation of Our Lady and what is strictly called philosophy. Even as she was called to offer up both her humanity and her feminine nature so that the Word of God might take flesh and become one of us, so also philosophy is called to carry out its rational and critical task in order to enable the fruitfulness and efficacy of theology considered as the understanding of faith. And as Mary, consenting to the message of Gabriel, lost nothing of her humanity and freedom, so too the discipline of philosophy in its accepting the superabundant truth of the Gospel loses nothing of its autonomy, but discovers that all its researches are propelled towards the highest perfection. This truth was clearly perceived by the holy monks of Christian antiquity, by whom Mary was called 'the table of intellectual faith'. In her they saw a suitable image of true philosophy and realized that they must *be philosophizing with Mary.*

> May Mary, Seat of Wisdom, be a sure haven for all who devote their lives to the search for wisdom. May their journey into wisdom, sure and final goal of all true knowing, be freed of every impediment by the interceding of her who, in giving birth to the Truth and treasuring it in her heart, has forever shared it with the whole of humanity. (*Fides et ratio*, §108)

I would like to conclude these remarks by drawing out two lines of implication from this passage. The first is that if, parabolically speaking, philosophy should be philosophizing-with-Mary, then it must not only acknowledge but also fulfil the feminine aspect of its nature or essence. Suppose, with Mary's openness to an angelic intervention in mind, we think of this as philosophy's passive or receptive moment. This finds expression in its acknowledgement of human finitude as that makes itself manifest in the various domains of philosophical reflection – in such limits or conditions upon our fantasies of utter self-sufficiency as our mind's fatedness to embodiment, the dependence of our knowledge upon (as opposed to its reduction to) what is given to us in experience, and the ineliminable situatedness of our freedom. Since, however, philosophy itself is an aspect or expression of humanity, and hence of the human condition, the receptivity of philosophy should also find expression in an acknowledgement of its own finitude, the essential conditionedness of its own autonomy in the intellectual economy of human culture. And if philosophy can, in this respect, find it possible to acknowledge its limits with respect to the natural sciences – to admit not only its dependence upon their existence for some of its most central questions, but also the existence of a point at which its own powers must cede ground to those of the scientist – then why not with respect to history, to literature, and even to theology?

But can we really take seriously the full reach of this incarnational parable, the full range of implications engendered by the thought that philosophy is the indispensable matrix for theology's incarnation? For this would suggest rather more than that philosophy's critical and rational faculties are essential if theology is to be as fruitful and efficacious as possible – as if philosophy were theology's handmaiden or underlabourer, so that theology without philosophy cannot become all that it might and should be. The analogy rather implies that a less-than-fully philosophical theology is not properly human or humanized at all – that it would essentially fail to incarnate a fully human understanding of faith, and hence fail utterly to fulfil its own nature. And it further implies that philosophy can fulfil its own nature only insofar as it responds to a divine address, and does so in such a way as to engender a mode of thinking that is both fully theological and fully philosophical. How might the summons to such an impregnation, and such a procreation, be made intelligible to its recipient without absurdity? Or is it rather the utter aversion of this address to everything that we presently understand by 'philosophy' that constitutes at once its validation and its attraction?

The second, closely related, line of implication arises from the conjunction of two characterizations of Mary employed in these passages – as 'Seat of Wisdom' and as 'The table at which faith sits in thought' (here I use the translation of the phrase from Pseudo-Epiphanius' homily offered in the first English version of the encyclical, at the risk of trading accuracy or truth for beauty and goodness). *Mensa* alludes not only to femininity (in its invocation of the monthly cycles of the moon) but also to sacrifice (in its primary reference to the top slab of an altar); *sedes* alludes not only to the appropriate location of a faculty or a soul, but also to the transformation of a nomadic form of life into one of continuous settlement. Hence, the encyclical's yoking of these titles suggests that philosophy's true vocation, the territory or *heimat* from which it endlessly wanders and towards which it endlessly returns, is to offer itself as the sacrificial site at which the human intellect is informed by faith, and thus at once utterly transformed and utterly fulfilled. Since the final line of the encyclical draws our attention to the fact of its being delivered over to us on the Feast of the Exaltation of the Holy Cross, it is clear that the notion of sacrifice being invoked here is one in which new life is attained only by a complete abnegation or denial of the old; the way to rebirth is through the death of the self. But can philosophy undergo, or even contemplate, such a crucifixion, its apparently annihilating reconfiguration as the matrix for the mutual acknowledgement of faith and thought, and still have faith in itself?

5. Redeeming Truth, Restoring Faith in Reason: A Feminist Response to the Postmodern Condition of Nihilism[1]

PAMELA SUE ANDERSON

Introduction: the concepts we live by

If women and men today are to redeem *truth*, restore *faith* in *reason*, and achieve change through *love* and *trust* in others, then we need to take a step back to reflect upon the concepts[2] which currently direct our lives. This imperative is supported by my reading of the encyclical letter of Pope John Paul II on *Faith and Reason*, newly translated in *Restoring Faith in Reason*, edited by Laurence Paul Hemming and Susan Frank Parsons.[3] To claim that the Pope's letter can function as a source for

---

1 I was invited to write this response to 'The Postmodern Condition of Nihilism', for a day conference held at Heythrop College, University of London, on 31 May 2003; the focus was on *Restoring Faith in Reason*, A New Translation of the Encyclical Letter *Faith and Reason* of Pope John Paul II, together with a commentary and discussion, edited by Laurence Paul Hemming and Susan Frank Parsons (London: SCM Press, 2002).

2 Roughly, a concept is that which is understood by a term (e.g. a predicate): 'to possess a concept is to be able to deploy a term expressing it in making judgements: the ability connects with such things as recognizing when the term applies, and being able to understand the consequences of its application' Simon Blackburn, *Oxford Concise Dictionary of Philosophy* (Oxford: Oxford University Press, 1994), p. 72. The use of language will show whether a person has or does not have a grasp of a concept; but this use is learnt in a particular human context. The possession of a concept is not only manifest in the ability to recognize which things fall under a concept, but shown in the ability to apply and misapply a concept, to extend it to new cases, to abandon it in favour of an alternative concept, to invoke the concept in the absence of things to which it applies, and so forth.

Also, for an original discussion on possession of 'action-guiding concepts' – in particular, 'thick' and 'thin' ethical concepts – in the context of an account of ethics, reflection and knowledge, see Bernard Williams, *Ethics and the Limits of Philosophy* (London: Fontana, 1985), pp. 140–55.

3 I am grateful to Parsons and Hemming for generating new understanding of faith, reason, meaning and truth with this edition of the Pope's encyclical, but

redeeming truth is an unusual act for a Protestant woman philosopher. Nevertheless, the Pope's realism about human life and philosophical reflection, as well as his desire for the objectivity of modern philosophy, have stimulated my reflections here.[4] In particular, I have been intrigued by the Pope's claim that: 'All men and women . . . are in some sense philosophers and have their own philosophical *conceptions with which they direct their lives*'.[5] My intention in this chapter is to reflect critically on the idea that we each have our own philosophical conceptions with which we direct our lives. I will rephrase this in terms derived from A. W. Moore's claim that 'to possess a concept is to live by it'.[6]

Moore's account of what it is to possess a concept includes an explanation of what it is 'to grasp a concept in an engaged way'. This will become highly significant for my overall argument: that is, to tackle the postmodern condition of nihilism, we need to make sense of our lives.[7] Moore admits to employing 'possess' as a term of art,[8] and I take a certain poetic licence with this admission, freely experimenting with possibilities not addressed by Moore himself. In particular, from a reading of Moore's most recent philosophical work on the moral and religious philosophy of Immanuel Kant, I suggest that Moore himself

---

also for their engagement with often untimely theological, spiritual and philosophical questions in the context of our contemporary postmodern culture.

4 Here I note my agreement with John Haldane that *Fides et ratio* is not a postmodern text (John Haldane, 'John Paul's philosophy', *The Tablet*, 7 June 2003, pp. 22–3). The assumptions of modern philosophy are crucial for the philosophical attractiveness of the encyclical. In the Pope's discussion of the relationship between theology and philosophy, he takes a modern (positive) view of the role of philosophical reflection; see *Restoring Faith in Reason*, especially §§64–5, 68–9, 73 and 75–7. The universal role given to philosophical reflection depends on a critical realism and the possibility of objectivity; also evident is the influence of Edmund Husserl's post-Kantian philosophy in the attention given to 'the ways in which persons and values are experienced' (Haldane, p. 22).

5 Janet Martin Soskice points out that the previous translation of this encyclical letter includes women with men as philosophers; see Soskice, '*Fides et ratio*: The Postmodern Pope' in Hemming and Parsons (eds), *Restoring Faith in Reason*, p. 294. Compare her quotation from the earlier to the recent translation in, *Restoring Faith in Reason*, p. 51, §30, which is also quoted in Soskice's footnote, p. 294, n. 10.

6 A. W. Moore, *Noble in Reason, Infinite in Faculty: Themes and Variations on Kant's Moral and Religious Philosophy* (London: Routledge, 2003), p. xv; cf. John Paul II, *Restoring Faith in Reason*, p. 51.

7 Moore, *Noble in Reason*, p. xv, 38–51, especially §8. The concepts, which I have in mind here include reason, faith and hope; but Moore gives other examples to illustrate what it is to possess a concept and grasp it in an *engaged* way: pp. 39–40 and 74–8.

8 More recently, Moore deliberately modifies his terminology, and replaces 'possessing' with 'embracing' a concept, in A. W. Moore, 'Maxims and Thick Ethical Concepts', *Ratio* XIX (June 2006), pp. 135–8.

demonstrates an engaged grasp of the concepts of faith and hope, and possession of these concepts creates certain possibilities for both philosophers and theologians in 'restoring faith in reason'.[9]

In his explanation of what it is to possess a concept, Moore makes an important distinction between an engaged and a disengaged grasp of a concept. In his words,

> I intend 'possess' in an unusually demanding way . . .

> To convey what I intend I need to draw a distinction. Many concepts, if not all concepts, can be grasped in two ways, an engaged way and a disengaged way. To grasp a concept in the disengaged way is to be able to recognize when the concept would (correctly) be applied, to be able to understand others when they apply it, and so forth. To grasp a concept in the engaged way is not only to be able to do these things, but also to feel sufficiently at home with the concept to be prepared to apply it oneself, where being prepared to apply it oneself means being prepared to apply it not just in overt acts of communication but also in how one thinks about the world and in how one conducts one's affairs. What *this requires*, roughly, is *sharing whatever beliefs, concerns, and values define the outlook that give application of the concept its point.*

> Take the concept of *the Sabbath*. Those who are not Jewish have no difficulty in grasping this concept in the disengaged way . . . But only a Jewish person recognizing an obligation to keep the Sabbath can grasp the concept in the engaged way. We might say . . . that such a person *lives by* the concept.[10]

It is significant to his philosophy and, I suggest, to his own outlook (on the world) that Moore's account of an engaged grasp of a concept is indebted to the ethical philosophy of Bernard Williams.[11] Here I am distinguishing between what Moore explains with his philosophical account of possession of concepts and what I discern to be his own grasp of concepts. So, Moore's philosophical account explicitly builds upon the philosophy of Williams; however, what I discern in Moore I do not discern in Williams' own grasp of certain moral and religious concepts. A fundamental difference exists between Moore and Williams.

---

9 Moore, *Noble in Reason*, especially pp. 51–2, 108–12, 166–9 and 170–96.

10 Moore, *Noble in Reason*, p. 48; italics added.

11 A. W. Moore, 'Williams on Ethics, Knowledge and Reflection', *Philosophy: The Journal of the Royal Institute of Philosophy* 78 (2003), pp. 337–54; and Moore, *Noble in Reason*, pp. 39–51; cf. Williams, *Ethics and the Limits of Philosophy*, pp. 140ff.

Williams himself does not have an *engaged* grasp of any theological concepts, whether derived from Kantian ethical ideals or a more direct product of Christianity.[12] Stated more strongly by Williams about himself and 'most of us':

> Most of us do not have . . . traditional religious reasons for thinking that the route from the fifth century BC to the present day had to take the course that it did take and, in particular, run through Christianity . . . The overwhelming role of Christianity in the transition from antiquity to the modern world is necessary, in the sense that if we try to subtract it, we cannot think determinately of an alternative history, and we cannot think of people who would be ourselves at all; but while the role of Christianity is in this way necessary, it might not have been.[13]

Thus, for Williams, Christianity is a necessary contingency in making us who we are today. That is, we might say that our lives have been directed by certain concepts which are determinate of our self-understanding, yet contingent in the sense of 'might not have been'. To understand our lives, our personal and social identities, we need to recognize those fundamental concepts, which have shaped our thinking and acting. Even if Christian concepts are necessary for our self-understanding, Williams does not think that Christianity had to be; and in fact, he does not share any Christian concepts, in Moore's terms, in an engaged way. If a sympathetic observer of the use of Christian concepts, Williams would be in a position to say that some of these concepts are false.[14] Yet the crucial point for my argument here is that Williams can only have a disengaged grasp of a Christian concept of faith. Employing Moore's terms, Williams does not share the same beliefs, concerns, and values which define the outlook that give the application of a

---

12 Williams explains the difference between someone who possesses an action-guiding concept and 'the sympathetic observer' who can report, anticipate and even take part in a discussion of the use made of the concept relating to religion, for instance, without being ultimately identified with the use of the concept: 'it may not be his' (Williams, *Ethics and the Limits of Philosophy*, p. 142). For more evidence of Williams' own disengaged use of concepts relating to Christianity, see Bernard Williams, *Shame and Necessity* (Berkeley, CA: University of California Press, 1993), pp. 10–12 and 91–5.

13 Williams, *Shame and Necessity*, p. 12. The 'us' certainly covers other analytic philosophers, but Williams may assume that 'us' covers other contemporary non-philosophers.

14 For a significant, however brief discussion of the possibility of recognizing true and fales ethical concepts as a 'sympathetic observer', see Williams, *Ethics and the Limits of Philosophy*, pp. 142–7; also, see footnote 12 above.

Christian concept of faith its point.[15] So, Williams differs from both Moore and the Pope in not having an engaged grasp of faith, love and redemption; and Williams would only have a disengaged grasp of these concepts insofar as he is a sympathetic observer. As for Moore and the Pope, although sharing certain philosophical and theological concepts (of modernity), they could not share all of the same Christian concepts, since Moore's Christian outlook is Protestant, not Roman Catholic.

In this chapter, I am most interested in the fact that, although Moore has a philosophical debt to Williams – whose account of truth will be explored later in this chapter – he is nevertheless unlike Williams in the nature of his (engaged) grasp of faith and hope. At the same time, it is important to recognize that Williams and Moore do share certain fundamental philosophical concepts: they both grasp reason and, as I will suggest, truth in an engaged way.

Modern philosophy and the postmodern condition

Before turning to the redemption of truth and faith in reason, it is necessary to say something about the definition of philosophy that is at play. On the one hand, I think that we need to be sensitive to recent changes in the philosopher's self-understanding.[16] The contemporary philosophers' increasing awareness of philosophy's own history and locatedness has been transforming philosophy's self-definition. Notably, feminism in philosophy has increased the growing consciousness of the social and material locatedness – including the impossibility of gender-neutrality – of philosophers and philosophy.[17] On the other hand, the particular sort of commitment to 'the truth' conceived as an absolute, or an absolute conception of reality, continues to dominate certain accounts of philosophy, especially philosophical theology.[18] The

15 Cf. Moore, *Noble in Reason*, p. 48.

16 Bernard Williams, 'Philosophy as a Humanistic Discipline', *Philosophy* 75, no. 294 (October 2000), pp. 477–96.

17 Miranda Fricker and Jennifer Hornsby, 'Introduction', in Fricker and Hornsby (eds), *The Cambridge Companion to Feminism in Philosophy* (Cambridge: Cambridge University Press, 2000), pp. 1–5; and Pamela Sue Anderson, 'Feminism in Philosophy of Religion', in Deane-Peter Baker and Patrick Maxwell (eds), *Explorations in Contemporary Continental Philosophy of Religion* (Amsterdam: Rodopi, 2003), pp. 189–90.

18 For examples of this commitment to truth, and at least the possibility of the absolute conception, in philosophy, see A. W. Moore, *Points of View* (Oxford: Oxford University Press, 1997), pp. 74–5, 79, 85–9. On the commitment to truth in philosophical theology, see Pope John Paul II, *Restoring Faith in Reason*, especially pp. 127–9, 135; and Eilert Herms, 'Objective Truth: Relations between Truth and Revelation in the Encyclical *Fides et ratio*, in *Restoring*

latter commitment to truth has been reasserted in recent years in direct reaction to current trends of nihilism in philosophy, while the former changes in philosophy's self-definition have been blamed for this trend. I hope to show that neither of these extremes will restore faith in reason nor achieve change through love and trust.[19]

Ironically, this tension in philosophy brings together the assertions of truth and of nihilism, which characterize two different extremes in contemporary culture. Certain postmodern followers of the philosophy of Friedrich Nietzsche have been accused of bringing about a culture of nihilism due to their Nietzschean denial of truth; or at least, the denial of truth's unity, simplicity and absoluteness.[20] Yet we will see that Williams recognizes another possibility: that is, the affirmation of truthfulness emerges in Nietzsche's critical work on genealogy.

To stipulate a few, more useful definitions at this stage, I understand nihilism in the contemporary terms of analytic philosophy as 'the loss of any hope of making sense of the world'.[21] I take 'making sense of things' to be one philosophical response to nihilism.[22] And I suggest that philosophers and theologians should learn to achieve 'a feminist standpoint', as a critical perspective, from which women and men today can come to grasp new, more inclusive concepts in an engaged way.[23] This feminist standpoint is both sensitive to the changes in the philosopher's self-definition and informed by recent philosophical writings on socially situated knowledge. It is also informed by feminist writings on the

---

Faith in Reason, pp. 206–24. In addition, for Moore's discussion of the nihilistic dangers of Nietzsche's perspectivism, see *Points of View*, pp. 103–14.

19 Consider Soskice's interpretation of the Pope's message, '[philosophers – men and women –] have contented themselves with philosophical trivia while the *big questions are left unanswered or unaddressed*. The philosophers have made themselves marginal in a world that more than ever needs their honest deliberations, and here we arrive at the nihilism' (Soskice, '*Fides et ratio*', p. 294).

20 Cf. John Paul II, *Restoring Faith in Reason*; Moore, *Points of View*, pp. 106ff.; and Bernard Williams, *Truth and Truthfulness: An Essay in Genealogy* (New York and Oxford: Princeton University Press, 2002), pp. 18–19, 126–8 and 135–40.

21 Williams, *Truth and Truthfulness*, pp. 267–9.

22 I appropriate this idea of making sense of things (or, the world) from both Williams (*Truth and Truthfulness*, pp. 232–69) and Moore (*Noble in Reason, Infinite in Faculty*, pp. xvi, 78–81, 87, 171). A potentially fruitful shift in analytic philosophy toward an awareness of social and material locatedness of our thinking and writing is evident if these passages in Williams and Moore are compared to bell hooks, *Remembered Rapture: The Writer at Work* (London: The Women's Press, 1999), pp. 12f.

23 On a feminist standpoint, see Pamela Sue Anderson, '"Standpoint": Its Rightful Place in a Realist Epistemology', *Journal of Philosophical Research*, vol. xxvi (2001), 131–54.

social and material locatedness of both philosophical and theological concepts. The crucial element of this feminist standpoint is the political imperative: that 'everyone must change' if sexist and racist oppression is to be overcome.[24] In brief, 'feminism is for everybody' at this moment in history when gender and its associated material factors of social locatedness are at the heart of our political struggles for change, for more truthfulness, trust and love.[25]

I maintain that the dissolution of 'the myth of patriarchy'[26] does not necessarily result in nihilism. In fact, just the reverse is possible, if we grasp the appropriate philosophical concepts of truth and reason in an engaged way. We have an engaged grasp of a concept, if the concept functions in overt acts of communication, as well as in how we think about the world and in how we conduct our affairs. Coming to possess concepts in an engaged way is, admittedly, not going to be a simple matter of learning new concepts or even of coming to employ them. What is crucial is giving the determinate content and truth conditions to those concepts which guide our lives.[27] Moreover, knowledge of how it is possible for us to employ concepts correctly remains ineffable; and on this, I agree with Moore that knowing how to use a language is a form of art.[28]

In 2003, Williams and Moore each offered their own significant responses to postmodern nihilism, explaining and developing their outlooks on truth and reason, respectively. In *Truth and Truthfulness: An*

---

24 bell hooks, *Feminist Theory: From Margin to Center*, 2nd edn (London: Pluto Press, 2000; 1st edn, 1988), p. 166. hooks quotes a fascinating passage from Susan Griffin, 'The Way of All Ideology', *Signs* (Spring 1982):

> A deeply political knowledge of the world does not lead to a creation of an enemy. Indeed, to create monsters unexplained by circumstance is to forget the political vision which above all explains behavior as emanating from circumstance, a vision which believes in a capacity born to all human beings for creation, joys, and kindness, in a human nature which, under the right circumstances, can bloom.
>
> When a movement for liberation inspires itself chiefly by a hatred of an enemy rather than from the vision of possibility, it begins to defeat itself. (hooks, *Feminist Theory*, p. 166)

25 I borrow this phrase from bell hooks, *Feminism is for Everybody: Passionate Politics* (Cambridge, MA: South End Press, 2000).
26 Pamela Sue Anderson, 'Myth and Feminist Philosophy', in Kevin Schilbrack (ed.), *Thinking Through Myths: Philosophical Perspectives* (London: Routledge, 2002), pp. 103–13.
27 Williams, *Ethics and the Limits of Philosophy*, pp. 146–51.
28 See Pamela Sue Anderson, 'Ineffable Knowledge and Gender', in Philip Goodchild (ed.), *Rethinking Philosophy of Religion: Approaches from Continental Philosophy*, series edited by John Caputo (New York: Fordham University Press, 2002), pp. 162–83.

Essay in Genealogy,[29] Williams writes in a spirit of creativity, which retrieves Nietzsche as not a denier of truth but an advocate of truthfulness. In *Noble in Reason, Infinite in Faculty: Themes and Variations in Kant's Moral and Religious Philosophy*,[30] Moore creatively weaves his concerns with pure practical reason through Kantian themes and variations on morality, freedom and religion. Moore demonstrates in Kantian terms that we all seek to make ethical sense of things. I suggest that Williams and Moore each seek to make sense of things both individually and collectively.[31] To quote Moore in support of this suggestion:

> Sharing possession of a concept is part of sharing a life. An individual, through possession of concepts, is enabled to make sense of things, and more particularly to tell various stories, and more particularly still to tell his or her own story, the telling of which is inseparable from acting it out – from living a life. But so too, a community, through shared possession of concepts, is enabled to make collective sense of things, and more particularly to propagate various stories, and more particularly still to propagate its own story.[32]

Yet as stated already Williams does not have an engaged grasp of either Christian or Kantian concepts, while Moore energetically writes variations on Kantian themes, upholding a realm of pure reason, as well as concepts of faith and hope which are compatible with at least one Christian story. It may also be surprising in this light that Kant, Williams and Moore – none of whom are either Roman Catholic philosophers or theologians – came to my mind when I read the Pope's account of a postmodern culture characterized by the diremption and, hence weakening, of faith and reason. Yet I would like to go some distance in demonstrating that if we accept this diremption, it undermines both theology and philosophy. And this is a crucial reason for including the Pope's outlook on theology and modern philosophy.

In response to the postmodern condition of nihilism, neither the Pope nor Williams call for a return to the Enlightenment philosophy of Kant with its elevation of human reason in making sense of things. In sharp contrast, Moore finds creative possibilities in variations on Kantian moral and religious themes. Despite this contrast, the Pope's allegiance

---

29 See note 20 above.
30 See note 6 above.
31 Williams, *Truth and Truthfulness*, pp. 15, 18, 267–9; Moore, *Points of View*, pp. 106–10; Moore, *Noble in Reason*, pp. 75–6.
32 Moore, *Noble in Reason*, p. 75.

to modern philosophy comes through even in his references to Thomas Aquinas, especially in his concepts of reason and philosophy.[33] This is reinforced by contemporary philosophers who are also rereading (Kantian like Thomistic) accounts of reason and morality in relation to, on the one hand, Aristotle and, on the other hand, Christianity.[34] Williams himself is forced to admit that 'modernity is not just a catastrophic mistake'; and that '. . . the formative influence of Christianity is something we owe to the way things turned out'.[35] Moreover, Williams showed a personal interest in Moore's work on Kantian reason;[36] and there is no doubt in my mind after reading his encyclical that the Pope would be intrigued by Moore's argument that as human we all have a rational drive to make sense of how things are.[37]

Could there be a similar sort of common ground for the two philosophers and the Pope on faith? No, is the answer which we would have to give for Williams. But for Moore this would be a different matter. He ends *Noble in Reason* with a definition of faith found in Kant's *Lectures on Ethics*:

We take faith . . . to mean that we should do the best that lies in our power, and this in the hope that God, in His goodness and wisdom, will make up for the frailty of our conduct . . . [Now] practical faith . . . lies in this, that we in no way prescribe anything to God through our will, but resign the matter to His will, and hope that if we have done what lies within our natural capacity, God will repair our frailty and incapacity by means that He knows best.[38]

---

33 On reason, philosophy and ethics, see John Paul II, *Restoring Faith in Reason*, especially pp. 23–57, 71–81 and 97.

34 Linda T. Zagzebski, *Virtues of the Mind: An Inquiry into the Nature of Virtue and the Ethical Foundations of Knowledge* (Cambridge: Cambridge University Press, 1996), pp. 18 n. 11 and 263; Nancy Sherman, *Making a Necessity of Virtue: Aristotle and Kant on Virtue* (Cambridge: Cambridge University Press, 1997); Robert Audi, 'A Liberal Theory of Civic Virtue', *Social Philosophy and Policy*, vol. 15, no. 1 (Winter 1998), especially pp. 155–167; Robert Merrihew Adams, 'Introduction', in Allen Wood and George di Giovanni (eds), *Religion within the Boundaries of Mere Reason and other Writings* (Cambridge: Cambridge University Press, 1998), pp. vii–xxxii.

35 Williams, *Shame and Necessity*, pp. 11 and 12; and see footnote 13 above.

36 Moore, 'Preface', *Noble in Reason*, p. ix.

37 Moore, *Noble in Reason*, especially pp. 170–72, 183, and 193.

38 Moore, *Noble in Reason*, p. 196; cf. Immanuel Kant, *Lectures on Ethics*, ed. Peter Heath and J. B. Schneewind, trans. Peter Heath (Cambridge: Cambridge University Press, 2001), p. 106–7; 27: 321–322. Note that Kant himself goes on to distinguish 'fleshy' and 'wise' trust: 'Fleshy trust is when we ourselves determine the worldly ends of our inclinations . . . in order that our trust may coincide with the plan of wisdom, it must be a wise trust, and unconditional,

I suggest that the Pope would agree with Kant (above) insofar as the Pope's life has been directed by concepts of practical reason and faith, while accepting that our 'natural frailty' is accompanied by hope in God's knowledge and grace. Moore, then, shares with Kant and the Pope concepts of practical reason and faith, precisely in seeking to make ethical sense of the world.

Yet, how can anything be claimed about Moore's and Williams' engaged grasp of truth when, in *Noble in Reason*, Moore does not explicitly discuss truth?[39] Perhaps, truth is an inappropriate concept in the context of Moore's making ethical sense of the world. To address this question of truth, let us turn more directly to Williams, the Pope and to a feminist practice, while staying close to Moore's contribution on faith in reason, on hope, trust and truth.

A redemptive practice: writing to tell the truth

The concept of truth appears in the Pope's definition of man and woman.[40] His conception of humanity in *Restoring Faith in Reason* depends upon the possession of truth:

[F]or all that they may evade it, the truth still influences life. Notwithstanding, even when fleeing from it, truth disturbs existence. Life in fact can never be grounded upon doubt, uncertainty or deceit; such an existence would be threatened constantly by fear and anxiety. Man [woman] may be defined, therefore, as *the one who seeks the truth*.[41]

The Pope also adds: 'Man [woman], the one who seeks [the truth], is . . . also *the one who lives trusting in others*.'[42]

For his part, Williams uncovers the values of truth and the concept

---

so that we believe in general that God, in His goodness and holiness, will both lend us His aid in regard to acting morally, and also allow us to participate in blessedness' (p. 107; 27: 321–322).

39 For background on this question, consider where Moore describes himself as a conceptual philosopher who aims to affirm truth. A. W. Moore, 'Arguing with Derrida', *Ratio*, vol. xiii, no. 4 (December 2000), pp. 357 and 366. Here Moore admits, 'a commitment to a certain paradigm of language use, namely that in which truths are affirmed' (pp. 365–6).

40 In the light of the Janet Martin Soskice reference (see note 5 above), I assume that we can translate the Pope's references to man and humanity in inclusive terms.

41 John Paul II, *Restoring Faith in Reason*, p. 49.

42 John Paul II, *Restoring Faith in Reason*, p. 53.

of truthfulness in Nietzsche's philosophy, for those philosophers who reject nihilism and resist self-deception:

> Although Nietzsche was keenly alive to what concerns the deniers [of truth], he was an opponent of them. The indifference to truthfulness which they encourage would be for him merely an aspect of nihilism. When he discovered that the values of truth and truthfulness, such as the resistance to self-deception and to comforting mythologies, were not self-justifying and not given simply with the concept of truth . . . [He aimed] to see how far the values of truth could be revalued, how they might be understood in a perspective quite different from the Platonic and Christian metaphysics which had provided their principal source in the West up to now.[43]

Williams both affirms and revalues truth, claiming to follow Nietzsche in this twofold task. He goes on to demonstrate that a new genealogical story, not dependent on Christian metaphysics, can be truthful.[44] Affirming the task of philosophy as a search for truth, the Pope also argues that men and women should seek redemption from the old ways of thinking, while re-establishing a trust in each other. The revaluations of truth by Williams and by the Pope connect truthfulness with trust and other virtues, moving the primary philosophical task to everyday truths (while also going beyond the everyday); this means moving the foundation of philosophy away from epistemology built upon philosophical scepticism about other minds or the existence of an external world.[45] Moreover, Moore's variations on Kant, if not Kant himself, and Williams' variations on Nietzsche are in substantial agreement with the Pope on the current need for *trust*. In the case of Moore, this is bound up with faith in reason as a common (Kantian) sentiment. Moore affirms the value of reason for us in making sense of things: 'One thing that I have been trying to accomplish . . . is a way of making sense of things, including our own yearning to make sense of things; that allows us to say, "Amen" to this sentiment in Kant.'[46]

The motivation to make sense of things rests on a yearning, implying a sentiment of hope. At the same time, reason shapes the nature of

---

43 Williams, *Truth and Truthfulness*, p. 18.
44 Williams, *Truth and Truthfulness*, p. 19.
45 On everyday truths, see Williams, *Truth and Truthfulness*, p. 10; and for Williams' revelation of the significant roles played by the virtues of truth, and especially the virtues of accuracy and of sincerity (which is bound up with the concept of trust), see pp. 11–12, 35, 83, chapters 5 and 6.
46 Moore, *Noble in Reason*, p. 196.

this yearning to make sense of our lives. In this way, a human being is characterized by a 'nisus for rationality', bringing together reason and human longing.[47] To build upon this rational account of yearning, I would like to bring in bell hooks from whom contemporary men and women can gain a new, concrete understanding of reason and truth. We will find that Moore's nisus for rationality becomes in hooks' terms a yearning for truth as a common human *telos*.

'bell hooks' is spelled with a lower case 'b' and a lower case 'h'. This is a pen-name for Gloria Watkins. Renaming herself was a deliberate act, marking the beginning of her writing life. bell hooks became known as the African-American feminist and cultural critic. It is highly relevant that hooks seeks to redeem truth 'in the mysterious place where words first come to be "made flesh"', that is, in the place of the everyday where she struggles to learn to trust in others.[48] I would like to focus upon the self-description hooks gives of her practice as 'a writing life'.[49] I will explore this practice both in terms of making narrative sense of life and in terms of the subversive practice of 'women telling tales'.[50]

For hooks, a writing life becomes not only a means to make sense of the world, but *a redemptive practice* characterized by truth-telling.[51] She seeks to transform fear into love and, ultimately, to overcome nihilism by evoking our yearning to tell the truth. In turn, this sort of truth-telling intends to heal wounds and to connect us with each other. To quote from hooks' account of redeeming truth:

After what seemed like endless years of journal writing about the past, I wrote a memoir . . . It was indeed the culmination of this effort to accept the past and yet surrender its hold on me. This writing was redemptive.

There are writers who write for fame. And there are writers who write because we need to make sense of the world we live in; writing is a way to clarify, to interpret, to reinvent . . . We do not write because we must; we always have choice. We write because language is the way we keep a hold on life . . . We communicate to connect, to know community. Even though writing is a solitary act, when I sit

---

47 Moore, *Noble in Reason*, pp. 183 and 193–6.
48 hooks, *Remembered Rapture*, p. 130.
49 For an example of this practice, see bell hooks, *Wounds of Passion: A Writing Life* (New York: Henry Holt & Company, Owl Press, 1997).
50 For background on my understanding of this phrase, see Pamela Sue Anderson, 'An Ethics of Women Telling Tales: Creating New Spaces', lecture delivered at the *Colloque international: Espaces publics, espace(s) privé(s)*, 27 October 2000, University of Cergy-Pontoise, France.
51 hooks, *Remembered Rapture*, p. 13.

with words that I trust will be read by someone, I know that I can never be truly alone.[52]

And on truth-telling:

To make community, we need to be able to know truth, to speak openly and honestly.

Truth-telling has to be a spiritual practice for many of us because we live and work in settings where falseness is rewarded, where lies are the norm. Deceit and betrayal destroy the possibility of community.[53]

At this point, it is useful to compare hooks' account of truth (and trust) with the claim of Pope John Paul II that: 'man [woman], the one who seeks [the truth], is . . . also *the one who lives trusting in others*.[54] And hooks connects truth, trust and love to a dramatic, unequivocal criticism of contemporary culture:

When men and women are loyal to ourselves and others, when we love justice, we understand fully the myriad ways in which lying diminishes and erodes the possibility of meaningful, caring connection, that it stands in the way of love . . .

[Today] widespread cultural acceptance of lying is a primary reason many of us will never know love. It is impossible to nurture one's own or another's spiritual growth when the core of one's being and identity is shrouded in secrecy and lies.[55]

The loss of truth renders our postmodern condition one of deceit, which, according to hooks, results in the loss of the virtues associated with truthfulness, especially love. To confront cultural and personal problems resulting from a lack of truth and the loss of a concept of love, hooks urges us to make sense of things. Unwittingly her project resonates with the Pope's concern with trust and truth, but with Moore's reconstruction of Kant's rationalism. As Moore himself explains, 'In th[is] reconstruction, rationality also demands that we seek concepts that enable us to make sense. We must realize that the world itself does not make sense: we have to make sense of it.'[56] He claims that this nisus

52 hooks, *Remembered Rapture*, pp. 12–13.
53 hooks, *Remembered Rapture*, pp. 120–1.
54 bell hooks, *All about Love: New Visions* (London: The Women's Press, 2000), pp. 42 and 46.
55 hooks, *All about Love*, p. 46.
56 Moore, *Noble in Reason*, p. xvi, §17.

for rationality motivates our search for concepts that enable us to make sense. Although hooks does not explicitly connect this search with rationality, her yearning to make sense of the world seems to embody reason's nisus.

Recall my opening quotation from the Pope that 'All men and women . . . are in some sense philosophers and have their own philosophical conceptions with which they direct their lives'. We can now ask, which concepts do we – and should we – live by? Truth? Faith? Reason? Hope in 'sense-making'? We must answer in the light of those persons with whom we share our world(s). As Moore explains,

> We do not and cannot possess our concepts *in vacuo*. We do not and cannot pick them up at will. Each individual comes to possess concepts by being immersed in a community, and each individual makes his or her contribution to telling the stories of these concepts, occasionally by helping to bring them to an end, occasionally by helping to initiate them, but most often by simply carrying them on.[57]

This leaves the question, how do we come to possess the (new) concepts, which make sense of all of our lives? And, in particular, how do (our) concepts prevent nihilism?

In the end, each of Pope John Paul, Williams, Moore and hooks presents answers to this line of questions. Each supports a serious alternative to nihilism. Each manages to resist despair in seeking to make sense of things, and so giving the ground for coming to truth. Such mutual support from very different points of view poses a challenge for all those women and men who acquiesce to the postmodern condition of nihilism and shrink from truth. The concept of truth – in telling 'the truth' and in giving a truthful account – becomes more and more central to our faith in reason.

Reason as authoritative (not authoritarian): trustworthy knowers

hooks seeks to restore *faith* in *reason* by way of learning to trust the knower (of everyday truths). Not only is truth, but reason is linked with trust. hooks' search can be shown to touch on similar points to those made already, in other ways, by Moore, Williams and the Pope on reason. The crucial difference is that all three of these men are respected, treated as authorities, as rational agents and credible knowers. In contrast, if hooks is trusted it is as a result of her life-long

---

57 Moore, *Noble in Reason*, p. 76.

struggle to write, in order to communicate to others whose lives are not like hers. It has not been easy for her words to be heard, let alone to be treated as authoritative. hooks' struggle has been *to write* to tell the truth, to be heard and to be trusted. For this she needs to be recognized as a knower who is also trustworthy.

Personally, I feel confident in asserting that not only is hooks' knowledge credible but she is trustworthy. What are the grounds of her credibility and trustworthiness? Too often these grounds are obscured by the biases and injustice in the epistemic practices by which we assert 'credible' and 'trustworthy' knowledge. These practices can act to exclude, creating mistrust of the trustworthy and credible on the grounds of racial, sexual or other social and material differences.

I would like to maintain, on grounds established elsewhere, that as readers of hooks' words, we need to develop a reflective critical openness.[58] That is, we must begin by openly and critically reflecting upon the social and material markers which, for us, have rendered a knower trustworthy or not. Consider the social markers of Gloria Watkins who was born in 1952, Kentucky, USA. She was born poor and, more crucially, black. As hooks herself points out, when white folks have a child the first thing they want to know is the sex; but when a child is born to a black woman the first thing that is noticed is the skin colour, and then the sex; colour and sex interlock, determining the child's fate.[59] Colour matters when it comes to trustworthiness. But should it? The crucial fact is that skin colour has marked out those who can be trusted to tell the truth and those who cannot be trusted. However, our sensibilities have been prejudiced by such markers; and we can see the devastation and loss of truth suffered because of this racism.

In 1981, Gloria Watkins published in her pen-name, *Ain't I a Woman: Black Women and Feminism*; this book by bell hooks quickly became a landmark text for challenging the authority of our concept of truth and in this context the related concepts of human(ity) and woman. In this 1981 book, hooks exposes white feminism's blindness to the difference that race makes to what it means to be a woman. hooks' act of writing is more important than either her historical identity or our questions about the author of her life. The woman who writes *Ain't I a Woman* seeks to derive her authority from social location within a matrilinear genealogy, going back to her great grandmother named

---

58 For my discussion of reflective critical openness as an intellectual virtue, see Pamela Sue Anderson, 'An Epistemological-Ethical Approach to Philosophy of Religion: Learning to Listen', in Pamela Sue Anderson and Beverley Clack (eds), *Feminist Philosophy of Religion: Critical Readings* (London: Routledge, 2004), pp. 87–92.

59 hooks, *Feminist Theory*, p. xii.

'hooks'. But this means that her writing aims to subvert the concepts (including 'woman'), which her readers possess, in order to change how they live, think and act. Established social and material markers determine whom we trust and who tells the truth. How can we (learn how to) possess a revised concept of truth?

With her conception of a writing life, hooks seeks to make sense of the world. She also explores the nature of truth as, in part, history and, in other part, fiction.[60] However, in using 'fiction' it must be understood this is an exploration of *truth* – of reality. So, the activities of making sense of our lives and of seeking new concepts do not aim to create, or promote, mere fabrications. We do not need to fabricate (our) traditions. Instead we need to grasp and understand human reality as well as possible, at the same time as recognizing how our lives have been shaped by the histories of philosophy and theology – disciplines which have sought to understand human finitude, as well as our relation to something infinite. hooks demonstrates that truth, history and its relation to what might be fiction, should matter to us. So, turning to fiction, or other literature, is not about fabrications – just the opposite. As Williams astutely explains about philosophy's use of literature and literary examples:

> It is not of course peculiar to [the] sort of inquiry, which aims at historical understanding, that philosophy should be concerned with literature. Even when philosophy is not involved in history, it has to make demands on literature. In seeking a reflective understanding of ethical life, for instance, it quite often takes examples from literature. Why not take examples from life? It is a perfectly good question, and it has a short answer: what philosophers will lay before themselves and their readers as an alternative to literature will not be life, but bad literature.[61]

And so I turn to the literary work, part fiction and part history, of bell hooks because she creates good literature – of life. The title of hooks' first book, *Ain't I a Woman*, is derived from a statement made by Isabella Baumfree, a black woman and former slave in 1852. At a meeting for women's rights in Akron, Ohio, Isabella challenges the public view of woman as fragile, and witnesses to the hard labour she has done; and then she asks, 'Ain't I a Woman?' She answers by calling

---

60 bell hooks, *Bone Black: Memories of Girlhood* (New York: Henry Holt Company, 1996), p. xiv. Also see Anderson, 'Myth and Feminist Philosophy', pp. 101–22.
61 Williams, *Shame and Necessity*, p. 13.

herself Sojourner Truth. Later this historical-fictional woman becomes a figure who appears frequently in hooks' own and other feminist literature. With her repeated appearances, Sojourner Truth becomes a mythical figure in stories of resistance.[62] She represents a definite challenge to the dominant concept of a woman as white, fragile and (so) untrustworthy. By treating the narratives about Sojourner Truth as an inter-text, hooks builds upon a tradition, not only of resistance, but of change. hooks helps to transform the ways in which black women are represented in literature, in private and public life; but more than that she challenges us to redeem the truth by telling stories about our private and public lives. She exposes the role of race and gender as factors in our social-material location. In this way, she seeks new concepts as words with flesh (again, not fabrication or lies, but real flesh) to make sense of our world.

As already suggested, hooks herself takes part in a tradition shaped by the epistemological power of naming. Not only does Gloria Watkins rename herself bell hooks, but hooks takes up a tradition in focusing upon Isabella Baumfree who renames herself Sojourner Truth. In so doing, she names truth as *located* in a shared tradition, yet *moving* in the sense of embodied in a sojourner.[63] Socially and materially located, yet free to move, truth is not meant to be contradictory.[64] In telling her own story, in renaming herself and in telling the story of Sojourner Truth, hooks reveals the imaginative power in naming, creating new realities in the sense of making the reality of our personal and communal lives more just – true to who we are. The particularity of our life stories matters – and it matters to the conception of philosophy being advocated in this chapter. This is supported by Williams' proposal that philosophy today should be understood as a 'humanistic discipline'.[65] His use of 'humanistic' implies location within a philosophical history. hooks could be read as participating in this discipline of philosophy by her act of disrupting its history with her insistence on truthfulness. She exposes what is false.

---

62 Anderson, 'Myth and Feminist Philosophy', pp. 115–17.

63 Williams also acknowledges that the practices of human life are both something 'we' *share* as 'local' or 'perspectival' and something 'we' question as no longer straightforwardly 'universal'. In other words, human practices are not universally determined yet as cultural practices, they reflect a remarkable human (evolutionary) success. For instance, the practice of philosophy becomes part of the shared activity of understanding ourselves and our other practices. See Williams, 'Philosophy as a Humanistic Discipline', pp. 484–5, 493–6.

64 Patricia Hill Collins, *Fighting Words: Black Women and the Search for Justice* (Minneapolis, MN: University of Minnesota Press, 1998), pp. 229–51.

65 Williams, 'Philosophy as a Humanistic Discipline', pp. 477–96.

hooks' use of the figure of Sojourner Truth disrupts and displaces the public and so-called universal category 'human' in a way that gives new content to the 'we' of humanity.[66] Not just any woman who stands up and asks, 'Ain't I a Woman?' would disrupt the relevant universals of race, gender and class. Sojourner Truth disturbs the fixed concept of truth, but also our application of the concepts of human and of woman which have assumed certain (false) beliefs about freedom.[67]

What ultimately distinguishes the story of Sojourner Truth from Western myths about our freedom in an original state of nature is the central figure of a black woman whose real life story – of un-freedom – is worth writing and retelling. The story illustrates the transformative power of telling the truth – our concepts are changed by recognition of falsehoods. In this way, Sojourner Truth gains an epistemic authority, while new social markers and concepts are tried out. This process constitutes the redemptive possibilities of hooks' writing life. The injustice and falsehoods of the past are revealed and surrendered to truth. In this way, the oppressive beliefs about human and woman are to be transformed, enabling the imagination of new concepts – of truth.

Clearly, hooks is not alone in seeking new concepts, or in telling new stories, in order to make sense of the 'we' of humanity. I would like to try to elaborate one way in which Williams' genealogical account of the story of 'the State of Nature' matters. It helps in telling the truth about very basic human needs and in revealing the values of our philosophical practices. To quote Williams:

In setting out my own State of Nature story, I shall invoke some very basic human needs and limitations, notably the need of co-operation,

---

66 For more on the 'we' of humanity, the hope of making sense, and the role of truth, see Williams, *Truth and Truthfulness*, pp. 266–9.

67 Donna Haraway summarizes the significance of this tale of gender identity for white and black feminism: '"Gender" was developed as a category to explore what counts as a "woman" to problematize the previously taken for granted, to reconstitute what counts as "human". If feminist theories of gender followed from Simone de Beauvoir's thesis that one is not born a woman, with all the consequences of that insight, in the light of Marxism and psychoanalysis (and critiques of racist and colonial discourse), for understanding that any finally coherent subject is a fantasy, and that personal and collective identity is precariously and constantly socially reconstituted, then the title of bell hooks' provocative 1981 book, echoing Sojourner Truth, *Ain't I a Woman*, bristles with irony as the identity of "woman" is both claimed and deconstructed simultaneously.' (Donna Haraway, 'Ecce Homo, Ain't (Arn't) I a Woman, and Inappropriate/d Others', in Judith Butler and Joan W. Scott (eds), *Feminists Theorize the Political* (London: Routledge, 1992), p. 96.)

For a variation on a modern (Kantian) account of freedom, see Moore, *Noble in Reason*, pp. 113–46.

and I shall consider ways in which they are related to discovering and telling the truth.

. . .

The State of Nature story is a fiction, an imaginary genealogy, which proceeds by way of abstract argument from some very general and, I take it, indisputable assumptions about human powers and limitations. In virtue of that, and in line with other examples we have considered, I take it to be an example of philosophy.[68]

This example of philosophy seems to serve a similar purpose to hooks' story of Sojourner Truth. And I suggest that the use of such examples is compatible with the Pope's idea that philosophy should be about the conceptions and the values that direct human lives. Williams employs a method of genealogy to conceive his 'State of Nature story'. His conception begins with very basic human needs not unlike hooks attempt to begin a new founding myth of humanity with the very basic need for freedom and associated common human passions. According to Williams, a 'genealogy' is a story, or narrative, that 'tries to explain a cultural phenomenon by describing a way in which it came about, or could have come about, or might be imagined to come about'.[69] (I might suggest roughly that hooks explains the cultural phenomenon of racist oppression – that is injustice, or lack of freedom – by describing a way in which slavery – that is falsehood, or denial of freedom – came about, excluding certain women from being conceived as women, or as human.) Williams admits that an imagined developmental story, or fictional narrative, aims to explain a concept or value 'by showing ways in which it could have come about in a simplified environment containing certain kinds of human interests or capacities, which, relative to the story, are taken as given'.[70] In his last published book before his death, Williams introduces a State of Nature story to ultimately establish a primitive basis of truthfulness.

Williams explains this as follows:

I use a method which I call 'genealogy'. It is a descendant of one of Nietzsche's own methods, but only one kind of descendant among others. Nietzsche himself was fully aware that the critique which he directed against old illusions might call in question some of what he said himself . . . But . . . in the end he only defends the idea of there

<hr>

68 Williams, *Truth and Truthfulness*, pp. 38 and 39.
69 Williams, *Truth and Truthfulness*, p. 20.
70 Williams, *Truth and Truthfulness*, p. 21.

being truths but also gives every sign of thinking that he has uttered some.[71]

Thus both Williams and hooks seek to tell truths, which will uncover old illusions, and generate the possibility of a new story. hooks imagines a new story with her narrative about Sojourner Truth. However, her story also becomes a political narrative of resistance and redemption, in creating something powerfully different from the old myth of patriarchy, which oppressed persons in very specific ways, according to the interlocking factors of race, class and gender. In particular, Sojourner Truth challenges the racist nature of representations, which have conceived sexist oppression in terms of the suffering of white women only, whether in the 1830s or today.[72] hooks' story of Sojourner Truth, a black female figure, takes on the significance of a new, founding myth in generating a narrative that represents the differences between what a general concept – for example, woman – signifies within a system of meanings and practices and what the general concept ought to represent; hence, suggesting a new concept.

More generally, hooks' writing seeks to make sense of life by generating socially situated knowledge. As hooks explains, 'I write as one committed simultaneously to intellectual life [and to the art of writing], which means that ideas are tools I search out and work with to create different and alternative epistemologies (ways of knowing).'[73] In this art of shaping words and writing to make sense of things which have not been known or trusted, hooks (re)creates and refigures those false universal concepts which have made up an arbitrarily fixed myth of humanity.

A rational passion for a common humanity

My own thinking has been decisively shaped by hooks' distinctive conception of yearning for a space in which needs and passions can be shared.[74] This would be a space where we might imagine one's and

---

71 Williams, *Truth and Truthfulness*, pp. 18; also see pp. 19, 21–2, 31ff.
72 For more theoretical background, see Toni Morrison, *Playing in the Dark: Whiteness and the Literary Imagination* (New York: Vintage Books, 1992).
73 hooks, *Remembered Rapture*, p. 16.
74 Drucilla Cornell also builds upon hooks' idea that, in retelling stories of slavery and oppression, feminist philosophers can generate a new conception of humanity for men and women who genuinely seek to uncover the particular conditions for their own freedom as passionate and sexuate beings. See Drucilla Cornell, *Beyond Accommodation: Ethical Feminism, Deconstruction and the Law* (London: Routledge, 1991; Oxford: Rowman and Littlefield, 1999); *At*

another's common humanity, in order to create new concepts by which we can live more truthfully. For hooks, knowledge of our shared sentiments is both socially situated and critically engaged and to express this knowledge hooks creates a new concept, yearning, which reappears again and again in various ways in her writing. Her initial conception is stated as: 'The shared space and feeling of "yearning" opens up the possibility of common ground where all [our] differences might meet and engage one another.'[75]

As already seen, hooks' imagination of the possibility in yearning resonates with Moore's account of the possibility of initiating new concepts, as well as Williams' account of the shared activity of philosophy as a humanistic discipline. My own attention turned to hooks' concept of yearning in, A Feminist Philosophy of Religion: The Rationality and Myths of Religious Belief,[76] where I state that

> I support an account of . . . a rational passion named 'yearning', as a vital reality of religion. [in hooks' words,] 'under the heading Yearning . . . I looked for common passions, sentiments shared by folks across race, class, gender, and sexual practice, I was struck by the depths of longing in many of us. Those without money long to find a way to get rid of the endless sense of deprivation. Those with money wonder why so much feels so meaningless . . . there are many individuals with race, gender, and class privilege who are longing to see the kind of revolutionary change that will end domination and oppression even though [our] lives would be completely and utterly transformed.'[77]

The distinctiveness of this yearning is, in part, a result of postmodern nihilism: life has lost its meaning for many. Yearning is, also, indicative of our human need to make sense of things with new stories by which we can live more just lives. The problem that renders necessary the mediating role of stories, as in part fiction and in other part history, is that the concept of human and beliefs about freedom, which have played a central role in the Western myth of humanity, are unimaginable for all women and some men in current, empirical terms. The category 'all

---

the Heart of Freedom: Feminism, Sex and Equality (Princeton, NJ: Princeton University Press, 1998).

75 bell hooks, Yearning: Race, Gender and Cultural Politics (Boston: South Bend Press, 1990), pp. 12–13.

76 Pamela Sue Anderson, A Feminist Philosophy of Religion: The Rationality and Myths of Religious Belief (Oxford: Blackwell, 1998), p. 22.

77 bell hooks, Yearning: Race, Gender and Cultural Politics (Boston: South Bend Press, 1990), pp. 12–13.

women' must cover a range of persons globally who differ economically, materially, socially, personally and in religious, ethnic, racial and sexual terms. The explicitly available concept of human in our culture today carries only certain accepted meanings and these disallow human freedom as a genuine possibility for women generally, although it is more likely to become a possibility for particular, privileged women. Precisely how the concept of human and beliefs about freedom can inform our practices to enable flourishing is not explicable in the terms of present culture(s). To the degree that the sexist, racist or ethnocentric character of a society itself precludes the possibility that the universal concept of a free human(ity) is adequate for all persons, the problem lies in the nature of knowledge more generally.

Again I would say that a solution to a problem – in this case, the problem of the nature of knowledge – depends on the possibility of grasping new concepts. A few years ago, I proposed an exploration of the ethics of 'women telling tales' as one way to initiate new knowledge of women's practices.[78] 'Telling tales' suggests the role of imagination, in imagining new possibilities. The ambiguity of the word 'tales' is pivotal to opening up possibilities for change. This allows us to explore a new concept of woman in the sense of a concept which would have new social and material markers rendering it possible that a woman can be a trustworthy knower. In this previous exploration, I attempted to play with the positive and negative connotations of tale. 'Tall tales', 'wives tales', 'telling tales' each have double meaning. Ironically, a negative sense can help to subvert fixed assumptions about the truth or falsehood of women's testimony. Do women take part in critical dialogue? Or, do they only 'tell tales' in a pejorative sense? The problem is often one of misplaced mistrust.[79] The struggle for less partial knowledge and new, more inclusive concepts necessitates the imagination of the impossible in tales which together aim to undermine the foundational myth of patriarchy.[80] So, for example, European feminist Luce Irigaray

---

78 Anderson, 'An Ethic of Women Telling Tales', see note 50 above.

79 Onora O'Neill discusses the problem of trustworthiness without trust, demonstrating that unlike misplaced trust, 'misplaced mistrust' cannot be simply eliminated by improving trustworthiness, see O'Neill, *Autonomy and Trust in Bioethics* (Cambridge: Cambridge University Press, 2002), pp. 141–2 and 165f. We see this problem of the refusal to trust authority in ethics today; cf. Anderson, 'An Epistemological-Ethical Approach'.

80 Susan E. Babbitt describes this well: '. . . [I]n a situation in which certain options are impossible even to dream, the bringing about of the imaginability of such possibilities can be personally empowering, even if such conceivability, as is often the case, itself entails suffering. For if it were to become possible for [the woman excluded on racist and/or sexist grounds] just to *dream* that which in other terms *is*, in fact, impossible, she might have been able to deliberate about herself and eventually to act in ways, and to influence others to act in ways,

contends that the truth about 'the overbearing power' of the patriar-
chal concept of God must be told.[81] We need a new concept of God
– of divine truth – which does not reinforce the mistrust of women by
their general exclusion from trustworthiness. An epistemology of hope
opens up the possibility of creating and possessing new concepts – yet
the possibility will necessarily involve both an ethical and an epistemological struggle.[82] Ultimately, a new concept of hope rests on the
willingness of men and women to imagine new possibilities.

The central problem with imagining the impossible as possible is *both*
epistemological and ethical. An epistemological question arises about
how it is possible to imagine and know more genuinely human possibilities than currently available in racist and sexist societies; this seems
to be impossible. An ethical question arises about the abuse (instead of
the use) of the imagination in creating, telling and retelling tales. Yet
this issue of abuse is not ultimately intractable. Justice can be brought in
as a practical ideal, which critically regulates both the epistemological
and the ethical dimensions of our rational passions for the possible.[83]
Again, Moore's contention that there is a nisus for rationality, which
motivates our search for making sense of things, could enable our grasp
of a concept of hope shaped by a regulative ideal of justice. Justice does
not exist for all of 'us'; hence, it must be hoped for, along with truth
and love, from – as I have maintained – a feminist standpoint.[84] The distinctiveness of this standpoint at this political moment of postmodern
nihilism results from a struggle for truth and truthfulness.

---

that expressed the possibility of such a dream.' (Susan E. Babbitt, *Impossible
Dreams: Rationality, Integrity and Moral Imagination* (Boulder, CO: West-
view Press, 1996), p. 195); cf. hooks, *Feminist Theory*, pp. xiv, xv, 5, 165; and
Patricia Hill Collins, *Fighting Words: Black Women and the Search for Justice*
(Minneapolis, MN: University of Minnesota Press, 1998), pp. 187–91, 198–
200, 229–40.

81 Luce Irigaray, *Elemental Passions*, trans. Joanne Collie and Judith Still
(London: The Athlone Press, 1992), p. 92. Contrast Irigaray's criticism of patriarchy with the Pope's account of Mary – who personifies philosophy as a love of
wisdom and submits to God, and so philosophy to theology, in *Restoring Faith
in Reason*, pp. 171–2, §108.

82 For an epistemology that resists the dualist danger of making science
(or knowledge) an exclusively masculinist domain, and for hope that seeks to
include women and men in knowing, whether this is scientific, ethical or spiritual knowledge, see Michele Le Doeuff, *The Sex of Knowing*, trans. Kathleen
Hamer and Lorraine Code (New York: Routledge, 2003), pp. 153ff.

83 For more discussion of the role of practical or regulative ideals, see Pamela
Sue Anderson, 'Gender and the Infinite: On the aspiration to be all there is',
International Journal of Philosophy of Religion, vol. 50 (2001), pp. 191–212.

84 Anderson, '"Standpoint"', pp. 132–3, see note 23 above.

Conclusion: from a feminist standpoint

Following bell hooks in this chapter, I have employed 'feminist' to describe the struggle to end sexist oppression. But this struggle at this historical moment is aimed at a general cultural transformation which would destroy oppressive dualisms, eradicate systems of domination, hence, seek the dissolution of patriarchy in its various global manifestations.[85] Elsewhere I have defined standpoint as 'an epistemologically informed perspective, that is achieved – but not without struggle – as a result of gaining awareness of particular positionings within relations of power, determined (but not definitively so) by both material and social reality'.[86] It is from a feminist standpoint, thus understood, that I conclude this chapter. From a feminist standpoint, men and women can seek to possess trust, love and justice, in order to redeem truth and restore faith in reason.[87]

The concept of truth is located, yet not fixed, as moving in the sense that our knowledge is changing or in process; what was once thought true has been shown to be false; old concepts are being discarded; new possibilities are being opened up, giving new meanings to concepts from which we had often become disengaged in any case. Ideally, the concept of faith would be neither irrational nor determined; and the concept of reason, neither authoritarian nor reductive. I maintain that any dualism that sets reason and faith in opposition can, and should, be collapsed through a struggle to transform our postmodern culture. hooks' strategy in writing is to create a space for critical dialogue which eradicates, however gradually, domination. This becomes a place for making sense of the world, but it also provides space for healing our wounds and enabling our trust in others. Yearning for a common humanity goes to the heart of truth, but also to the depths of our embodiment, individually and collectively.

hooks arouses her readers to touch the pleasures of the body, mind and soul. She also exposes the wounds of sexist oppression caused by racism and white supremacy. hooks performs words in writing, in order to create a place for the transformation of our personal, social and racial passions. Her act of writing is a gesture of political solidarity in a standpoint that is ever restless, that is, there is always a spiritual yearning for truth and love. However, it has been my argument here that change, love and trust can only take place by the creation of new possibilities, new beliefs and concepts with which we can (re)direct our lives.

---

85 hooks, *Feminist Theory: From Margin to Center*, pp. xiv, 5, 163, 165.
86 Anderson, '"Standpoint"', p. 145.
87 Also see Collins, *Fighting Words*.

In particular, the postmodern diremption of faith and reason, theology and philosophy, runs deep among privileged philosophers and theologians. For those of us with less privilege, and a sense of responsibility for our global world, we experience a keen sense of injustice. In addition to sexist oppression there are wide-ranging injustices generating global conflicts: injustices of race, ethnicity, class, social and material inequalities. Today a very basic human need for freedom – for freedom to know and speak truth, to trust and to love – are at the heart of what needs to be transformed in our personal, social and spiritual lives. With hooks, I suggest that we seek new ways to express our spiritual desires, in making narrative sense of suffering, hope and love. As she herself says,

> As a writer, I seek that moment of ecstasy when I am dancing with words, moving in a circle of love so complete that like the mystical dervish who dances to be one with the Divine, I move toward the infinite.[88]

The political solidarity represented by 'a circle of love' is implicit in writing from a feminist standpoint. This circle creates a vision of possibility for actual change, remembering that everyone must change. This political vision aims to resist postmodern excesses and divisions, especially the extremes, which reject reason completely as always authoritarian and so totalitarian. Instead we recognize the way in which reason informs our passions for change as expressed, on the one hand, in the theologian's faith and hope, and on the other hand, in the philosopher's yearning for truth and trust; ultimately, love needs to become a common passion of both philosophers and theologians. Much more needs to be thought, written and done about love and our all too human vulnerabilities. However, for the moment, I end with a twofold claim about philosophy and theology. If we are going to move beyond the postmodern condition of nihilism, then our yearning must bring us together in order to make (better) sense of our world philosophically; and if we aim to complete this sense-making project, then theologically speaking we need to grasp the possibility of understanding ourselves in relation to the infinite – always struggling as human, yet never quite expressing the desired oneness with the divine.[89]

88 hooks, *Remembered Rapture*, p. 38.
89 Anderson, 'Gender and the Infinite'.

6. Giving Way to Nihilism: A Response to Pamela Sue Anderson

SUSAN FRANK PARSONS

I am grateful to Dr Anderson for her chapter and in particular for the way in which it brings out two dimensions of the question that concerns us in this book, the question of redeeming truth. Taking up an explicitly feminist response to this question by drawing attention to the configuration of gender in which women's thought and experience has been constructed and from which the various forms of feminism seek to liberate women, her chapter calls to mind the dilemmas that attend the understanding of being human which this difference reveals in the fabric of modern thought. By recalling this difference of gender and by summoning it to help in the project of the redemption of humanity, a work in which she is indebted to bell hooks, Anderson's is itself a brave attempt at overturning the limitations of this heritage by means of 'the passion to make and make again – where such unmaking reigns', as Adrienne Rich expresses it in her poetry.[1] There is a special role for women that takes shape here, as the ones in whom this yearning for the freedom of truth finds its place, its 'locatedness' as Anderson calls it, and so as the ones out of whose imaginative envisioning of a new universality, out of whose dreaming of dreams and telling of tales, the bringing of humanity into its own authentic truth will be accomplished. In this way she understands the challenge of *Fides et ratio* to be a call for a better concept of being human by which all people, women and men, may direct their lives, and she has shown us how this call might be obeyed.

It is certainly the case that the being of being human is very much at the heart of this encyclical, as indeed it has been a recurring theme of so much of the Holy Father's teaching for the past quarter of a century. His intellectual roots in phenomenology and in personalism, and his profound pastoral concern for what is happening to humanity in the

---

1 Adrienne Rich, 'Natural Resources', in *The Dream of a Common Language* (New York and London: W. & W. Norton, 1978), pp. 65–6.

devastations of war, of unbridled technology and of a globalized economy – these are themselves indications of his bearing of the Church's mission into these places of anguish to make manifest God's love there. He shows us that the way we understand our being human and the way in which that understanding is enacted in the world today are properly and urgently the concern of those who would witness to Christ. What is not to be taken for granted, however, in this matter is that this understanding requires a concept or indeed a cluster of concepts in which the being of being human can be grasped and set out before us as the context to which we are ordered and within which we can then take up our individual places. Such is a uniquely modern way of approaching human being, of thinking *about* human being as though it were an object of intellectual attention and of moral evaluation and certainty. It is this way of thinking that finds its fullest expression in anthropology, that science which posits the conditions of our being human as prior to our appearance and so as the ground of our subjectivity, and that is reproduced in feminism by the demand upon women to locate themselves at the rifts of anthropology's most perplexing conundra and to secure their own being as subjects there.[2]

So while I am in sympathy with Anderson's recognition of the fissure of gender which is our Western inheritance, I am less sure of the crossing of this aporia by means of concepts, more inclusive and persuasive though they be made. For we are the consequence of the unmasking of modernity's pretension to establish the foundations of human being, a disclosure that is of the essence of postmodernity and that leaves exposed the discomforting position of the human subject whose projection this is and whose need for certainty drives its continual reprojection. Thus the way in which we are to understand the being of being human is rendered all the more problematic in our time, and may be heard then with special poignancy in the text of this encyclical.

Which brings me to the second dimension of our question to which her chapter draws attention, and that is to this matter of making sense of things, making sense of our lives, making sense of the world, a phrase which has entered common parlance as the urgent task of humanity today, which Anderson herself understands to be at risk in the 'condition of nihilism' and which again she seeks to restore to us through a more noble effort of reason, a loftier work. Here what is asked of us

---

2 A good example of this would be Carol Gilligan's study of the fracture in the psycho-social development of moral thinking along which women's identity is formed as distinctive to men, a fissure that derives from Kant and the anthropological concepts that are at work in his philosophy. See her *In a Different Voice: Psychological Theory and Women's Development* (Cambridge, MA: Harvard University Press, 1982).

is twofold. On the one hand, there is to be a continuation of the work of Kant, in whom faith as basic trust and reason as the action of a subject in bringing meaning to the world enter into a kind of co-operative partnership. But there is also to be a determined response to Nietzsche, whose revaluing of truth as the truth of beings-in-particular rather than being-in-general overturns the unhealthy Western inheritance of absolute eternal ideas. These strands come together and find their focus in a project of myth-making, of writing 'a new founding myth for humanity', of setting out a 'state of nature story' in which the good things we value today – trust, love and justice in solidarity – can be given pride of place, and in which endeavour, women and men are of one mind in providing for themselves the ground of their being.

Surely the question that disturbs this project and that requires a more radical critique is: What need is there for such fabrications, and to what end? What is going on in the emergence of this necessity? For this project seems entirely to be founded upon a belief that, as everything in the tradition of thinking thus far is already fabricated, multiplying these versions of truth is a way of living up to reason's expectations upon us to be authors of our own lives. And this work as a whole is further situated by the positing of an apparently limitless horizon of possibilities from out of which this diversity can be generated, a wide open space for representation upon representation which is nothing other than a virtual nature or the world of late capitalism – it makes no difference. The necessity for these narratives, and I would venture for narrativity as such, is born of Nietzsche's uncovering of the nihilism that has been unfolding since the beginning of philosophy and that is the last scene of this beginning to be played out in the age we call postmodern. But to find that the nihilism he noted has now become itself the reason for the creation of stories that will make sense of our lives is surely not to overturn this nihilism in any way, but rather to instantiate it by repetition of the very form of power it has proclaimed to be always already at work. I cannot see a way out of this difficulty in Anderson's paper, which is intended to restore faith in reason, and to do a good and a redeeming thing thereby, which indeed must bear a *will* that reason recover its power of telling a good story, and yet in the very bearing of this will and its enactment discloses only the posturing of subjects, valiant and worthy though they may be, that is the end to which philosophy thus far conceived has brought us.[3] For after Nietzsche, does not the

---

3 Anderson sets out this project explicitly both in her *Feminist Philosophy of Religion* (London: Routledge, 2003), and in her contribution to Susan F. Parsons (ed.), *The Cambridge Companion to Feminist Theology* (Cambridge: Cambridge University Press, 2002), entitled 'Feminist theology as philosophy of religion'. In the latter, she says that the ground that 'needs to be broken

awareness of will to power mean both that there is no longer any inno-
cent reading of the tradition and at the same time that we are driven
to the edges of what can be thought, to that Archimedean point that
Bernard Williams has elsewhere described as the ultimately inaccessible
place of the philosopher?[4] To stand in recognition of this place and
its very closedness to us is the heroic undertaking of the philosopher
after Nietzsche, and Williams knew that the only work for ethics that
awaited us there would be to engage in internal critique without end.

To speak of these things is to understand the dimensions of our question which have been brought to the fore in Anderson's paper to be
an expression of the problematic that lies both within nihilism after
Nietzsche and in the concept of human being as this is passed on to us
through Kant. And if it seems that the last avenue that would safely
take us through this problematic and bring us out on the other side
as the victors over its most painful consequences has just now been
closed off, then it is necessary even to take one further step along the
path of this destruction in order that we may attend to what is going
on here. For what is at work in this response to nihilism is the breaking
up of the logic of moral thinking that has been bequeathed to us in the
Western tradition, a disintegration that can no longer, I think, be called
a diremption because even its two constituents are no longer what they
seem. The task of moral theology and philosophy in this time is deeply
troubled by this event that rumbles so uncomfortably through it, still
seeking as it does to respond to the anguish of humanity by carrying
us across from where we are to where we ought to be, even as the very
banks that contain and so define this gap are collapsing ahead of it. The
fruitlessness which pervades the ever-growing industry of ethical debate
today and the easy disillusionment with which even its best promises
are received are signs of this demise of the moral that leave us without
a hope of redeeming in this way.

It is in Kant, of course, that moral thinking takes shape as the exercise of self-sufficient reason, which he understood to be the reasoning

---

by feminist philosophers' requires 'a transformative awareness' and 'an epistemological strategy for reinventing ourselves as other. The strategy requires
philosophers of religion to struggle to achieve a feminist standpoint, in order to
tackle the problem of a hierarchy of values in which reason is valued over desire,
male over female, upper class over working class, infinite over finite, power over
weakness, centre over margin, and other similar (value) combinations, inherent in philosophical texts' (p. 56). We are asked to 'rebuild philosophy at the
level of fundamental presuppositions', and to 'create an alternative sketch of
philosophical conceptions of reason and belief' (p. 54), sustained by reason and
desire.

4 Bernard Williams, *Ethics and the Limits of Philosophy* (London: Fontana,
1985).

of a subject, a self, a human subject to whom the world is now referred after Descartes. Reason's work is to govern the will of this subject in its freedom, and so to provide for the will reasons for what it wills that serve to guide the will towards the fulfilment of its own nature. To discharge its service here, reason lays out the fundamental principles in accordance with which the will may be disciplined by duty and saved from the loss of its own unique place in human being, a loss that happens when the will lets itself be a thing determined from outside of its own intention (by feelings for example, or by predictions of likely consequences, or indeed by the will of another), and so is ruled by laws of nature rather than by laws of freedom. The will is thus underpinned in its free movement through the world by founding itself upon reason's principles, by taking as the ground of its decisions and choices in particular situations what reason has laid down as a priori, as the already prior laws or imperatives that govern all human subjects and so are universally applicable and effective.[5] The will submits itself to these laws, and it does so because its own nature, its purity (*ein reiner Wille*) is entirely ordered to the Good. It is the Good itself, and here is Kant's reading of the ἰδέα τοῦ ἀγαθοῦ, the idea of the Good of Plato, which stands above the will, and is the highest, the supreme idea, in relation to which and only insofar as it continues to hold itself in this relation, the will itself is to be called good. Kant accords to the will the utmost place in relation to Good by saying that it is impossible to think, to conceive of anything that could be taken to be good but a good will,[6] and so the will is given value in itself, shining as a jewel for its own sake by the light of the Good.[7]

Kant's *Groundwork of the Metaphysics of Morals* makes it clear that this fundamental project is entirely comprised of the rational formation of concepts, *Begriffe*, and so his interpretation of Plato's idea of the Good renders this idea as the outcome of a productive reason, of human

---

5 See Immanuel Kant, *Groundwork of the Metaphysics of Morals*, in *Practical Philosophy*, the Cambridge Edition of the Works of Immanuel Kant, ed. and trans. Mary J. Gregor (Cambridge: Cambridge University Press, 1996), 'Preface', §§387–392. [Originally published in German as *Grundlegung zur Metaphysik der Sitten* (Riga: Johann Friedrich Hartknoch, 1786), and available as Bd. 11 in the *Bibliothek der Philosophie* series (Essen: Phaidon, 1996).]

6 Kant, *Groundwork*, 'It is impossible to think of anything at all in the world, or indeed even beyond it, that could be considered good without limitation, except a good will' §393. [*Grundlegung*, 'Es ist überall nichts in der Welt, ja überhaupt auch außer derselben zu denken möglich, was ohne Einschränkung für gut könnte gehalten werden, als allein ein guter Wille.']

7 'Kant, *Groundwork*, '. . . then, like a jewel, it would shine by itself, as something that has its full worth in itself', §394. [*Grundlegung*, ' . . . so würde er wie ein Juwel doch für sich selbst glänzen, als etwas, das seinen vollen Wert in sich selbst hat'.]

thinking working out what is necessary for the freedom of the human subject whose best and highest interests it guards and governs. So, with Kant, we are presented with an understanding of the will which, by thinking of it in this way and so holding it before us, preserves what is uniquely human in human being and bestows upon human being the intrinsic value of being human. The concepts that Kant works out here on this basis – the concept of happiness, the concept of a rational being, the concept of an unconditioned necessity, and so on – these provide for the human subject the rational foundation upon which it can be secured in being and the entire context which is the domain of the Good within which horizon the freedom of the human subject in making decisions can be exercised safely and led to completion.

For Nietzsche to show that there is nothing at work here but will to power is not to impugn any individual motives or assign responsibility – moral assessment is not appropriate here – but to attend to the genealogy of moral thinking from which this way of thinking has come, fathered he suggests by Plato's idea of the Good as the valiant, the giver of power, handed over then to the masses by Christianity whose God sustains the place of this Good by divine will, and that has lately been taken up as the defining project of human being since Descartes and Kant, with whom the valiant is now located in and as the will of a subject. It is also correct I think to say that Nietzsche did not overcome this genealogy[8] but rather played into the middle of it, carrying out its logic in his writing and in his life, and, by his own recommendation of the revaluing of values as the way by which the Good is to be knocked off its perch as the highest, Nietzsche gives no exit from the logic of moral thinking so understood. It is then not surprising to find that moral philosophy and theology after Nietzsche has been consumed by the problem of finding the Good as that which reigns supreme, as that which transcends this disordered muddle of choices and styles and bright ideas and values with which the world is now awash, and so which gives us again the ultimate reason for which we are here. That its best efforts are haunted by what it has heard in Nietzsche and thus are trapped by the recycling of its own constructions, each meant to be better than ones previously, is the condition of nihilism he foretells.

This problematic resonates through the work of A. W. Moore, cited by Anderson, which is constructed as a set of themes and variations in response to the question, 'How is it possible for us to make ethical sense of things?'[9] His emphasis on 'the possession of concepts' as 'what

---

8 As Bernard Williams, among others, noted.

9 A. W. Moore, *Noble in Reason, Infinite in Nature: Themes and Variations in Kant's Moral and Religious Philosophy* (London: Routledge, 2003), p. xiii.

makes possible the autonomous, unconstrained (except by the constraints of rationality) creation-cum-discovery – in a word, the *making* – of sense' is a confident affirmation of the use to which Kant's practical reason can be put today, updated as it were to new circumstances.[10] Yet in the contemporary awareness of the social construction of knowledge the free self-legislation that Kant took to be the very foundation of rational human community has collapsed. Already such postmodern suspicion of the exercise of reason means that today we are constrained to think in terms of the possible, reflecting on what have been and are existing forms of life, in ways that are alien to Kant's thinking.[11] This contextualized empiricism is one step in the 'reconstruction' of Kant's rationalism, and it is balanced by an emphasis on the exercise of imagination. To imagine possibilities is both to reflect upon 'what might have been' and on 'what may yet be', but to do so in expectation of 'an innovative element', which Moore describes as 'an element that needs to be capable of yielding something that is, in the deepest sense of the word, new'.[12] Here Moore believes the human person is pointed towards and grounded in the infinite, not only because both our concepts as well as our maxims are constantly to be held up for moral assessment, but because we are to understand ourselves as having 'an unlimited capacity, not just to apply concepts, but to create new concepts; to develop extant concepts; to contemplate different forms of life; to respond to whatever befalls us, both by making sense of it and, correlatively, by making sense in the face of it'.[13] Thus the 'new' becomes the focal point of human hope for authentic life, as for Anderson it bears human yearning for the good, and concepts or the possession of concepts are believed to be the way of its appropriation.

If there is one section of *Fides et ratio* that especially could be commended for closer consideration of these things, it would be §90 in which the Holy Father describes this condition. Each of its phrases is thought-provoking and so takes us into the centre of our dilemma and points to what is happening in it, and inspires our thinking and our prayer most earnestly to seek out that of which it speaks. Two things are being suggested in this section that may be briefly described. The first is found in the statement that many philosophies 'have deserted the meaning of being', that indeed this desertion 'seems to dominate the shared view' of these many philosophies, and that something of this desertion and this domination lies within what is called nihilism. Indeed the desertion of the meaning of being continues to happen in

10 Moore, *Noble in Reason*, p. 73. Emphasis in original.
11 Moore, *Noble in Reason*, see esp. §§13–14, pp. 66–71.
12 Moore, *Noble in Reason*, p. 72.
13 Moore, *Noble in Reason*, p. 79.

our midst as human being too is configured, and that means situated and explained and understood, only and entirely within its parameters. What this points us to is that the essence of nihilism has something to do with being, and therefore with that *of which* nihilism is itself a phenomenon of Western thinking, and with that *to which* human being too is directed. To think this is not to be led towards a higher idea or a transcendent being that lies somehow apart from nihilism and that would trump whatever hand it has played, but it is to be led rather to what is to be found *in* nihilism, in what nihilism itself is about and thus what it reveals to us, and it is this – what nihilism is the appearance of, what it is saying to us and what can be heard in this saying – that we are asked to begin to think.

Martin Heidegger would teach us that what is going on in nihilism has to do with the coming near and the receding of being which is time, and thus that nihilism may be heard as the summoning of us into time. His description of nihilism as 'the abandonment of being', as *Seinsverlassenheit*, is suggestive of the way in which being has given itself to us to be known and so has let itself be revealed in thinking and speaking, but also of the way in which, in this very revealing, there is withdrawal that cannot be held or fixed in what is said or thought.[14] To say that there is abandonment of being in nihilism is to draw us into our own timeliness and to ask how we have come to be here and so to follow the movement of being in the tradition that has handed us on. But more than this it is to listen out for the way in which being has stayed away, *ausbleiben*, even where it has been disclosed in particular beings, because the tradition thus far has forgotten being's own timeliness in its overwhelming concern to establish what is eternal and permanent and so altogether beyond time. To hear that being is staying away, that it has abandoned us in the unfolding of nihilism that is metaphysics, is for us also to be beckoned to come towards it and so to come into being ourselves, to become transcendent not as ones who reach out to take hold of being, but as ones who are touched by being's own movement and led into its necessity. Heidegger understood that to 'heed the essence of nihilism as an essence of the history of Being itself' means that 'the plan to overcome nihilism becomes superfluous, if by overcoming we mean that man independently subject that history to himself and yoke it to his pure willing. Such overcoming of nihilism is also fallacious

---

14 Martin Heidegger, *Nietzsche*, Vol. IV, Pt. 2, 'Nihilism as determined by the history of being', trans. Frank A. Capuzzi (San Francisco, CA: HarperSanFrancisco, 1991), pp. 199–250. [Originally published as 'Die seinsgeschichtliche Bestimmung des Nihilismus', in *Nietzsche II* (Pfullingen: Verlag Günther Neske, 1961).]

in believing that human thought should advance upon the default.'[15] Rather are we to know ourselves as the ones with whom or the places where being dwells, and so as 'the there' where being comes and will come to be disclosed. And it is in awaiting this advent, in letting being be with us in the manner of its own unfolding that we are transcending. For we step back to let arise what comes to be known.

Is this a way in which we may understand the second thing that is suggested in this section of the encyclical, namely that what is at risk in nihilism is 'the denial of the humanity and the very identity of man'? If this is most often read as the call for a resistance to nihilism by means of the conceptual formulation of a more expansive and securely grounded humanism, might it not also be heard as a requirement upon us to give way to nihilism, to be taken through its being as a withholding of being, and in that way to undergo the passion of which human being is constituted? For being itself and the being of being human are intimately bound together, the desertion of the one belonging with the denial of the other. In their dwelling together of which this encyclical repeatedly speaks, something of God is revealed in the face of man, because it is in this place of encounter that the essence of man comes most alive in itself as what it is given to be, and is most utterly taken up into a future it cannot of itself produce, but which can only come to it from without because it must be crossed over in death. This being handed on into a future that is not of our making takes place in time and so in our own comportment to time as we live only and entirely on the promise of God. If the understanding of nihilism may bring us closer to being in its very withdrawal into the future where we cannot follow, and if we may know ourselves anew as ones to whom this understanding has been entrusted, then philosophy, reason, will have been stretched out to its furthest reach and will find there that in revealing the conditions for the coming of being, it will have also prepared the way for faith. For faith is beholden to a knowledge that must be received in time, a knowledge that is already but not yet, and that is itself a summons into the life of God 'when', St John says, 'we shall be like him because we shall see him as he really is' (1 John 3.2). In this is the redeeming of truth.

---

15 Heidegger, *Nietzsche*, p. 225. ['Achten wir auf das Wesen des Nihilismus als einer Geschichte des Seins selbst, dann wird das Vorhaben einer Überwindung des Nihilismus hinfällig, wenn damit gemeint ist, daß der Mensch von sich aus je diese Geschichte unter sich bringe und in sein bloßes Wollen zwinge. Eine Überwindung des Nihilismus ist auch in dem Sinne irrig, daß menschliches Denken gegen das Ausbleiben des Seins anginge', p. 368.]

7. Truth and Identity: The Thomistic Telescope

JOHN MILBANK

Truth and identity

The question of truth is deeply related to the question of identity and stability. If we think of truth as saying 'what is the case', as in 'it's true that there's a cat perched on the windowsill', then the cat has to stay still long enough for one to be able to verify this. And there has to be something distinctly recognizable as a cat. Too fast a flash of mere fur would undo everything.

However, we do not necessarily have to have anything to do with cats, who may be too elusive for the cause of truth. We can invent something stable for ourselves by making it sufficiently rigid and treating it always the same way (more or less), like a table that we eat on. Then it seems that we can be sure of saying some true things about the table. Still we may wonder if the table is really as it appears to us to be, securely shaped and coloured, and some people may use it to sit on, thereby re-defining it. A more radical recourse is to invent something more abstract like the number 1. This seems more certain and controllable – until we realize that we can only define it in relation to 2, but 1 as twice exemplified in 2 does not seem to be the pure 1 that cannot be multiplied or divided. It quickly appears that the most fundamental self-identical thing is elusive and inaccessible: it would have to be immune to participation and multiplication, but the 1s we know about can be divided and so multiplied into two halves and so forth. Then we resort to a further abstraction: turning from arithmetic to algebra and logic: whatever 1, the self-identical is, we do at least know that it cannot be *as* 1 also zero – even if, as 1 it can also be 2, 3, 4 and so forth. This gives us the law of excluded middle or of non-contradiction: 1 cannot be at the same time zero, and *no* 1, no single thing, can be and not be what it is at the same time and in the same respect. If this *were* possible, then even tautologies would not be true, but we do at least know that a standing tree is a standing tree is a standing tree, recursively, *ad infinitum*.

94

Since the ancient Greeks, just this law has been seen as the foundation of all logic, and so of all truthful discourses. Here at least one has a *formal* truth: modern thought, starting long ago with certain medieval currents, has often hoped to build on this formality towards a secure epistemology and even an ontology. But here a doubt must always persist as to whether one can cross the chasm between logical possibility and given actuality. Is anything more than a thin formal truth available to us?

For the ancients and much of the Middle Ages, things stood otherwise. The law of excluded middle only ruled actuality because there were real stable identities out there in the world. Ralph Cudworth, the seventeenth-century English philosopher and theologian noted that in Plato's *Theaetetus*, Socrates' sceptical interlocutor, Protagoras, by arguing that reality is only material particles in random flux, entailing that our knowledge of them is only the contingent *event* of our interaction with them, renders the law of non-contradiction inoperable.[1] For Socrates points out that if reality and knowledge consist only in sequences of events, then a affecting b must presuppose a_1 affecting b_1 and so on *ad infinitum*. Every item at the same time and in the same respect would already be *not* this item, and our knowledge of something could only be knowledge of this knowledge and so on recursively, such that either we could never stay still long enough to be subjectively aware, or else our staying still must be an illusion – the illusion of being a subject. Likewise, Aristotle in his *Metaphysics* said that without stable substance the law of non-contradiction cannot hold.[2] One can at least read this assertion to mean that, without stable essences, stable formed matters or *eide* out there in the world, the law of excluded middle cannot be applied to a deprived reality which would then be, like Protagoras's reality, somehow 'really contradictory'. However, I suspect that Aristotle's doctrine of the priority of act over possibility means that, more radically, he thinks that only the actuality of ontological substance makes it true in the realm of logic, which ponders possibilities, that the law of non-contradiction really does hold.

At the very least though, one can see that if this law applies only in the realm of logic, this gives us but a meagre doctrine of truth. It certainly will not allow that things in so far as they 'are' are somehow also 'true', but also it will not allow us to make truthful statements about things as they are, or even as they appear to us to be. So can we be assured that there are real, actual self-identical items in the world? Plato, it seems, was

---

1 Ralph Cudworth, *A Treatise Concerning Eternal and Immutable Morality*, ed. Sarah Hutton (Cambridge: Cambridge University Press, 1996), Book I, ch. II, p. 17; Book II, ch. II, 1, p. 33.
2 Aristotle, *Metaphysics*, 1007 a–1035 b.

half in agreement with sceptics like Protagoras: the material world was in itself a temporal flux; if it nonetheless exhibited relative stabilities we could rely on, this was because it participated in eternal and immutable archetypes of everything: trees in the *eidos* of tree, just acts in the *eidos* of justice and so on. Aristotle, by contrast, thought that the *eide* were perfectly stable within the material, temporal world, without participation in transcendence. These two views of the forms or *eide* were then synthesized in different ways by later commentators on Aristotle, by the Neoplatonists and then by Islamic, Jewish and Christian thinkers. To say that the world contained *eide* and participation in those supreme *eide* that were divine ideas, was to say that even if the world does not itself think (and most people affirmed even this in the case of the celestial realm, beyond the lunar orbit) it is nonetheless composed of thoughts or the reflection of thoughts, which are meanings. Beings themselves are also truths, because they only exist as manifesting themselves in ordered patterns related to ends they seek and the ordered proportions and relations they enter into with other beings.

This view also implies that there is an ordained proportion between things as they exist and our knowledge of things. As knowers we are not like visitors to this solar system from an altogether strange galaxy, making observations and taking notes that reality never intended us to be capable of taking. Instead, for the Platonic-Aristotelian tradition, forms in things exist in order that they may finally be known. For this reason knowledge is not a mirroring of things, a 'representation' of them, but rather it is the process by which forms themselves migrate from matter to a higher mode of being that is intellectual existence. Thus an act of thinking, for Aristotle, was identical with the realization of an objective *eidos* as a thought.[3] But inversely, to have a thought and realize an *eidos* also further fulfilled and unfolded the active capacity of thinking itself. The transition from passive reception to active formation by mind was often debated: did the passively received form really become the active form, or did it rather occasion the sympathetic emergence of the latter? Respectively, these positions can be seen as more Aristotelian and more Platonic. There were many sub-variants, and yet they all rang changes on the same shared theme. Thought, for this model was possible, not on account of the accident of mirroring, based on the example of the eye mirroring light, but rather on account of an arcane ontological proportion, or ordering, or 'convenience' between things as existing and things as known.[4]

---

3 Aristotle, *On the Soul*, 429b20–30, 430a5–10.

4 See John Milbank and Catherine Pickstock, *Truth in Aquinas* (London and New York: Routledge, 2001), pp. 1–60.

Realism and nominalism

Already in the Middle Ages however, beginning as far back as the twelfth century with people like Roger Bacon and Gilbert Porreta, this started to seem unsatisfactory.[5] On the traditional model it appears that one can only teach someone to know by sage advice to attend to one's inner light which intuits and judges by nature and without other reason. One could not, under this jurisdiction, teach a fundamental *method*, which says 'accept only the transparently clear and what can be measured and proved and shown to work in a repeated fashion'. So in a long process culminating in the seventeenth century, various thinkers suggested that knowledge was not a kind of communion with being and realization of being, but instead was logical certainty, representational measure and technological experiment.

Often these recommendations were accompanied by a theology which said in effect: 'God has laid down the world with an order that is radically contingent, according to the decrees of his freely willed charity: this order does not necessarily reflect the divine ideas, and embodies no relative necessities of essence. For this reason, our minds do not operate by gathering the ways in which the world symbolizes and participates in God, nor by abstracting out and unfolding pure essences. Instead we are to observe God's gift of creation in a detached manner (indeed like investigators from another galaxy), and to respond to the divine freedom with free usage of the world for pragmatic ends that we invent and contract with others to observe.'

What was seen as especially mysterious and unnecessarily obscure in the older view was the idea of universal essence: surely besides trees, one does not need to suppose that there is a real *eidos* of tree, even if this only exists *qua* universal in our minds? Isn't our idea of a tree just a generalization from trees, which then functions as a cognitive *sign* for trees? This getting rid of universal essences is usually known as 'nominalism' or 'terminism': universals are just conventional names or terms, not natural subsisting realities.

However, we have already seen that the *eide* were traditionally seen as the guarantors of truth, and of the operativity or even reality of the law of excluded middle. How could one now have truth without them? Well, first of all, the entire Platonic-Aristotelian tradition had always hesitated between – or tried to include both – the idea that stable substance resides in a general *eidos* on the one hand, or in an individual

---

5 See Olivier Boulnois, *Être et Représentation: Une généalogie de la métaphysique moderne à l'époque de Duns Scot* (xiiie–xive siècle) (Paris: PUF, 1999), pp. 17–107.

substance on the other, be this material or angelic (God was taken to be beyond the contrast of individuality and generality). The nominalists chose exclusively the latter fork: arguing that the sameness of an individual tree (for example) belonging to a particular species, grown bent in a particular way and so forth, was much more secure than some vague essence of 'treeness'. In the second place, however, they tended to declare (William of Ockham is the best instance) that actually universal essence as much as flux violates the principle of non-contradiction. For the traditional 'realist' (meaning here the opposite of nominalist) view, the tree *as* individual tree always shows something universal, not in an aspect but *in toto*, and not in terms of a parcelled-out share, because there is (at least for Aquinas and even to a degree for Scotus) no self-standing essence out there in the world apart from individual trees. Concomitantly the universal form 'tree' in my mind as universal also *is* the fulfilled-as-comprehended individual trees. In either case 'universal' and its opposite, 'individual' seem to coincide. Nominalism was in part a strategy for a purged Aristotelianism fully following through on the law of excluded middle.

Ockham and others also suggested that notions of participation and analogy of attribution likewise violated this law: something cannot be at once like and unlike a higher thing, not simply in some isolatable aspect – for then one could parcel out analogy between univocity and equivocity – but truly *as* its whole self. Something similar applied for the nominalists to ideas of real relation: something cannot be *intrinsically* and not just externally and accidentally related to something else without it being itself as not itself.[6] One can notice here how close real relation and universal are to each other as concepts: a real relation implies something in common shared between two things, rendering them what they are. Inversely, if trees embody a universal form of treeness, even though this form does not stand like a totem in the middle of the forest (like a mutant golden fir, as occurs very occasionally in North American evergreen forests), then it means something like the hidden relational community between them. Likewise, the really universal tree in the mind only exists as the really relational (real for the mind's relation to the thing known) intention of all particular trees.

Universal, analogical participation, real relation. These were the three essential components of the realist idea that the world holds together as a kind of arcane harmony ordained by God. In God, the source of this harmony, order was at once actuality and knowledge; the creation echoed this by a reciprocal interplay between being and knowing. Being

---

6 William of Ockham, *Quodlibetal Questions*, 4.12; 5.11; 5.12; 6.9; 6.12; 6.13; 6.14; *Summa Logicae*, 1.16.

urged towards knowing; knowing could be distilled from being, but knowing always had to return to the surplus of harmony and potential knowledge that finite being contained and that could be encompassed only by God's infinite awareness. Such an outlook in effect claimed that, as Balthasar today puts it (building upon, but improving Descartes), only the awareness that we participate in the divine understanding, which always understands more of his creation than we do, ensures that we do not think of our thoughts of things as merely solipsistic elaborations of our own being.[7]

As we have seen, this scheme of cosmic harmony was once seen as guaranteeing the operation of the law of non-contradiction, and so the presence of identity, and therefore the presence of truth. Now the nominalists in effect declared that this was, after all, half pagan myth of mysterious and ungraspable fluxions: far from guaranteeing truth, it actually violated the law of excluded middle itself. They proclaimed a disenchantment in the name of logic, or evidence, or experiment, or human political freedom, but also in the name of the divine freedom and the priority of the divine will, which as self-giving was the will to charity.

So if two accounts of truth were at stake here, so also were two accounts of Christianity – so different that they almost seem like different religions. For the old realistic account, in actuality there is no *bare* being; actual being is accompanied always by value – it shows itself as meaningful truth, just as it communicates itself as goodness. As Hans Urs von Balthasar *almost* says (but see later) in his *Theologik Volume 1*, for Aquinas and others truth was more than just representation of being, because it was also being manifesting itself as beauty; likewise the good was more than fulfilment of selfish desire, because it was an aiming for the Beautiful that is objectively loveable in itself.[8] Balthasar (now followed by Gilbert Narcissse) thus rightly draws out the crucial yet latent aesthetic character of the older vision: beauty as 'taking care of herself' (as the English Catholic artist Eric Gill famously put it) was little mentioned, just because it was so fundamentally presupposed and was the real link between being, truth and goodness.[9] Thus in the realist vision, being as value was a free gift, but also a gift of reciprocal exchange of gifts between being and knowing, knowing and willing.

---

7 Hans Urs von Balthasar, *La Théologique I: Vérité du Monde*, trans. Camille Dumont S.J. (Namur: Culture et Vérité, 1994), p. 54. In some ways Descartes is a transitional figure; the 'modern view' of knowledge is more emphatically elaborated by Locke.

8 Balthasar, *Vérité du Monde*, pp. 229–34.

9 Gilbert Narcisse, *Les Raisons de Dieu: Arguments de Convenance et Esthétique Théologique selon St. Thomas d'Aquin et Hans urs von Balthasar* (Fribourg: Editions Universitaires Fribourg Suisse, 1997).

For the new nominalist account, by contrast, the only being one can securely and entirely know is *represented* being, which is the bare fact of an individual possession of being as self-identical: 'one is one and all alone and ever more shall be so'. A finite thing can now be considered in logical abstraction from its createdness, simply as existing. Already, beginning with Scotus and later extended by Ockham, this bare logical minimal consideration of being nevertheless informed a new minimalist ontology: each thing as existing fully possesses its own being. If it did not, if as existing it only borrowed its existence from a supreme *esse* whom it resembled (as for Aquinas) then *as being* it would also not be, and as *being* finite its actual existence that it possessed would also be infinite. Already Scotus declared that analogy and participation violated non-contradiction.[10] The result was that, for Scotus, while God, as infinite, created finite beings in respect of their particularity and caused occurrence, he did not (as for Aquinas) as *esse* create general abstracted being (in the mode of finite *ens commune*) as such. So being was no longer regarded as intrinsically and ineluctably a gift, and being as finite being no longer reflected the divine infinite harmony which ensured that it was always really an exchange of reciprocities.

However, this did not mean that gift was abandoned. Modern Franciscan theologians characteristically argue that this rather allowed the gift itself to be deontologized.[11] Since being is not the gift, *finite* being is pure free gift beyond any supposed existential necessities. Reciprocity is lost, but this is not to be regretted: instead the divine gift to us is purely gratuitous and does not 'return' to God (even though God as replete does not really 'receive' anything for Thomistic theologians either) by way of a created reflection of the divine order.[12] Likewise, since the created return is in no way naturally elicited, humans make an entirely free response from within a freedom more ontologically outside divine determination than it was for Aquinas. Meanwhile, within the created order, reciprocity and teleology is replaced (already with Scotus) by formal contract and a moral law valuing primarily free personhood.[13]

So now we can see that the debate about truth, which concerns the question as to whether identity resides in the individual only, or also in the essence, is also the debate about the gift. Does the gift arise as

---

10 Duns Scotus, *Ordinatio*, I d. 3 Q. 2 art. 2.26; I d. 8 Q. 3.121; *Collatio* 24.24. See also William of Ockham, *Quodlibetal Questions*, 4:12.

11 See Orlando Todisco OFM, 'L'Univocità Scotista dell'Ente e la Svolta Moderna', in *Antonianum* LXXVI (Jan.–March 2001) fasc. 1, pp. 79–110; Isiduro Manzano OFM, 'Individuo y Sociedad en Duns Escoto' in the same issue pp. 43–78.

12 See also Jean-Luc Marion, *Étant Donné: Essai d'une Phénoménologie de la donation* (Paris: PUF, 1997).

13 See Manzano, 'Individuo y Sociedad'.

free and unilateral beyond being, or does being without the gift lose the reciprocal dimension of the gift, the dimension of gift-exchange which *complements* free unilaterality, just as essence for Aristotle and Aquinas *complements* the self-standing individual? The debate about truth then, is simultaneously the debate about the nature of goodness and of charity. Those who find essences, analogy and real relations to be contradictory, will most likely find the idea of a free gift that expects or hopes for a return to be also contradictory – as likewise violating the law of excluded middle.

Names against nominalism

So which side is right? And perhaps this is the most fundamental debate within Western culture. We can call the Scotist and nominalist way 'Modern Christianity' and suggest that it is in large part responsible for modernity as such (its legacy eventually merging, in Hobbes and Spinoza, with the neo-pagan legacy of Machiavelli). However, 'Modern Christianity' and modernity (the child it has half-parented) has increasingly run into conceptual problems. These are primarily problems with nominalism itself. All its key strategies eventually turned sour. Let me try to summarize this in three instances.

First of all, the idea that a universal is a sign. As John N. Deely's researches have shown, building on the labours of Jacques Maritain in this regard, the Iberian Thomists in the Baroque Era, especially those of the school of Coimbra in Portugal, and supremely the Portuguese theologian Jean Poinsot (John of St Thomas) produced an effective counter-riposte.[14] Not only is a universal a sign, but a thought as such in its character as an inner word (as Aquinas already taught), is itself a kind of sign. A first encounter with one's first tree would already think it under the sign 'tree' without explicit reference to other trees; one would only see it as an individual tree through the inchoate recognition that there might be other trees of different shapes and sizes that were still trees. Because we only grasp the individual tree via sign of tree in general, the relation of tree to sign of tree must be a *real relation*: we cannot think of a tree without its sign and merely bring the two together *ad placitum*. No, since the tree is only invoked through the sign, the sign must be really and not accidentally related to the tree.[15]

---

14 See John N. Deely, *New Beginnings: Early Modern Philosophy and Post-modern Thought* (Toronto: University of Toronto Press, 1994), esp. pp. 53–86.

15 Jean Poinsot (John of St Thomas), *Cursus Philosophicus*, I, qq. 1–6, 646a 9–41 – 693a31. [John Deely (ed.) *Tractatus de Signis; the Semiotic of John Poinsot* (Berkeley, CA: University of California Press, 1985), pp. 116–219]

This circumstance does not then apply only to our *concept* of the tree; it applies also to our percept and mental image of the tree. Hence whereas the nominalists said that 'a concept is only a sign', the Coimbrists declared that even a percept and a mental image is a sign. It followed for them that if the rawest material of all thinking still involves a sign-relation, then it can never be a question of 'only' a sign, nor of a merely stipulated relation. If a percept or image is itself a sign, it is in a sense already a faint adumbration of a concept; in consequence a concept as a more abstract and reflexive sign is also indispensable for a more fully developed knowledge even of individuals and is therefore never a 'mere' sign only.

Moreover, for Poinsot we negotiate the actual world in terms of natural signs: the sight of a track and a break in the trees suggests a way through the forest and so forth. Without these natural signs we would be lost, doomed to pure sylvan errancies, since we cannot recognize the path as path in treading it, unless we first grasp it as sign of a continuous way. These natural signs are therefore instances of cognitive real relations latent in nature herself.

There is also an important further point: while mind is less substantive, as less self-standing, than a physical reality like a tree, its relations to things via concepts which are signs is as real as the tree's relation to the ground on which it depends. This applies *both* to conventional 'stipulated' signs (like the 'King's Head' on an inn-signboard) which are said by Poinsot to be 'materially transcendental'(conventional) *and* to natural signs: both types are 'formally' speaking ontological rather than merely 'transcendental' relations, because in both cases the sign-relation is indispensable for thought. Poinsot noted that being and knowledge coincided in God precisely in the mode of relation, as the doctrine of the Trinity finally explicates.[16]

Nominalism's very names therefore are names on its tombstone: we cannot after all obtain proper descriptions before attaching names of a general type.

---

16 On the real relation of stipulated signs, see *Cursus Philosophicus*, I, q. 2 658617–659633 [*Tractatus de Signis* 141–2]. For the reference to the Trinity, see *Cursus Philosophicus* q. 17 a 1, 575a19–b28 [*Tractatus de Signis*, p. 83]: 'in God relations are not extrinsic denominations but intrinsic forms'; a 3 585a1 – 588b11 [*Tractatus* pp. 103–108]. See John of St Thomas, *Cursus Philosophicus*, q. 17 a2 579b35 – 580a28 and John Deely, *Four Ages of Understanding* (Toronto: University of Toronto Press, 2001), pp. 382–5.

The elusive individual

Let us look in the second place at problems which have emerged with the idea of individual substance.

William of Ockham thought that he had reduced the list of categories to substance and quality.[17] However, if there only exist individuals, the notion of qualities 'attaching' to individuals, and the often accompanying idea that we only perceive individuals in terms of these qualities, seems problematic. Just what is this mysterious 'attachment'? It seems just as occultly sympathetic as essence, real relation and analogy. Qualities ought simply to *be* the individual substance, or else other individual substances accidentally attaching to it, like limpets to a rock. One can read aspects of Leibniz's work as trying to rectify this situation: if a thing and its qualities are the same, then they can be substituted for each other *salva veritate*.[18]

The full reductionist programme however awaited the twentieth century. Then Frege and Russell attempted to reduce every 'is' of predication to the 'is' of pure identity: 'x is y' as in 'this apple is red', is then only comprehensible as x = y where 'equals' spells identity. There must be no obscure and impenetrable attachments. However, as the American Catholic philosopher and religious solitary (educated partly in France) Claire Ortiz Hill has recently well shown, this radical programme is unsustainable.[19] One cannot reduce all the qualitative aspects under which individual things appear to us simply to the things themselves in their bare extensional existence. The tree comes to us sighing, creaking, resistant, concealing, growing and so forth. If we tried to identify all these things we would soon produce nonsense. And why? Because the referent, the tree, is *only* available to us under an infinite multitude of senses or aspects, which in attending to, we also *intend*. For this reason, the collapse of the attempt to reduce quality to equality with individual substance entails also the problematization of individual substance as such.

So just as that seeming ally of nominalism, the sign, led back to universal and real relation, so also, as phenomenology has realized, its other seeming ally, the individual substance, proves intrinsically multiple and self-concealing (like the back of the tree that always remains however

---

17 William of Ockham, *Quodlibetal Questions*, 7.2 resp: 'qualities of the third species differ in reality from substance' (unlike relation, action and passion, position, etc., etc.).

18 See Hidé Ishiguro, *Leibniz's Philosophy of Logic and Language* (Cambridge: Cambridge University Press, 1990), pp. 17–43.

19 Claire Ortiz Hill, *Rethinking Identity and Metaphysics: On the Foundations of Analytic Philosophy* (New Haven, CT: Yale University Press, 1997).

many times we run round it). Instead of it being the case that there are only atomic things, it turns out that (as George Berkeley already taught) there are only multiple qualities (in fact multiple shared essences) since the tree has no monopoly on sighing. Just how it is that we perceive through all this annual flurry but one tree, is the real mysterious thing: what else can one say but that the mind constructs a kind of analogous holding together that enables it intentionally to reach the real tree? Once nominalism self-deconstructs, it seems that analogy lies not only between things but within things as before them, so allowing them to be. Another way of putting this would be to say that there can be no access to ontology without a complex phenomenological detour.

The problem of aspects (as first opened up by Husserl and later considered by both Heidegger and Wittgenstein) seems therefore to ruin individual substance and to disclose the analogical infinity of the particular thing in a way that even older realism had not seen. I hope that we are beginning to realize then, how the collapse of nominalism does not simply *take us back* to the older realism. It is actually the same with signs: Poinsot already saw that if thoughts are signs, then the signs of culture are lived thoughts and real relations. Beyond Thomas, as Maritain suggested, he started to see human historical culture as essential to the unfolding of our thought and participation in the divine *logos*.[20] (Poinsot's thoughts on intellectual being and signs can supplement attention to the Thomist metaphysics of *esse*, even though – dissenting from Deely here – one can agree with Gilson against Maritain that Poinsot like most of the Baroque Thomists misunderstood this metaphysics.) Deely has plausibly argued that C. S. Peirce linked signs and real universals in a fashion like that of Poinsot, and to a degree indicates that his claimed kinship with Scotus rather than Aquinas was mistaken.[21] But Peirce added to the counter-nominalist reaction the point that if a universal as real is still a sign, then indeed it is only partial and so *aspectual*, and must always be interpreted by a formally 'third' position which 'abducts' to an absent indicated thing. Although Aquinas also knew that one cannot ever 'survey' the interval between thought and thing, Peirce adds again a more temporal dimension: not only does the *eidos* arrive in the mind like an event, it must always be further interpreted, in a hermeneutical process that runs to infinity. What guides this interpretation? It can only be for Peirce the will towards more realizations of the Good in the world, which yet

20 Jacques Maritain, *Distinguish to Unite or the Degrees of Knowledge*, trans. Gerald B. Phelan (Notre Dame, IN: Notre Dame University Press, 1995), pp. 75–145.
21 Deely, *New Beginnings*, pp. 39–109, 183–245; *Four Ages of Understanding*, p. 385.

assumes that this unfolds further a *real ontological bond* between the sign-universal and the absent original which it conveys to us. In a comparable fashion, Balthasar rightly suggested that already for Aquinas truth was not just Greek *aletheia,* the disclosedness of being, but also Hebrew *emet,*[22] truth as bond or fidelity, or *troth* as one could so nicely say in Old English. One helps to reveal truth in plighting one's troth to being. But the semiotic perspective accentuates this plighting as a renewal through variation of ontological vows in the course of historical time. Truth as event echoes onwards and never quite, in time, fully occurs.

So signs and aspects have started to undo nominalism, and to insinuate a reborn and extended realism: a kind of Thomistic Telescope – the same *organon,* but drawn out and allowing us to see further and more clearly.

Sets or essences

Now I want to suggest a third new lens for the telescope and this has to do with the question of numbers and sets. As Claire Ortiz Hill reminds us, Frege sought a way out of his reduction of predication to equality via Cantor's mathematical set-theory.[23] Thing and quality could be identified in so far as a qualified thing is one example of a single set of kinds of things: the red apple is identical with the apple since the red apple falls within the set of all apples. One can say that in order to handle qualities, nominalism must turn to sets instead of essences; more suspiciously, one might say that sets are the minimum obeisance that nominalism is forced to render to essences. Already though, it had emerged with Cantor himself that sets are afflicted by paradoxes not entirely remote from the third man argument that supposedly undermined the Platonic theory of forms. This is doubly significant, because set-theory not only deals with numbers which are, as we saw, the most primitive paradigms of identity, but also, by treating even natural numbers as primarily sets and instances of sets, seeks to logicize arithmetic and not mystify it as necessarily a revelation of 'real' numbers. Although Cantor in fact made realist affirmations regarding number, he did not consider these to be essential for his formalist account of mathematics. In this account numbers are sufficiently defined by their distinctness and insertion into a linear series; as such they are 'intersubjective' for Cantor. While he also considered numbers (outside the bounds of pure arithmetic) as 'transubjectively' imaging physical real-

22 Balthasar, *Vérité du Monde,* p. 39.
23 Claire Ortiz Hill, *Rethinking Identity,* pp. 2–3, 57–73, 111–16.

ity, he nonetheless thought that they only enjoyed a fully real status in themselves in so far as they existed in the mind of God. (Here he cited Augustine; yet for Augustine as for other genuinely Platonizing thinkers, our numbers can only be analogically akin to the divine ideas in their eminently 'quantitative' aspects.)

Thus if nominalism began by saying that universal essences violate the law of excluded middle, now it is threatened by the vaunted discovery (in the paradoxes of set-theory) that so do *individuals* in their most paradigmatic arithmetical and logical instances.

Already in the Middle Ages, Robert Grosseteste and later Gregory of Rimini and others noted the existence of what we today call transfinites. Thus 1 + 1 + 1 is an infinite series, and so is 2 + 4 + 8 + 16, yet the latter seems infinitely to grow bigger than the former. Or again, the series of all even integers seems paradoxically to be the same size as the series of all even and odd integers, when both are extended to infinity, even though the continuum of the latter series must from another perspective be considered greater. Cantor, however, argued that this kind of example does not show radically incommensurable transfinite infinities, since the drawing of endless lines across the two infinite series between each respective member establishes the same infinite cardinality which he named aleph-zero.[24] Here he appeared arbitrarily to ignore the increase factor in the medieval examples, or the 'escaping' factor of every next even integer in the modern one (2 is more than 1, 4 than 3, etc.), and he did so because he rejected the idea that the equality or else inequality of two or more series could be a matter of pure choice. The increase factor was thus inconsistently relegated by Cantor to the realm of pure indefinite possibility, even though this factor alone constituted the difference between the two sets which allows one to talk of two 'different' cardinalities that are then deemed to be 'equal'. This opposition to choice in the field of pure arithmetic was also exhibited in his equally dubious rejection of Guiseppe Veronese's claim for the reality of actual infinitesimals.

The Cantorian set-theoretical paradox emerges from his treatment of the problem of the transfinites. His own example of transfinitude depends upon multiplying or subdividing whole digits with different finite quantities to produce different series. A posited increasing or decreasing difference of an individual digit (by fractal multiplication

---

24 Robert Grosseteste, *De Luce, passim*; Georg Cantor, *Contributions to the Founding of the Theory of Transfinite Numbers* (New York: Dover, 1955). See in addition for most of the details regarding Cantor in this paper, J. W. Dauben, *Georg Cantor: His Mathematics and Philosophy of the Infinite* (Cambridge MA: Harvard University Press 1979), pp. 108, 122, 128–31, 143–8, 233–5, 296.

or division) is alone what allows 'diagonalization'. The latter concept indicates the fact that, however far one infinitely subdivides in turn the infinitely subdivided units of a numerical interval, one can still construct diagonal lines across the vertical lines of the subdivisions to produce an infinite sum of the subdivided units higher than the total infinite sum of all these subdivisions, since any diagonal line drawn across a set of verticals will be longer than any single vertical line. In the situation of infinitely continuous division, this is the case because the diagonal is always one unit ahead of the previous position on the vertical that it has just crossed. This ensures that even the infinite diagonal is always longer than an infinite series of verticals that it has actually traversed. To the seemingly exhaustive sum of the infinite, the infinite diagonal therefore endlessly adds 'one more'.

This diagonal, usually termed C, is said to diagonalize out of a set which might appear to contain it: C is in this way somehow greater than aleph-zero. Such a set thereby becomes 'non-denumerable'.

It should be noted here that, since aleph-zero denotes a cardinal sum, it indicates an actual and not merely potential infinite; hence the contrast between aleph-zero and C cannot be approximated to that between a finite potential infinite and the real actual infinite in Aquinas's thought. Cantor's relationship to scholastic mathematics was in fact highly ironic: against Aristotelianism he affirmed actual mathematical infinites, and against materialistic determinism he rejoiced in the indeterminism of transfinites. Yet in common with scholastic tradition, he, as a devout Catholic, feared any validation of an immanent, material eternity. Thus Cantor vigorously and incoherently denied that transfinites confirm the existence of infinitesimals, on the basis of the Archimedean principle that a number is a number if a finite or infinite group of them can be added together to produce yet another linear magnitude. Cantor claimed that this principle was demonstrable, thereby denying its traditional status as a pure axiom, which it clearly is, since it aims to define the concept of ordinary number as such and cannot therefore itself be proven within such a linear system.

Cantor sincerely believed that transfinites could once and for all banish such spectres as the infinitesimals. Thus even though they were a form of mathematical actual infinity, he still hoped that they would *take over* the older metaphysically restrictive function of the mathematical potential infinite. By showing the measurable order of actual infinity in the immanent world, they would rule out of play an infinitely divisable continuum, real infinite magnitudes and real numbers smaller than any arbitrarily small real numbers yet more than zero (infinitesimals). He hoped thereby to confine the immanent actual infinite to the cardinality of aleph-zero and the linearity of increasing or decreasing transfinite cardinal sets. Yet as we have seen, he evades the situation where an advancing or diminishing series simultaneously constitutes and disturbs cardinality, in such a way that one can regard a set equally in terms of a relatively cardinal or a relatively ordinal aspect. Infinitely large or infinitely small numbers are then in the same undecidable case as the transfinites: one can think of the greatest of the infinitesimals simply as having an infinite cardinality, or alternatively one can think of it as linearly advancing to the number 1 in terms of multiplying itself by the imagined smallest of the transfinites (the cardinality of the lowest 'diagonal') which stands in linear contrast to multiplying itself by the next smallest of the transfinites and so forth.

But a similar consideration applies to diagonalization itself. Cantor thought that he had insinuated a kind of order into disorder, since C is the infinite plus 1. However, Kurt Gödel later rightly declared that it was undecidable whether C was greater than aleph-zero by a kind of leap, or whether there were an infinity of mediating diagonals between them – that is to say, between the diagonal and the set of all the verticals.[25] This ensures that C is both greater *and* not greater than aleph-zero – that a set contains and does not contain itself – violating the law of non-contradiction. The same can in fact be said for Grosseteste's paradox: 2 + 4 + 8, etc. is and is not bigger than 1 + 1 + 1, etc. Furthermore since, in the case of a numerical set, the set is defined by a numerical series and contains such series, there is recursion here of much the same kind as afflicts Bertrand Russell's famous set of all sets that do not contain themselves. For Russell the set of all apples is clearly not itself an apple – else it could not be claimed to contain all apples – in a way that is less clear for the Platonic form of an apple. And the set of all sets of fruits is likewise not itself a set of fruits. However, the set of all sets of this kind (sets not containing themselves as members) appears to lapse back into the condition of a Platonic form after all. It would seem that, once again, the set of all sets not containing themselves is not itself an example of what it contains, else it could not be exhaustive and fulfil the very condition for being a set. But on the other hand, if it is not contained by what it contains, it follows that it *is* itself an example of a set not containing itself as a member. An ineluctable but contradictory conclusion then ensues: this set includes itself as an example of itself precisely *because* it does not do so.

These paradoxes only intrude when one invokes the infinite: 'all sets' and 'all sub-sets', etc. Graham Priest plausibly argues that diagonalization has always lurked, whenever it has been seen that the finite can

25 See Brian Rotman, *Mathematics as Sign: Writing, Imagining, Counting* (Stanford, CA: Stanford University Press, 2000), pp. 73–4.

be infinitesimally fractalized – whenever one thinks of a finite thing as actually containing infinite divisions within itself.[26] Hence the infinite presumed set of divisions inside a grain of sand exceeds the grain; more subtly the inside of a tree is an organic series with infinite potential that could exceed the whole tree like a cancer. Likewise, we cannot say which hybrid of the infinite sub-sets of types of apples will ultimately mutate into another kind of fruit altogether. Much more profoundly, for Aquinas the 'accident' of participated infinite *esse* exceeds the finite essence of a creature.[27] One might say here that Being 'diagonalizes out' of createdness. Or again, Kant resumed and complexified an ancient conundrum – if one imagines a totality, one can immediately imagine the breaching of that totality. Hegel pressed this point against him: all categorial limits can only be established insofar as they are transgressed.[28] Critique based upon the bounds of an available set can always be trumped by a metacritique which points out that the bounds are violated in their very establishment. It is the same it seems with every law, theoretical or practical; it is itself within the law, yet must be above it in order to establish it. It must be implicitly the exception to its own rules, and so its anarchy keeps pace with and ceaselessly crosses out its own legitimating measure.[29]

Attempts have been made to evade these paradoxes. They all involve an attempt to escape recursion and vicious circularity by treating sets as qualitatively different from what they contain. Russell suggested that aporetic master sets are somehow of a higher *type* than the straightforward set, and that the first horizontal numerical series in Cantor's proof of transfinitude is of a different 'type' from the enclosed vertical sub-series.[30] Claire Ortiz Hill today suggests that sets are more like phenomenological aspects or ontological essences.[31] But this move in Hill's version in effect tends to 're-platonize' mathematics and logic in the sense that it bends sets back into essences, into kinds of things-in-

---

26 Graham Priest, *Beyond the Limits of Thought* (Cambridge: Cambridge University Press, 1995). See Milbank and Pickstock, *Truth in Aquinas*, p. 34; Marion, *Étant Donné*, 'Adveniens extra', pp. 17–21.

27 See Milbank and Pickstock, *Truth in Aquinas*, p. 34; Marion, *Étant Donné*, 'Adveniens extra', pp. 17–21.

28 See Priest, *Beyond the Limits*, pp. 79–123.

29 See Giorgio Agamben, *Homo Sacer: Sovereign Power and Bare Life*, trans. Daniel Heller-Roozen (Stanford, CA: Stanford University Press, 1998).

30 Claire Ortiz Hill, *Rethinking Identity*, pp. 91–111.

31 Claire Ortiz Hill, *Rethinking Identity*, pp. 136–53. On aspects in phenomenology, see Robert Sokolowski, *Introduction to Phenomenology* (Cambridge: Cambridge University Press, 2000), pp. 17–22. For a fine demonstration that Wittgenstein was also centrally concerned with the question of aspects see Stephen Mulhall, *On Being in the World: Wittgenstein and Heidegger on Seeing Aspects* (London: Routledge, 1993).

themselves existing in a sphere of pure noetic constitution without any necessary reference to actuality (even if it seeks to evade the Platonism involved in recursion and the problems of the third man argument).

Thomism, psychologism and phenomenology

But should we not simply rejoice – is this not nominalism's self-dissolution and our return to the ancient world of real numbers and real logical essences and so forth? But to rejoice would be to accept the unstable truce of much twentieth-century mathematics, logic and philosophy.[32] In this truce, philosophy has its own proper field of possible logical or phenomenological items to investigate, without having to venture upon philosophical speculation about transcendent being outside eidetic appearances, or else outside the consequences of propositional logic. At the same time, the 'Platonic sphere' of Fregean logical items or Husserlian pure phenomena supposedly gives philosophy a task beyond naturalistic science, whose investigations of the brain might otherwise be taken as displacing the need for philosophy altogether.

Such a prospect was indeed often proposed before the advent of Frege and Husserl, and is again often proposed today. Yet we forget that a non-naturalistic psychologism was entertained by the originally Catholic Aristotelian Brentano, as by the early Husserl himself.[33] For Aristotle as for Aquinas's actualism, logic is a property of actual thoughts, of the *psyche*, if not of the mere material brain as for J. S. Mill. Thomism therefore has no stake in simplistic anti-psychologism, nor in possibilistic and supposedly timeless universal essences that are extra-mental – indeed this mode of immanent Platonism (as found in Frege, Husserl and even in Peirce) is really more Scotist in flavour and long-term inspiration. For Aquinas, by contrast, essences are present as universals only in the *psyche*, and for this reason do not escape the materially grounded *temporality* of the specifically human *psyche* – a temporality that is accentuated when we realize that the noetic essence is also sign, aspect and aporetic set. (And indeed for Platonism and Neoplatonism numbers are but conjectured shadows, in a way that is actually *compatible* with non-Euclidean geometries etc: it was in fact Proclus who first stressed the constructed, contingently 'problematic' character of Euclid's geometry.)[34]

---

32 See Rotman, *Mathematics as Sign, passim.*

33 See Martin Kusch, *Psychologism: A Case Study in the Sociology of Philosophical Knowledge* (London: Routledge, 1995).

34 Proclus, *A Commentary on the First Book of Euclid's Elements*, trans. E. R. Morrow (Princeton, NJ: Princeton University Press 1970).

Just for this reason, a telescopically extended Thomism outman-oeuvres pure phenomenology (phenomenology claiming to be the whole of philosophy) by showing that even its most radical effort at reduc-tion is, as Eric Alliez puts it, 'impossible'.[35] For the temporality of the given phenomenological event ensures that there can be no immanent gnoseological security. No manner of appearing to a consciousness can be permanent or final, since, as Protagoras says in Plato's *Theaetetus*, it cannot escape the way in which our knowing, which is expressive of a unique situated perspective and selective response, has always already altered what appears to it. This applies also to the case of all categorial arch-phenomena postulated as general conditions of possibility for appearing in general – like the ontological difference (Heidegger), the saturated adonation of the subject or the aesthetic object (Marion) or auto-affection (Henry). These overarching frameworks also only appear to awareness in the course of time and if they present to us something that is, indeed, always unavoidable, then at the same time they present us with something that is inherently problematic and irreducibly sub-ject to radically different interpretations.

So when phenomenology claims to be able to present such transcen-dental phenomena as reductively given to analysis, it can only do so by virtue of a dogmatic treatment of the bounds of finitude, which ignores the fact that the boundary between the finite and the infinite is not itself a clear and given border within finitude. Thus being is seen as the authentic nullity that lies within and beyond mere finite beings; the saturation of the gift within beings is understood as the non-appearing 'call' of the invisible to an equally radically concealed subjectivity, and the auto-affection of the subject is understood as an immediate presence of self to self in the very act of awareness which involves no detour via corporeal sensing or reflexive imagining. Essentially, phenomenology's dubious claim to displace metaphysics is here itself rooted in hidden assumptions derived from a Scotistic metaphysics by way of the Kantian legacy: within the field of being taken as univocal one can posit a clear boundary between finite and infinite, such that the finite is fully com-prehensible within its own terms.

Thomism however, or an 'extended' Thomism, still offers in the face of this 'modernism' an alternative hermeneutics of being and know-ing in general that is at once 'pre' and 'post' modern. The grammar of 'finite' suggests that it can only be known in conjunction with the infinite; the phenomenology of finitude suggests that (as for Aquinas) it is at once radically 'finished' and yet also 'incomplete' insofar as it

---

35 Eric Alliez, *De l'impossibilité de la phénomenologie: sur la philosophie française contemporaine* (Paris: Vrin, 1995).

limits both actuality and possibility; a speculative apprehension of finitude (after Eckhart, Cusa, Bruno and Pascal) suggests that the finite
is always hollowed out by infinitude, just as a grain of sand is endlessly divisible, and moreover that a limited thing is only definable by
its relations to what lies outside itself – relations which are themselves
potentially infinite in scope. Accordingly, one possible interpretative
response to the grammar, phenomenology and logic of the finite is to
argue, after Aquinas, that since, according to our human *modus cogno-
scendi* it is always the finite instances of being, truth, goodness beauty
or spirit that make most sense, and since, nonetheless, it is also clear
that these instances do not furnish any exhaustive experience of the
transcendentals or the quasi-transcendentals (spirit, knowing, desiring,
etc. which coincide with being, truth, etc. in God but not in all finite
things), we always experience a partial apprehension of realities whose
true home is in the infinite. This hermeneutic ontology remains truer,
one might argue, to the irreducibly murky character of the boundary
between finite and infinite by not allowing that the finite is comprehensible simply in its own terms, or that one can distinguish infinite from
finite merely in terms of an infinite quasi-quantity or else by a hypostasized negation of all bounds (as with Heidegger). Instead, this ontology
seeks to safeguard the judgement that we consistently experience or
in some sense 'see' a *mediation* between the visible and the invisible.
Such a judgement and such an experience remains ineffable: yet the
dogmatic claim for such an ineffability can only be ruled out by the
counter-dogmatism of the Scotist-Kantian legacy within whose horizon
pure phenomenology still stands.

This counter-dogmatism which arbitrarily shelters the finite from
the infinite (or vice versa in the case of Levinas and Marion) grounds
pure phenomenology as a 'rigorous science'. Once this dogmatism is
exposed as such therefore, one can see that such a project is in reality
impossible. And given this impossibility, a radical scepticism seems to
open to view. The very reasons that render phenomenology impossible,
also ensure that its critical bracketing of transcendence is metacritically
abolished: since no stable *noemata* appear within the realm of noetic
appearing, bracketing loses its alibi and *raison d'être* in terms of any
secure, isolatable, self-appearing categorical framework. Without the
alibi, the investigative assumption must be that bracketing can never
have been where it claims to be according to the witness of a supposed
reductive clarity, and instead that our intentions, via signs, directly
reach but modify, objective worldly realities.

And this presumption, despite its proximity to a hyper-scepticism
(because of the presumed modification involved in all knowing), may
reopen the path to a genuine security for knowledge grounded in eter-

nal realities, as opposed to the immanent security that is illusorily offered by the foundationalism of most twentieth-century philosophy – a security that, after all, secures only a 'human' knowledge that could be nothing more than perspectival illusion.[36]

Number and the dynamic universal

We have seen that the logical and phenomenological 'essences' that reappeared in twentieth-century thought were actually at once too static and at the same time too little psychic, since they were but whimsically placed beyond the limited naturalness and subjectivity of the human mind. Yet just because this presumed psychologism was suppressed, a 'third realm' of logical beings and *noemata* could be substituted for the assumption that such essences are ontologically real, which follows (one could persuasively argue) from the natural intentional bent of the human mind. Essences could be newly deployed as a barrier against the need for any metaphysics evoking transcendence only because they themselves were the prime counters within a dogmatic metaphysics of immanence.

One can argue that Clare Ortiz Hill is therefore wrong in her Husserlian desire to substitute this sort of essence for the notion of a set. One needs instead something like a new sort of hybrid 'set-essence'. The notion of 'essence' would return because that of 'set' turns out to be aporetic, yet 'essence' remains 'set' because the notion of 'essence' alone does not successfully banish every *aporia*.

For at this point we need to acknowledge what was *valid* in the nominalist critique of essence, as also of analogy and real relation. Surely they *do* tend to violate the principle of non-contradiction, and we can reconstrue this in terms of the way these concepts involve numeration and the interference of the infinite in the finite. In fact, Aristotle already declared in the *Metaphysics* that the basic paradigm of generic essence is number – which is metaphorically akin to the *stoicheion* of geometry which is an ultimate part of matter (that which remains formally the same however further subdivided).[37] To this degree Western philosophy

---

36 This was grasped by Derrida for phenomenology and by Rorty for analytic philosophy: both writers though lapse into a scepticism that pays negative tribute to what they comprehensively deconstruct. This is because they fail to see that they have deconstructed the 'metaphysical' (or onto-theological) barrier against 'metaphysics' if one takes this term (anachronistically) to mean the tradition of analogical ontology which referred being to God and not God to being (the Cappadocians, Dionysius, Augustine, Bonaventure, Aquinas, Eckhart, Cusa, Pico, Bérulle, etc.).

37 Aristotle, *Metaphysics*, 1014 a 26–1014 b 15.

remained Pythagorean. Even if the universal of a tree is not a tree, even if it is only in the mind, is a sign, conveys an unfolding series of aspects and manifests the event of the arrival of *eidos* in constantly renewed interpretation, it still, in all these modes, sustains a dimension of numeration and inclusion. Whatever else we are doing in thinking, we are always doing mathematics: distinguishing, dividing, uniting, including, excluding, denumerating, subnumerating, and so forth. The set conceived as type or essence is supposed to evade the breaking of the law of identity thrown up by set-theory, but the nominalists already showed that the notion of essence appears also to violate this law, and in any case the notion of essence has never been free of the notion of number and number entails the idea of a set.

So one should not say that the (paradoxically) recursive set must be replaced by premodern essence, but rather that the recursive set is revealed in its contradictoriness as once again essence, which *in turn* we must now reconceive in terms of number and recursive set, as earlier we reconceived it in terms of sign and aspect. Since essence is newly grasped as dynamic, as appearing only in a series of infinite aspects that must always be interpreted as signs of further aspects, essence now possesses in its constitutive multiplicity and eventfulness, an inescapable numerical aspect (in terms of both natural integers and transfinite sets and other actual infinites).

Already, in the seventeenth century, Ralph Cudworth had somewhat renumerized the notion of essence. He sought to reintegrate the new mathematicized physics into Platonic-Aristotelian tradition by introducing a new, non-negative fundamental quasi-matter consisting in mathematical and geometric basic elements whose essence lay in pure logical form, not mere material extension. Higher forms of active power (exhibited in the motions of magnetism, planets, plants and animals) beyond this basic level displayed the presence of other ontological realities besides the mathematical *ogkoi* or 'bulks'. These higher forms Cudworth named *dynameis* or 'active principles'.[38] And yet these were for him manifest primarily in the harmonious and self-sustaining aesthetic patterings of the static 'bulky' mathematical elements. These patterings for Cudworth constituted *real relations* that he termed *scheses*.[39] When we understand the truth, our mind reproduces or sometimes artificially originates such *scheses*. Here a new acknowledgment

---

38 Ralph Cudworth, *The True Intellectual System of the Universe*, Vol. *II* (Bristol: Thoemmes, 1995), pp. 390–4; Vol. II, p. 619: here nature bestows 'a kind of life' in everything; *A Treatise Concerning Eternal and Immutable Morality*, Book III, ch. I, 3–4, p. 51; ch. II, 4, p. 57; ch. III, 1, p. 57; Book IV, ch. 7, 1, p. 73–4 and in particular 5.
39 Cudworth, *A Treatise*, Book IV, ch. II, 4–13, 86–96; ch. III, 11, 111.

of the mathematical building blocks of reality goes along with a more flexible and still more relational understanding of the categorial organization *common* to mind and the world, as compared with medieval scholasticism.

Cartesian dualism is thereby, one might argue, benignly plundered by Cudworth. There are two basic kinds of finite being: the bulks and the active principles. However, even the inert and mutually external bulks are the deposits of vital activity, and this activity has hierarchical degrees culminating in human understanding. The latter (foreshadowing Peirce) does not just fully elaborate forms under the guiding lure of the Good (which for Cudworth is identical with the Divine Father as single source of the multiple 'comprehension' of the Son-*Logos*),[40] but *anticipates* the discovery and invention of new forms. For Cudworth as later for Balthasar, the more the mind is self-elaborative, all the more is it receptive.[41]

A modern integration of mathematicized physics, and grasp of the numerical dimension of essence is important, since it reminds us that the most 'bulky', seemingly 'material' level is in fact the level most clearly subject to fractal vanishing: the point and the triangle are simply not materially 'there'. It also allows us to realize how higher forms arise through dynamically active and harmonious rearrangement of things. Thereby it renders *eide* both in nature and in us more innovative and productive – nearer in character to forms that are always forming or thinking than just abiding or being thought. That same integration also allows us to see that supposed 'secondary qualities' like colours, although they are as truly there as quantities (we should here modify Cudworth, who was proto-Lockean in this respect) nonetheless arise as 'events' in the relatively stable habits of our interaction with reality.

Quantities arise in the same way, but unlike colours they involve, as Aristotle realized, our 'common sensing', since no single sense directly grasps quantity. Cudworth insisted that the new atomistic and mechanical physics did not favour either Hobbesian materialism or Cartesian dualism, because both the quantitative and the relational ('schetic') most basic aspects of reality can only be grasped by the mind, not immediately by the senses. Only the mind grasps the *scheses* of thing to thing, part to whole and vice versa, and the ineluctably relational notions of cause and effect, equality and inequality, sign and thing signified, besides the more aesthetic realities of order and proportion which are judged to exist by our minds under the ultimate lure of the Good. In consequence, these realities are ultimately intellectual in character – yet while Cudworth

---

40 Cudworth, *A Treatise*, Book I, ch. III, 8, pp. 26–7.
41 Balthasar, *Vérité du Monde*, p. 48.

rendered the *eide* in the world closer in character to a kind of eidetic thinking process as compared with scholasticism (although this was still only the trace of transcendent divine thought, and he refused the notion of an *anima mundi*) this did not at all mean that he verged towards an idealist subjectivism, even of a Kantian variety. The 'intellectual' character of numerical quantities and real relations was not for him a sign that we ourselves construct apparently given reality, but rather a sign that the universe is 'an intellectual system', since it is created. The understanding of this system more by active mind than by passive sensing does not then point to a pre-organized a priori of mental structure, but rather to the 'anticipatory' power of the mind both with respect to the discovery of nature and the invention of culture. The mind actively grasps the given cosmos, because the obscure signs arising in sensory events provoke a renewed participation in the light of the divine *Logos* that expresses the Paternal goodness and is the creative source of both the cosmos and our finite minds (see note 38 above).

So to see essence as also number can dialectically reinforce one's sense of the dynamic character of *eide* and the closeness of the activity of thought to the changeful character of the cosmos. However, I have said that with number comes also recursive set. This destroys the principle of non-contradiction. So now it seems that realism has failed to secure identity and thereby truth, but nominalism has failed just as dismally. Neither essences *nor* individuals submit to the law of excluded middle. So must we be sceptics? Yet if so, how is it that there appears to be relative identity? As Plato indicated in the *Theaetetus*, the idea that there is only flux and appearance must *also* appear within the flux, and seems thereby to identify a contradictory stable flux and true appearing of this flux to knowledge.[42] As today with supposed 'redundancy' theories of truth, one cannot really cross out truth, or deny the interval between being and truth which being itself opens up, in favour of a reduction of knowledge to one more ontic 'event'. Indeed as Balthasar pointed out (like Adorno), we are only immediately in contact with being because of simultaneous mediation (as in the situation of physical touch). We *know* something is there only to the measure that it resists our knowledge and we also know that there is more to be known, like the back of the tree.[43] We can only speak of being because it shows itself or gives itself as true, and yet in this showing also presents a certain palpable reserve. Thereby, in giving truth it also gives that gap between truth and being which is the never closed future horizon of understanding.

---

42 Plato, *Theaetetus*, 161 D 1–161 E 5.
43 Balthasar, *Vérité du Monde*, pp. 122–3. On redundancy theories see Milbank and Pickstock, *Truth in Aquinas*, pp. 1–6; on touch, see *Truth in Aquinas*, pp. 60–88.

Either, then, the relatively stable identities of *eide* are true realities, or else the one paradoxically stable form and truth is the form and truth of formless flux – which finally lacks identity because what it both shows and reserves is an ironic lack of reserve, a concealed as unconcealed nullity. But in neither instance can we any longer appeal to the absolute sway of the law of non-contradiction.

Identity beyond non-contradiction

It seems then, that the Thomistic telescope must incorporate the perspectives of Nicholas of Cusa. Cusa sought to salvage the Proclean/ Dionysian tradition especially associated with the Dominican order, by *admitting* that universals, real relations and participation violate non-contradiction. He also tended to see universals as signs opening up endless perspectives or aspects. Likewise, finite truth was for him (like Cudworth and Peirce) also a continuous task for human artisanal construction, since he also effectively stole from the nominalists the theme of human sub-creation. Whereas, for Ockham, finite spirits, like God, can at least in principle cause finite being,[44] since being is a bare univocal existential that can be posited outside divine creation, in Cusa's writings for humans to create is also to receive something and to surprise themselves, since they only *share* to a limited degree in the divine capacity absolutely to originate.[45] And while we can for Nicholas create triangles or spoons, we nonetheless can only create these as essences: for we must thereafter observe the infinitely unfolding constraints and possibilities of triangles and spoons, which as our own fabricated offspring endlessly take us by surprise and cannot be law-lessly manipulated at our pleasure, just as when we divide or modify things in nature we cannot really change essences – we can cut down trees and genetically modify them; we cannot get rid of the idea of tree that has appeared to us only through real trees growing. The point that even artificial things exhibit essences is elaborated more specific-ally by Cudworth, who notes that an invented thing like a *horologe* or watch contains certain regular *scheses*, and has a certain regular nature because it is a contrivance of mind – even if the mind that has contrived it cannot at once fathom all the implications of its regular-ity. (Inversely, for Cudworth, relational regularity in the natural world betrays a certain artificial 'intellectuality', precisely because he has

44 William of Ockham, *Quodlibetal Questions*, 1:1; 2:1; 2:9; *Reportatio* 2:6.

45 Nicholas of Cusa, *Idiota: De Mente* in *Opera*, ed. P. Wilpert (Berlin: De Gruyter, 1967), pp. 236–42.

dynamized essence as formation rather than simply form.)[46] This is in fact another disproof of nominalism: the idea that there can be a 'pure construction' entirely within our control from entirely discrete brutal elements. No, the most basic element, the geometric point, contains the direst mysteries and most inescapable ambuscades.

In sign, aspect (late medieval or renaissance 'perspective'), number and *poesis*, Cusa, like Pascal later, recognized the impinging of the infinite at the heart of the finite. (By contrast, Aquinas did not acknowledge an actual as opposed to a possible – or else privated, actual but negatively valued – infinite as truly but contradictorily involved in the finite itself.) Truth, for him, as for the tradition, is the identical, the *non aliud*. But only the finitely identical is subject to non-contradiction, since as bounded it cannot violate its own bounds. In the infinite this does not apply: here the minimum is also the maximum, the hottest the coldest, etc.[47] Here, since the infinite God is all things, including all opposites and yet *simple* as well as infinite, he must be at the same moment and in the same respects these opposites – notice that Cusa needs to affirm in the strongest possible terms, like Aquinas (and unlike Scotus), God's simpleness as well as infinity in order to arrive at the *coincidentia oppositorum*.

However, since the finite is itself invaded and upheld by the presence of the infinite (both in logic and within our phenomenological experience) contradiction collapses identity here also: the point is the circumference of the circle and its centre; the tendency to the infinitely small is also the tendency to the infinitely great and so on.[48] For this reason our mathematics, in contrast to the later view of Galileo, cannot really attain to the real components of the divine *mathesis*: perhaps one can suggest, supplementing Cusa and following Grosseteste, that transfinites (besides other actual infinites and irrational numbers) hint

46 Nicholas of Cusa, 'On the Summit of Contemplation' *(De Apice Theoriae)* in *Nicholas of Cusa: Selected Spiritual Writings*, trans. H. Lawrence Bond (New York: Paulist Press, 1997), p. 302. Cudworth, *A Treatise*, Book I, ch. III, 4, p. 25; Book IV, ch. II, 4, pp. 85–6.
47 Nicholas of Cusa, *On Learned Ignorance (De Docta Ignorantia)* in *Nicholas of Cusa: Selected Spiritual Writings*, trans. H. Lawrence Bond (New York: Paulist Press, 1997), Book One, chs. 13 to 22, pp. 102–20 and *passim*. On the infinite see also Antoine Côté, 'Infinité' in *Dictionnaire Critique de Théologie*, ed. J-Y Lacoste (Paris: PUF, 1998), pp. 572–5. (It should also be said that the infinite for Nicholas, unlike Scotus or Descartes, is not something positively thinkable by us, even though it indicates, as for Gregory of Nyssa, a positive and non-relative unboundedness in God himself. Nor can one for Nicholas think God's infinity without or prior to his other perfections such as goodness, as one can for Scotus.
48 *Nicholas of Cusa: Selected Spiritual Writings*, and Book Two, ch. 12, pp. 160–66.

at the successive propagation of the actually finite from the true actual simple and qualitative infinite.[49]

As for the Catholic Platonico-Aristotelian tradition in general, so for Cusa, finitude is in flux, and can only borrow relative stabilities of essence and individual substance from the infinite divine ideas, uttered in the *Logos*. However, he adds to this that participation in perfect identity is also participation in perfect non-identity, for the ultimate ontological scenario can always be envisaged the other way round. Only when apparent finite identities collapse in the unbounded is there a stable reality. And then these two metaphysical schemes paradoxically combine: only when the One is itself other to the One and so is Many is it also the One returning to itself as origin. Trinitarian theology allows Cusa to put this in more dynamic terms. The actively possible One is the generation of the actual Many: the Spirit displays this reciprocal bond where absolute becoming and absolute unchanging being are further coinciding opposites.[50] But only in the infinite is there perfect coincidence, including of the limited and unlimited; between this true infinite and the created, explicated, finite infinite there is *no* coincidence, as later there is for Hegel. The latter hypostasizes a contradiction that remains contradictory, so that in a way finite and infinite ceaselessly cancel each other out, rendering each a void, and one has (as Hegel admits) a mode of nihilism: Cusa instead invokes a mystery of contradiction which is at the same time its own incomprehensible resolution, and so after all an infinite identity.

It may nonetheless seem troubling that for Cusa the finite, 'explicated', non-simple infinite is still an actual and not merely possible infinite; as such, despite the term *explicatio,* it possesses a cardinality. At this point, the shadow of materialism, monism and pantheism that had hovered over a positive actual infinity ever since Greek antiquity (most of its advocates prior to Plotinus were materialists) seems to re-intrude. However, for Nicholas, every immanent actual infinity is a) only aspectual, abstracting out some quantitative or else virtual dimension of reality and b) is always complex and never simple. Nevertheless, it must be recognized that the infinitesimally small and the immeasurably large, together with undecidable factors in sets and diagonals, do indeed 'instantly fade' towards absolute simple infinity, without of themselves in their own peculiar aporetic nature truly encompassing it.

---

49 See Grosseteste, *De Luce.*

50 Nicholas of Cusa, *On Actualised Possibility (De Possest)*, trans. Jasper Hopkins in *A Concise Introduction to the Philosophy of Nicholas of Cusa* (Minneapolis, MN: Minnesota University Press, 1978), pp. 65–9, 93, 121. See *On the Summit of Contemplation (De Apice Theoriae)* in *Nicholas of Cusa: Selected Spiritual Writings*, pp. 293–303.

In consequence they can be read, or even for a certain insight demand to be read, not as the traces of pantheism, but rather as signs of the creature's created nothingness in itself, and of Augustine's closeness of God to us that is closer than that of ourselves to ourselves.

On this understanding therefore, finitude reveals itself as a contradictory mystery. Only two rival truths are now possible, even if they can appear alarmingly akin to each other. There is first of all the truth of non-truth of nihilism that will require a mode of faith in nothingness if it is to evade the recursivity of the truth of non-truth. Second, as an alternative, there is the at once conjectured and experienced truth of transcendent metaphysics or theology: this alone now offers us the truth of truth, of a fully ontological truth. For the latter position, every creature exists by diagonalizing out of its finitude through participation in being; humanity is the site of conscious awareness of this exit. A human being can be the living self-aware diagonal, or else can perversely choose to suppress this contradictory reality. Like Cantor's C, humanity is the infinite plus 1, beyond yet not beyond even the infinite aleph-zero extension of the universe. One can try futilely to construe this plus 1 in functional terms as useful to an animal – yet mere *assertion* of non-functionality (as Jean-Luc Marion has often indicated) frustrates any such demonstration and sustains the diagonal excess, while the constant creative eccentricity of the diagonal means that totalizing functional explanation must forever struggle to keep pace with its innovations.

Truth then requires identity. But this is only found in incomprehensible infinite non-identity in which this world incomprehensibly participates. This infinite non-identity is itself the Trinitarian play between the infinite *peras* of the One and the equally infinite *apeiron* of the 'complicated' and so simple and ordered Many expressed in the *Logos*. This play spins off from both as their arising unity without surpassing them, in the form of the Holy Spirit which is at once the bond of desire and the freedom of charity. Truth in the creation reflects this infinite exchange, and is to a degree present in the constitutive relational interplay between individuals and universals, and between being as substantial and being as intellectual. This interplay runs also, as we can now see, thanks to the Thomistic telescope, along a temporal axis between nature and culture, and between essence and event, sign and number, substance and aspect.

Truth as the bond of being

Balthasar, rather like Cudworth in this respect, affirms that such inter-play concerns the Good and the Beautiful as well as the True. To be more precise though, he actually says that the True is not mere repre-sentation, because it is communication of the Good, while the Good is not mere fulfilment of desire because it is the expression of self-giving Being.[51] The Beautiful is supposed for him to be involved in both these excesses. Yet it is hard in a way to see where it finds a place in this scheme. In the end, Balthasar's aesthetic and his presentation of Aquinas's *De Veritate* gives way before a lingering Bonaventuran stress on the priority of the will and the Good. Indeed perhaps because he bases his aesthetics too much upon subjective phenomenological intuition, and too little upon speculative judgement of an ontology, the excess of the invisible in the visible which constitutes for him the lure of beauty is in danger of reducing the notion of visible beauty to a mere sign of an infinite otherness and gratuity. Then indeed it will seem that the True is the manifestation of Being beyond the mere mirroring of Being, because it also communicates the Good, while goodness is no mere fulfilment of need because it receives the infinite sacrificial one-way gift of Being, which is pure gratuity. One can appreciate how, like Augustine and Cudworth, Balthasar preserves the Platonic notion of a primal Good that sustains even judgements of the True, rendering them in the end precipitations of true desire. However, he at times allows this to mean that the will outruns the ordered distributions of judgements. He ends *Theologik* Part I by saying that while we cannot comprehend divine truth, truth remains our element, whereas before divine love our cognitive and willing efforts must fall silent and we must simply adore. Love, he says, is more ultimate in God than truth.[52] But are they not co-equal? And is not *theoria* fulfilled in liturgy rather than abandoned by it?

A love beyond even our inkling as to the nature of love sounds like a pure imparticipable manifestation of will. Similarly, Balthasar says that love makes mercy outrun the justice of truth. However, for Aquinas infinite justice as justice was mercy, and mercy remained the infinite just placing or distribution of the reconciled in peace.

By contrast, a lingering Scotist and Kantian conception of mercy as mere subjective gesture persists in Balthasar here. And the same set of positions means that finally for him the one-way unilateral gift triumphs: beyond even the exchange of Father and *Verbum* in the truth,

51 Balthasar, *Vérité du Monde*, pp. 229–34.
52 Balthasar, *Vérité du Monde*, pp. 285.

the *Donum* is the excess of free offering in God and to us. It is significant that Balthasar declares that Being is communication of the Good *before relation* – that is to say, before a kind of binding (or *troth*) of Being to this manifestation that would obligate Being in its very freedom.[53] Instead he wants Being to be radically free. But how can this be consistent with the Trinitarian giving of the Truth and the Good, of *Verbum* and *Donum* by the Father who is *esse*, since this *is* a relational communication that is free always as bound in truth?

Here one wonders about the status of Balthasar's metaphysical prolegomena – for in this case starting with the metaphysical transcendentals seems to engender a conflict with the perspective of the theological Trinitarian transcendentals which are 'word' and 'gift'. Balthasar rightly says that what is necessary participation from our point of view is free 'revelation' from God's point of view,[54] and one can add that one should be able to say this of revelation *tout court*, since even the revelation in Christ and the Church heightens human participation, and this is necessary to us beyond necessity, in terms of our real supernatural end. He also rightly notes that Aquinas says that every human cognition is an obscure cognition of God – yet by this, as von Balthasar knows, Aquinas also means that every human cognition is an obscure anticipation of the beatific vision only re-offered to us by redeeming grace.[55] Therefore, for Aquinas, all participated knowledge occurs remotely by virtue of such grace. This would suggest that metaphysical prolegomena are at best ambivalent, except as conscious anticipations of a Trinitarian ontology. It is clear that *in reality* Balthasar's metaphysics would not in general have the shape it does were it not exactly such an anticipation. Yet in this specific instance it seems that the metaphysics of the transcendentals whereby Being gives before relations *governs* the theological ontology of *Verbum* and *Donum*, such that something in the Holy Spirit is in excess of its substantive relation to the relation of Father to Son. This excess is still the modern 'free gesture' of will, whose background is a Being that is otherwise reduced to a gift-less existential inertia.

However, one can repair Balthasar. He is not consistent in this tendency and at times refuses a Bonaventuran pneumatology.[56] Rightly he stresses, unlike Jean-Luc Marion, that the *Donum* is both the manifestation of the prior reciprocity in truth of Father and Son *and* that

53 Balthasar, *Vérité du Monde*, pp. 39.
54 Balthasar, *Vérité du Monde*, pp. 238–55.
55 See Milbank and Pickstock, *Truth in Aquinas*, pp. 19–60.
56 Balthasar, *La Théologique II: Vérité de Dieu*, pp. 177–9. *III: L'Esprit de Vérite*, pp. 152–4.

this reciprocity is in itself a passing beyond itself.[57] Without this passing beyond (one can elaborate), the reciprocity between Father and Son might appear to involve a mere symmetry, since the Father *is* engendering and the Son *is* being engendered, according to the logic of substantive relation. Yet since the latter properly implies mutual ecstatic being and not a mutually reflexive self-confirmation through the mirror of the other (a 'doubling' inconsistent with the divine simplicity), the passage of Father to Son and of Son to Father is not just an immediate return in either case, but also a sustained exceeding of any return and so of any merely complicit mutuality. This exceeding of one towards the other therefore is immediately also the exceeding of both by both which gives rise in actuality to the Holy Spirit as the space of possibility for an infinite sharing by infinite others of their mutual love. In this way, the purely relational dyad is only constituted by a constant escaping of the dyad and the symmetry of the Father/Son relation is endlessly renewed by the asymmetry of the third. The third continuously interrupts the circularity of two and yet this circularity nonetheless entirely pivots about this interruption.

Hence although the Father only gives to the Son what the Son returns to the Father, the Son forever receives something new by the excess of the Spirit's spiration in which the Word is breathed out from the Father's mouth. Similarly, although the Father only receives from the Son what he has given to him, he endlessly receives back something newly inspired by the Spirit's mediation. This constantly renewed asymmetry within the reciprocal relation of Father and Son therefore constitutes the 'moment' of unilaterality that renders the *Donum* truly *Donum* and not just formally equivalent exchange, and at the same time a *Donum* (as Augustine declared) receivable by us as the 'extra' and yet necessary (if we are to realize our supernatural end) gift of deifying grace – just as the Spirit within the Trinity is at once superfluous and yet fundamental.[58] This unilateral moment corresponds, as we saw in the realm of knowledge, to the moment of valid individuality and individual identity that is not exhausted by universal essence.

To sustain this balance regarding the *Donum* however, one needs to say more emphatically than Balthasar that what exceeds mere representation in the truth is the Beautiful, as this retains the character of truth as measure and yet ensures that truth *as* truth, not as communicated will, exceeds mere copying. Likewise one needs to say that what exceeds satisfaction of desire in the case of the Good is also the Beautiful,

---

57 Balthasar, *La Theologique I, Vérité du Monde*, pp. 46, 78–9; *III: L'Esprit de Vérité*, 216–29; *Theo-Drama Vol. V, The Last Act*, trans. Graham Harrison (San Francisco, CA: Ignatius Press, 1998), pp. 105–9.
58 Augustine, *De Trinitate*, Book XV, ch. 5, 27–39.

because then one can allow that the Good exceeds satisfaction in itself in so far as it is the realized mutual co-dwelling of human or angelic persons, and not merely as the passive receiving of a gift from the excessive source of Being. This ensures that the moment of unilateral giving does not surpass but rather allows mutual reciprocity through asymmetry, since such asymmetrical reciprocity is fundamentally beautiful. In turn, the aesthetic so conceived (here following Balthasar) as balancing a measured manifestness (classicism) and the lure of desire beyond appearance (romanticism) cannot reduce beauty to a mere sign of the sublime beyond of the supreme other. Instead, as Balthasar often seems to indicate (when he transcends mere personalism) the invisible here truly is *in* the visible, by another coincidence of opposites (although they only perfectly coincide in the infinite, where the *Logos* is a boundless image).

Repaired in this way, Balthasar's understanding of how truth is aesthetically established in the desire for goodness – the desire to give – blends very well with the Thomistic telescope that newly stresses how truth as realized *eidos* is also truth as anticipation, truth as made, truth as continued event, truth as interpreting signs, truth as receptivity of new aspects.

Together these perspectives suggest that truth is that which opens us to contemplation of the infinite just in so far as it is also that which prepares us for a more harmonious human and cosmic future. Beyond contradiction and non-contradiction, truth only begins to disclose to us an infinite integral identity in so far as it also begins to realize in our finitude the measured exchanges of hope and love which ceaselessly and incomprehensibly blend the same with the different. Truth as disclosure is also troth, the bond of being.

8. Is There a Thomist Hermeneutic?

OLIVIER-THOMAS VENARD OP

If, in a first attempt at an etymological definition, hermeneutics is understood as the art of interpretation, the question can be analysed in various ways depending on how the adjective 'thomist' is read. First, grammatically speaking, a *subjective* understanding of 'thomist' gives rise to two possible senses:

1 Did St Thomas develop his own 'art of interpretation' (we may refer to this more precisely as a Thomist hermeneutic)?[1]
2 Is there an 'art of interpretation' implicit in St Thomas's works which his disciples would be able to make explicit? (This would be, more precisely, a thomist hermeneutic, a reconstruction performed by us which is sympathetic towards his wisdom.[2]

The response to these two questions is positive, and we could all cite works to illustrate this.

Second, grammatically speaking, an *objective* understanding of the adjective 'thomist' makes the question far simpler: Is there a hermeneutic of which Thomas is the object? Here, under the title 'thomist

---

1 Cf. Thomas's commentary on the *Peri Hermeneias*. [ET: *Commentary on Aristotle's* On Interpretation, ed. and trans. Jean Oersterle (Notre Dame, IN: St Augustine's Press, Dumb Ox Books, 2006).] Editors' note: Throughout this paper, the adjective 'Thomist', beginning with an upper case 'T' is used to mean St Thomas's own 'art of interpretation', while the adjective 'thomist', beginning with a lower case 't' is used to mean the 'art of interpretation implicit in St Thomas's works'.

2 Cf. the chapters in the major classical introductions describing St Thomas's concern with having access to authentic texts and his fidelity to certain types of literary criticism; past researches on the structures and methods of St Thomas's writings (e.g. Ghislain Lafont, *Structures et méthode dans la 'Somme théologique' de Saint Thomas d'Aquin* (Paris: Desclée de Brouwer, 1961)); or present works that look to explicate the grand principles of his biblical exegesis (e.g. G. Dahan, *L'Exegèse chrétienne de la Bible en Occident medieval [XX– XIV siècle]*, 'Patrimoines: christianisme' (Paris: Cerf, 1999), which updates and completes the work of Henri de Lubac).

hermeneutic', the interpretative techniques developed by the disciples of Thomas on the entire corpus of his works would be gathered. Application of the historical method is then necessary, although it is remarkable how the simplistic hermeneutic of the scholastics was so fruitful when, at times, it lacked a historical relativism. Their approach made it possible nevertheless for Thomas to remain a contemporary of the generations separating us from him!

The importance of thomist works in the Anglo-Saxon tradition, highlighting the actual contexts (in particular religious and linguistic) of St Thomas's thought, must be emphasized. The key text from this tradition has been Burrell's *Aquinas, God and Action*.[3] They enrich the historical approach adopted by 'Old Europe', drawing on the more pragmatic preoccupations of the New World which are completely at home with the theological approach adopted by St Thomas. It is to be hoped that one and the other traditions will meet.[4] The presence among us these days of John Milbank and David Burrell is perhaps as important as the content of the papers we set out!

If the term 'hermeneutic' is understood in a more historical and blurred way, in the sense that it is possible to speak of a 'hermeneutic turn' in contemporary theology, the question becomes more complex. Hermeneutics, as the rigorous interpretative art of texts in fields where it is necessary to research content that is not experientially verifiable, has extended itself, little by little, to all disciplines, claiming today a universal status beyond any particular specialism.[5] But the practice of hermeneutics is rooted in preoccupations that were gradually developed by a kind of hermeneutics (h) squared (h²), until their eventual blossoming, in the course of the last century, into the various hermeneutics of 'philosophy' or 'theology'. The latter pose great problems for theological thought, that of the hierarchy of knowledge and their truths.

---

3 David B. Burrell, *Aquinas: God and Action* (Notre Dame, IN: University of Notre Dame Press, 1979).

4 The meeting has already taken place at the Saint Thomas Institute in Utrecht: see *inter alia* Wilkhelmus G. Valkenberg, '"*Did not our heart burn?*", Place and Functions of Holy Scripture in the Theology of Saint Thomas Aquinas', dissertation, Publications of Thomas Instituut te Utrecht, 3 (Utrecht, 1990) (reviewed by S-Th-Bonin: *Revue Thomiste* 92 (1992), p. 899–901); and Henk J. M. Shoot, '*Christ the "Name" of God, Thomas Aquinas on naming Christ*', Publications of Thomas Instituut te Utrecht, NS 1 (Leuven: Peeters, 1993).

5 The hermeneutical master of the last century, Hans-Georg Gadamer has been vigorously criticized for claiming a universality for hermeneutics: cf. Jürgen Habermas, 'La prétention à l'universalité de l'herméneutique', in *Logique des sciences et autres essais*. Translated from German by R. Rochlitz, 'Philosophie d'aujourd'hui' (Paris: PUF, 1987).

Theological hermeneutics has developed progressively into a general philosophical hermeneutic which is not without dogmatic consequences, in particular the possibility now of a 'Word of God' utterly dependent on the problem of interpretation. It is then a fundamental question that is posed: there is a real risk that the Word of God, inexpressible outside the discipline of hermeneutics, will end up on a Procrustean bed of the prevailing secular philosophy. The Judeo-Christian experience of truth as encounter, and not as a possession to be grasped, seems to be put in jeopardy.[6]

In fact, the idea of an independent hermeneutic is itself a problem for the Catholic theologian. As Marie-Joseph Le Guillou has made abundantly clear, the idea emerged from the need to direct the course of free thinking introduced by the Reformation.[7] Given this, one is perhaps tempted to answer with an uncompromising 'no' to the question of whether or not there exists a 'thomist hermeneutic'. Aquinas, no more than his disciples, would share in keeping the ecclesiastical Magisterium and Tradition at a distance, a first principle of modern hermeneutics.[8] It is this argument from prescription which prevents getting to the bottom of the question. Being contented with this, would not be faithful to the theological mission as St Thomas conceived it. A thought which appears to be false should not be judged only from the exterior. Rather, as he says at the beginning of *Summa contra Gentiles*, there should be a wrestling (*impugnare*) with such a thought, not using the tweezers of principles which it does not recognize, but hands and fists. As to what we perceive to be truth, this needs to be 'pronounced meditatively (*meditatem eloqui*)'.[9] It is not only dishevelled German romantics who can detect a certain fecundity in the human word, and who notice that a truth, even one that is very ancient and perfectly established, nevertheless gains something from being (re)told![10] The charity of truth does not consist in giving our contemporary neighbour a few well thought out judgements concerning his errant ways, but rather in finding out the things that are so important to him that he clings to them so vehemently. Even if it means letting go of Aquinas in the process, sometimes, as the Gospel tells us, he who loses everything,

---

6 See Paul Toinet, *Le problème de la vérité dogmatique, Orthodoxie et l'hétérodoxie* (Paris: Téqui, 1975), p. 57.

7 M. J. Le Guillou, *Le Mystère du Père, Foi des apôtres, gnoses actuelles*, 'Le signe' (Paris: Fayard, 1973), pp. 16–17.

8 Le Guillou, *Le Mystère*, p. 16.

9 St Thomas Aquinas, *Summa contra Gentiles* (*SCG*) I, ch. 1.

10 Cf. O.-Th. Venard, *Thomas d'Aquin, poète-théologien*: vol.1, *Littérature et Théologie, Une saison en enfer* (Genève: Ad Solem, 2003), pp. 286–8: theological *inventio* in the teaching act.

gains all! It is in this spirit that we would like to raise here the problem for thomist thought posed by a contemporary hermeneutic.

A Thomist counterpoint to certain core hermeneutical themes in their (post)modern mutations

Hermeneutics as problem or solution: modern terms of the problem, and why St Thomas does not belong

Hermeneutics is a discipline which tries to make clear *what is happening in the act of understanding.* This endeavour is rooted principally in the 'fact' of the remoteness, of the distance (metaphysical or physical, temporal, cultural, mental . . .) which exists between the understanding of the producer and of the receiver of the information in question. Because of the distance, this whole enterprise is accompanied by a pessimistic reflection on distance itself.

Common sense had for a long time believed that *understanding* occurred more frequently than non-understanding, which was seen to be abnormal. In this case – and in this case only! – a research method was invoked in an attempt to illuminate that which was obscure.[11] But we have gradually come, in the course of a history which it is impossible to detail here, to consider non-understanding as primary to the extent that, at the beginning of the twentieth century,[12] successful understanding appeared as an asymptote, often approached but never reached, in the Kantian sense of these terms.[13]

Basically, all transmission of information, and not only the passage from one language to another, appeared as a translation: the person who expresses 'translates' into exterior signs a content of interior thinking, reputedly of another order. Interpretation distinguishes itself from understanding, as loud speech is distinct from interior conversation.[14] Put otherwise, the philosophy of hermeneutics was closer to

11 See H. G. Gadamer, *Vérité et méthode, les grandes lignes d'une herméneutique philosophique*, the whole edition revised and completed by P. Fruchon, J. Grondin and G. Merlio, 'L'ordre philosophique' (Paris: Seuil, 1996), pp. 198–9. [Originally published as *Wahrheit und Methode: Gründzuge einer philosophischen Hermeneutik* (Tübingen: Mohr, 1960); ET: *Truth and Method*, trans. William Glen-Doepel (London: Sheed & Ward, 1975).]

12 F. Schleiermacher had stated that communication is not naturally easy and that misunderstanding is most common; it is Dilthey (1833–1911) who completes the movement.

13 Cf. Raymond Aron, *La Philosophie Critique de l'Histoire*, Points Essais, 18 (Paris: Seuil, 1969), p. 84.

14 Cf. F. D. E. Schleiermacher, *Herméneutique,* trans. C. Berner (Paris: Cerf/Lille, PUL, 1989), ' Discours de 1829'.

being an interrogation of language (and in particular of signs, of relations between signifying and signified) and of its servile or parasitical
relation to truth.[15] One might well have thought that, on the dial of
truth, the hands of reality and interpretation had made a complete turn:
in saying that 'everything is interpretation' one might just as easily say
that 'everything is objective', or finally that new confidence should be
kindled in a certain common-sense communication with others. There
has not though been a rekindling of this confidence, as we shall see.

What is this brief reworking of the givens of the modern hermeneutical problem able to suggest to a thomist? Thomism would have rejoiced
at the turn we have just described because, for Thomas, *interpretatio*
indicates from the outset, not a problem, but the ability to resolve a
problem; or the capacity of language itself, in particular the verbaliza-
tion of thought with a view to oral expression.[16] Nevertheless, it seems
difficult to speak of a Thomist hermeneutic in the modern sense of the
term.

Why there is no Thomist hermeneutic

First of all, I believe that St Thomas would not subscribe to the hermeneutical view that the distance between the one who speaks and the one
who is spoken to is difficult, if not impossible, to overcome. He receives
it simply as a fact.

1 On a metaphysical level, distance for him turns out to be a condition for understanding.[17] In being-in-its-entirety, there is a difference
between being and spirit, and therefore a 'distance' (the term *distantia*
is used on several occasions by St Thomas to express difference, most

---

15 In a certain sense, the etymology contains a plan for the conquest of all
knowledge by hermeneutics, since the Greek word, ἑρμηνεύω, means not only
to *interpret* (to explain) and to *translate* (or to serve as an interpreter), but also
and principally to *express* (to enunciate, to say).

16 Following Aristotle, St Thomas explores this distance between things, the
thinking of things and their linguistic expression, in *Peri Hermeneias*. In the
tradition of logic, since Boethius, *interpretatio* has been synonymous with *vox
significativa*, or *enunciatio*. Everyone is endowed with an expressive faculty,
or *interpretatio*. The faculty of speech is presented as a given in human nature
in the same way as the capacity to move: *potentia interpretativa est naturalis
homini*. But Thomas has the wisdom to describe both its immanence (it is natural
for man to speak) and its transcendence (as it engages non-material intellectual
activity). See St Thomas, *In Peri Hermeneias*, Lib.i, lect. 6 (Marietti, p. 33,
§80). The expressive faculty is natural to man. Cf. Aristotle, *De Anima*, II, 8,
420 b 5 and Irène Rosier-Catach, *La Parole comme acte, Sur la grammaire et la
sémantique au 18th siècle*, 'Sic et non' (Paris: Vrin, 1994), p. 125.

17 Cf. Pierre-Ceslas Courtes, *L'Etre et le non-être selon Thomas d'Aquin*,
Croire et savoir, 27 (Paris: Téqui, 1998), chs. 3 and 4.

notably in *De potentia*). Because being, which is at the source of the life of the spirit, is anterior to any actual knowledge, being is not being-known but is being-in-itself, *per se primo*. The spirit has knowledge of being and knows itself, at least habitually, as intentional being.[18] Knowledge in its true essence is therefore both a movement to over-come distance and to assimilate difference.[19] Knowledge is itself remote from itself as it is only through the mediation of being that we experience that we are, feel, think, want and act. This knowledge requires movement in action that is faithful to the wisdom of being, and of being according to being (simultaneously being-as-such (*res*) and one's own being).[20] Truth, an exigency beyond that which has been acquired, is distance surmounted and the surmounting of distance.

2 On a pragmatic level then, Thomas spontaneously tends to assimi-late those who engage in the act of communication to an academic discipline. He straight away understood human understanding in terms of *doctrina* (that is of *teaching* in the operative sense of the word), with a master, a disciple and a fashioned word. In the philosophical order, the theory of pedagogy[21] allows him to clarify a number of noetic problems,[22] including even the difficulties associated with communica-tion. Indeed it is through the art of pedagogy that Thomas is able to speak of the metaphysical impossibility of one man illuminating another.[23] In the theological order, the metaphor of God-as-teacher structures his approach to revelation as such;[24] again the image of God-as-Teacher explains the need for Scripture to recover its *modus symbolicus*[25] and underpins prophetic theology.[26] This image is epitomized in the descrip-tion of Christ as the Doctor *par excellence*.[27]

---

18 In *De Veritate*, Q. 10 and in his commentary on *De causis*, St Thomas develops the theme of spiritual substance, by nature *conversiva ad se*.

19 St Thomas defines distance as ontological difference and distinct being.

20 See *Summa Theologiae* (*ST*), Ia–IIae, Q. 94, art. 2, which states that prac-tical reason follows speculative reason as good follows being; and *De Veritate*, Q. 1, art. 1, ad 3.

21 Cf. S. Thomas D'Aquin, *Questions disputées sur la vérité*, Question XI. *Le maître (De Magistro)*, Introduction, translation and notes by Bernadette Jollès, Bibliothèque des textes philosophiques (Paris: Vrin, 2, 1992).

22 See *ST* Ia, Q. 117, art. 1.

23 *De Veritate*, Q. 9, a. 5 (Marietti, p. 188).

24 *ST* Ia, Q. 105, art. 3; IIIa, Q. 12, art. 3.

25 See *ST* Ia, Q. 111, art. 1; Q. 117, art. 1, ad 3; IIIa, Q. 12, art. 3, ad 2 on the need for symbolism in human teaching.

26 See *ST* IIa IIae, Q. 174, art. 2, *in fine*.

27 See *ST* IIIa, Q. 42 ('De doctrina Christi'); IIIa, Q. 7, art. 7: 'In Christo fuerunt excellentissime omnes gratiae gratis datae, sicut in primo et principa-li Doctore fidei'; IIIa, Q. 9, art. 4, ad 1; and *In Ioan.*, cap.1, lect. 11 (§215, p. 44).

3 On an epistemological level, it is necessary to emphasize how the various disciplines communicate with one another within the framework of *sacra doctrina*. John Milbank and Catherine Pickstock, in the early chapters of *Truth in Aquinas*,[28] place strong emphasis on St Thomas's integration of the noetic with the ontological.

Here are some examples. It is the discourse provided by creation and participation theology which enables his rigorous analysis of the teaching act, despite the semiotic occasionalism in which it could seem to result. (We are thinking of the objection that no man can call himself *magister* since God alone is such.)[29] This mutual enrichment between the theological and the noetic reinforces the engagement of the noetical with the metaphysical. Biblical exegesis likewise displays similar exchanges between disciplines which today are opposed to one another.[30] One such exchange reappears in the distinction Thomas makes between two different kinds of word, illumination and locution.[31] In distinguishing, *within the representational function of language*, that which ontologically strengthens the intellect and that which brings nothing to it, he shows how, for him, the noetic is integrated into the order of being in general. And he shows this once again in the exciting notion of *ordo disciplinae*.[32]

In his treatise on divine names, he sometimes makes a detour through linguistic analysis in order to respond to a question that concerns the state of things.[33] Never in his responses does he parenthesize discourse so as to cling only to the 'real'. It is as much the detour through logical and linguistic analysis as the *res* itself that allows Thomas to avoid verbal exaggeration; a paradox exists, though only from a modern point of view where object is dialectically opposed to subject, reality to its perception and real being to its linguistic expression. As for Thomas, he often deploys a logic of a priori perfections, a whole axiomatic and semiotic Neoplatonic inspiration which transcends all orders of being, and which perhaps has not been sufficiently studied. As soon as an axiom like 'natural forms are similar to immaterial forms' is admitted, the question of *linguistic* semantics appears to be resolved: it is accidental

---

28 J. Milbank and C. Pickstock, *Truth in Aquinas*, Radical Orthodoxy series (London and New York: Routledge, 2001).

29 See *ST* Ia, Q. 117, art. 1, ad 1.

30 A few examples can be found in our *Littérature et théology . . .*, 'Le principe de causalité', pp. 178–85, and 'La colombe de saint Thomas', pp. 210–22.

31 See *ST* Ia, Q. 107, art. 3, ad 1.

32 Cf. our *Littérature et théologie . . .*, pp. 157–62.

33 Cf. Thierry-Marie Hamonic, 'Ratio, intellectus, intuitus et contemplation philosophique selon saint Thomas d'Aquin', typed theology thesis, Human Sciences, University of Strasbourg, 1992, p. 59.

to the sense communication between two intelligences.These incessant exchanges between the noetic, the metaphysical and the theological are simultaneously the cause and the effect of a positive appreciation of the detour through language to arrive at truth:[34] speech for the scholastic is an instrument of vision.[35] Human discourse is therefore not belittled, because 'the imperfection of reasoning knows its imperfections and corrects itself'.[36]

This leads us to consider an aspect which, properly speaking, is linguistic. As for language itself, Thomas has received from Aristotle a certain optimism and a sense of the transparency of language (or rather of the illuminating of its obscurities).[37]

1 On a verbal level, the sign, before being a problem as it has become in contemporary hermeneutics, is for St Thomas a solution: joining together the signifier with the signified to produce a *discursus* which moves from the sensible of the signifier to the spiritual of the signified,[38] the sign is an adequate answer to the problem of corporeal grossness (*grossities*) which obscures a clear vision of the soul nevertheless informing it.[39] The sign, which really ought to reach the unknown through the intermediary of the known, is made in this way for man.[40] As the means of interpersonal communication,[41] the sign is less something known than an *object* through which other things are known.[42] Within such a framework, words appear as signs par excellence, because they have been specifically instituted with a view to signification.[43] The same optimistic thought characterises Thomas' reflection on the written word, presented as the solution discovered by incarnated intelligences, to transcend spatio-temporal distances[44] by means of a language which, however, has been formed from transitory sounds. Finally, language

---

34 Reasoning for scholastics is 'a different view' (*regard différé*). Cf. Jean-Louis Chrétien, 'La connaissance angélique', in *Le Regard de l'amour* (Paris: DDB, 2000), pp. 125–39 (p. 130). Refer also to words attributed to Saint Thomas when he stopped writing the *Summa*: 'What I have written is nothing compared to what I have seen . . .'

35 Cf. *SCG 1*, cap. 57, *in fine*.

36 J. L. Chrétien, 'La connaissance angélique' . . ., pp. 130–31.

37 A flowing λέγεται stresses in that way every part of the metaphysical view of language expressed in his very first work, *Topica*. Aristotle, following most other thinkers, believes that the multiple accepted meanings belonging to a notion can be enumerated coherently.

38 See *De Veritate*, Q. 9, art. 4, obj. 4.

39 See *ST* Ia, Q. 117, art. 1.

40 *ST* IIIa, Q. 60, art. 2.

41 Cf. *ST* IIIa, Q. 60, art. 4.

42 *ST* IIIa, Q. 60, art. 1, obj. 2; art. 4, ad 1; q. 63, art. 2, ad 3.

43 *ST* IIIa, Q. 60, art. 6, *tertio*.

44 See *Peri Hermeneias*, Lib. 1, lect. 2 [§2, p. 10].

turns out to be the semiotic system par excellence, to the extent that it provides a necessary interpretative model for all others: the symbolism of natural things themselves ends up being thought through the model of the word.[45] Incidentally, it is worth pointing out that the two founding laws of semiology, according to Emile Benveniste, are present in St Thomas's theological stance.[46]

2 On a more general semiological level, being both an essential relation of measure (regarding the signified *in recto* and referring to the epistemic faculties *in obliquo*), and a measure of being and representation (of an object by another less-well-known object upon which it depends), signification goes beyond just the linguistic sphere. Apparently, everything seems to be simple: words are the *signs* of concepts, themselves in a relation of *similitude* with the real.[47] Words enter into relationship with things through the intermediary of an *operation*, one of the intellect which conceives and which judges. There is a relation of similitude between things and their intellections and a sign relation between intellections and words. For Thomas, the sign is not therefore the occasion of double-sided or allegorical thought because it can not be analysed into two separate entities, substance and signification. Rather there are three: substance, signification and *supposition*.

What is at stake, here, is that thought and language isomorphize reality. Actually this linguistic optimism ends up posing questions for our modern mind, accustomed as it is, since Saussure, to take the thesis of the arbitrariness of signs as given. Finally, that which constitutes the 'problem of language' for contemporary thought – the question of the marriage of meaning with verbal material – is not likely to show up in St Thomas. Let us have a more thorough look at this question, returning once more to contemporary hermeneutics.

The history of hermeneutics as the deepening of the being of language: a question posed to Thomism

We pointed out above that the generalization of hermeneutics has not resulted in a new confidence in common sense. Rather, since the advent of romanticism, the distance between interiority and exteriority, between thought and its expression, which is a fact, is still understood fatalistically. Today, through a symmetrical excess of romantic subjec-

---

45 *ST* Ia IIae, Q. 102, art. 6.
46 Cf. E. Benveniste, *Problèmes de linguistique générale*, Vol. 2, 'TEL 47' (Paris: Gallimard, 1974), pp. 60–62.
47 Cf. *ST* Ia, Q. 13, art. 1.

tivism, postmoderns privilege exteriority – the trace, the text, the Word or Language hypostasized by a capital letter. What hermeneutic could explain the consequent talk of the 'disappearance of Discourse'?[48] The hermeneutic circle in which 'each sign relates to all others, except in a fuller sense'[49] is *wrong*, from the perspective of absolute truth. The text no longer calls for further explanation: textuality's everlasting echo itself answers back.[50]

During this evolution, hermeneutics has rediscovered and breathed new life into the philosophical question of language. Two factors have contributed to this: first, the displacement, beginning with Heidegger, of the hermeneutical problem, of epistemology with ontology (what is the mode of being of the being who comes into existence only in the process of understanding?);[51] second, the de facto re-establishment of an ontology of language, linked to the rising success of linguistics, has given formal recognition to the dualism at the heart of language initiated, from the Middle Ages, by Ockham.[52] I shall give a single example of this: linguists of the twentieth century have gradually substituted the traditional pair 'artificial sign/ natural sign' with 'intentional sign/ attentional sign'. From now on, putative 'natural' signs are simply 'clues', open to subjective interpretation, which actually, or not, signify, depending on the kind of attention they arouse.[53] They no longer result from an intention to communicate (which could only be that of a creator through nature and her laws), but from a desire to interpret. Is this not an inversion of the theology of the Word?

The question is one of the 'hermeneutical leap',[54] not only from language to reality, but from thought to language; and, in words them-

---

48 Cf. Michel Foucault, *Les Mots et les choses. Une archéologie des sciences humaines*, Bibliothèque des sciences humaines (Paris: Nrf Gallimard, 1979 (1966)), p. 59. [ET: *The Order of Things: An Archaeology of the Human Sciences* (London: Routledge, 2002).]

49 Geneviève Trainar, *Transfigurer le temps, Nihilisme. Symbolisme*. Liturgie (Genève: Ad Solem, 2003), p. 54.

50 Cf. Jacques Derrida, *La Dissémination* (Paris: Seuil, 1972). [ET: *Dissemination*, trans. Barbara Johnson (London: Athlone Press, 1981).]

51 Cf. Martin Heidegger, *Unterwegs zur Sprache* (Pfulligen: Neske, 1959), translated into French by J. Beaufret as *Acheminement vers la parole*, W. Brokmeier and F. Fédier, TEL (Paris: Gallimard, 1976). [ET: *On the Way to Language*, trans. Peter D. Hertz and J. Stambaugh (New York: Harper & Row, 1971).]

52 See William of Ockham, *Quaestiones in librum secundum Sententiarum (Reportatio)*, II, 14, *Opera theologica*, V (St Bonaventure, NY: St Bonaventure University Press, 1981), p. 315.

53 Cf. Oswald Ducrot and Jean-Marie Schaeffer, *Nouveau dictionnaire encyclopédique des sciences du langage* (Paris: Seuil, 1995), pp. 214–15.

54 We borrow this phrase from G. Dahan, *L'Exégèse chrétienne de la Bible en Occident médiéval . . .*, p. 435.

selves, from their signifying exterior to what is internally signified. The dialectic of the sign likewise transpires to be a linguistic rendering of the fundamental noetical problem: that of the 'bridge' between the sensible (what is perceived) and the intelligible (what is understood). The 'oversight/omission of language', denounced by Gadamer and other postmoderns, is a genuine question posed to metaphysicians and theologians. Through ignoring 'the essential connection of thought with the texture preceding language',[55] a large part of Western thought has accustomed us to think of 'being as an absolutely attainable objectivity',[56] ruining any chance of a realistic metaphysics. Worse still, for Christian theology, the notion of the exteriority of thought and language is a typically Gnostic insight, contrary to the mystery of the incarnation which positively promotes the relationship between spirit and matter. The incarnation is not a diminution of God, but rather his salvific revelation to mankind.

Now, if the Thomist approach to language is far from being simply idealistic or materialistic, because it refuses to confuse *intentio animae* (the intended) with *signum* (the signified), it remains however the juxtaposition of a formal conception or ideal of language – as the transfer of information – with a prosaic understanding of language as a conventional instrument or, more crudely, of language as the discursive work of thought. I will illustrate this remark by two examples of this approach which is not problematic for language.

Theory of the language of angels, or how to explain a 'sublime and unknown'[57] way of talking or to think a language without speech and a speech without words

First, to explain the communication between two pure spirits, it is necessary to be rid of all corporeal language, which implies the rejection of the *locutio vocalis*[58] and the sign (one immediately thinks of a sort of thought transference). Second, so that the distinct personality of the angel is respected, and the reduction of language to a mechanical transfer of information is avoided, we should imagine the intimately interior language of an angel, oriented towards another, as a certain type of exterior language. Again, the communication between a high-ranking

55 Jean Grondin, 'L'universalité de l'herméneutique et de la rhétorique: ses sources dans le passage de Platon à Augustine', in *'Vérité et méthode'*, *Revue internationale de philosophie* 54 (2000), pp. 469–85 (p. 470).

56 H. G. Gadamer, *Vérité et méthode* (Paris: Seuil, 1976), p. 438 (*Wahrheit und Methode*, p. 418).

57 Gregory the Great, *Moralia*, II, VII, cited in *ST* Ia, Q. 107, art. 1.

58 Cf. *ST* Ia, Q. 107, art. 1, ad 2 ; also *De Veritate*, Q. 9, art. 4, ad 3.

angel and a lesser one presupposes accommodations and distinctions (cf. *De Veritate*, Q. 9, art. 5) which it is difficult to imagine without signs! To avoid transforming angelic communication into a purely mechanical transfer of information, and so that the distinct personality of the angel is respected, Thomas invents a sort of intelligible 'sign',[59] a 'spiritual virtue', for intellectual meaning. The obscure expression *aliqua virtus spiritualis* is testimony to the fact that thought cannot be reduced to language. Might it pertain to the angels – all the more as it recalls to mind the expression *quaedam vis spiritualis*, by which Thomas designates the presence of meaning in the human voice which allows the incarnation of the Word or the spiritual efficiency of the sacraments to be appropriately represented.[60]

Theory of the language of Adam

On the one hand, St Thomas privileges intuitiveness in Adam's consciousness to such an extent that the noetic detour of sign seems to be almost superfluous;[61] on the other, because Adam had a body, he needed signs to speak[62] and to understand that someone was speaking to him.[63] There was therefore a language before original sin, not as 'dull' then as it has since become, weighed down as it is by the sedimentation of sememes (units of meaning) in spoken or written material. Again, if Thomas places the omniscience of Adam before all abstract thinking, it is precisely because Adam spoke from the beginning:[64] his argument is perfectly circular. So, what language did Adam speak? Thomas, although not particularly interested in that question, simply proposes, in passing, an opinion hazarded by Saint Augustine: God spoke to Adam in much the same way as he speaks to the angels!

We can conclude that, before and after the original fall, there were two modes of the *same* language; and that there must still be today, even if very blurred, two types of knowledge accessible to man: a more intuitive mode, consistent with reading the spiritual effects contained within sensible things or sign images, and another mode, consistent with abstracting the intelligible from the sensible[65] (that is, that which can be perceived). Without going into it more thoroughly, let us just

---

59 See *ST* Ia, Q. 107, art. 1, ad 3.
60 See *ST* IIIa, Q. 62, art. 4, ad 1, for an analysis of voice; and Q. 6, art. 6, ad 3, for a comparison between incarnation and phonation.
61 See *ST* Ia, Q. 94, art. 1; and *De Veritate*, Q. 18, art. 2 *in fine*.
62 See *ST* Ia, Q. art. 3, ad 1.
63 See *ST* Ia, Q. 111, art. 1, ad 3, *in fine*.
64 *ST* Ia, Q. 94, art. 3, sed c.
65 *ST* Ia, Q. 94, art. 1.

note that in a passage of St Thomas's treatise *De Prophetia*, the irreducibility of the sensible into the communicable comes across as a kind of illness (how true it is that the sign in this case is a medicine!).[66] It would be possible to make analogous remarks a propos theology which concerns itself with the inspiration behind Scripture, dependent on a sufficiently 'mentalist' conception of knowledge.[67]

Finally, is not St Thomas tempted by what George Steiner calls a 'pre-fall semiotic'?[68] In those times, 'signifier and signified, word and world, semantic sign-post and *Logos* were concordant in a way they have never been since . . .' In concrete domains such as teaching,[69] St Thomas appears to be dreaming of a transparent and purely spiritual language on the one hand, and on the other the pedagogue has a lively conscience concerning the being of language, the obstacles it puts in the path of pure intelligibility and the practical necessity of rendering an account. Thomist realism thus does not ignore a certain ontological consistency within language although it appears to refuse to treat of it per se.

Let us ask ourselves the simple question: why does Thomas not pose the question of sign?

First, for logical reasons. Speculative grammar makes available to Thomas several distinctions (between signification and the mode of imposition, and between the mode of signification and supposition), allowing him to do his best with the so-called arbitrariness of sign.[70] Thomas makes use, not so much of a demonstrative logic as of a logic of *suppositio*. Between logic, psychology and metaphysics, *suppositio* is both an intra-linguistic phenomenon (as a mode of signifying) and the actualization of the very intentionality of intelligence. Thus, if he is not committed to demonstrative logic in his neglect of the dialectic of the sign, it is less because it is an insoluble problem and more because it has *already been solved* in a use of signs which *supposes* a theological life and maintains a symbolic vision of creation in its entirety.

Second, for metaphysical and theological reasons. For Thomas, intelligence invents things as (already) signifying and thinkable. In a certain sense, reality speaks for itself, because all noetic mediation is not, properly speaking, spoken (nor are signs generally instituted). For

---

66 *ST* IIa IIae, Q. 174, art. 2, ad 2.

67 *ST* IIa IIae, Q. 171, art. 1.

68 Cf. George Steiner, *Passions impunies*, trans. P. E. Dauzat and L. Evrard, with an original chapter in French from A., 'Nrf-essais' (Paris: Gallimard, 1997), p. 114. [Originally published as: *No Passion Spent: Essays 1978–1996* (London: Faber & Faber, 1996).]

69 See *ST* Ia, Q. 117, art. 1, ad 1.

70 Cf. H. J. M. Shoot, *Christ, the 'Name' of God*, pp. 40ff. (see note 4 above); and I. Rosier-Catach, *La Parole comme acte* (see note 16 above).

example, *figura*, as the natural expression of substance, is also a noetic mediation. Signification is even rooted in this fundamental fact: it is the radiance of the substance through its accidents – a substance that remains hidden from our senses, which know only accidents.[71] If the order of meaning is not severed from the order of being in general, and is not made into an object of specific consideration, it is because both are founded *theologically*. The interaction of being and meaning, which enables any speculative discourse claiming to be 'realist' (this has since been illustrated with regards to metaphor and analogy)[72] is *supposed* by faith in creation.

Third, for liturgical reasons. The transcendent and the immanent, which give to human nature its humanness and which structure and authorize *sacra doctrina* (because it is in the order of meaning that divine wisdom 'impresses' subordinated human sciences),[73] are communicated in the diverse *practices* of sign. Counted among these practices, the sacraments of the Church or the reading of Sacred Scripture are the most obvious in an age which has secularized even the cosmos. According to G. Trainar 'ritual memory has the capacity to destroy the vicious hermeneutic circle' of signs returning indefinitely to one another.[74]

Does the world-view, which St Thomas shares with his contemporaries, thus resolve the question of sign? If the legacy of philosophers, and in particular teachers of the *artes liberales*, allows him to explain *how* language functions, the nourishment derived from Scripture when received productively in an ecclesiastical (sacramental) setting, explains *why* there is meaning in speech. The hermeneutical dialectic between truth and its expression is surpassed in the symbolic mentality (*pansemiosis*, as Umberto Eco would put it) which results from faith in a God who creates through and in the Word; that of event and meaning is surpassed through faith in a God who saves only through the diffusion of revelation.[75] St Thomas no more attempts to de-emphasize the part played by mystery in speech than he does in anthropology or noetics.[76]

---

71 Cf. *ST* IIIa, Q. 75, art. 2, ad 3.

72 Cf. Lucien Martinelli, *Thomas d'Aquin et l'analyse linguistique*, Conférence Albert-Le-Grand (Paris: Vrin/Montreal, Institut d'Études médiévales, 1963), and P. Ricœur, *La Métaphore vive*, L'ordre philosophique (Paris: Seuil, 1975). [ET: *The Rule of Metaphor: Multi-disciplinary Studies of the Creation of Meaning in Language*, trans. R. Czerny with K. McLaughlin and J. Costello (Toronto: University of Toronto Press, 1977).]

73 Cf. our *Littérature et théologie*, ch. 14. '"Convenances": les consequences littéraires de la théorie de la théorie de la subalternation des sciences', pp. 429–56.

74 G. Trainar, *Transfigurer le temps*, p. 54 (see note 49 above).

75 *ST* IIIa, Q. 42, art. 4.

76 Etienne Gilson, 'Propos sur l'être et sa notion', in *San Tommaso e il pensiero moderno*, Studi tomistici, 3 (Rome: Académie pontificale Saint Thomas d'Aquin, 1975), p. 14.

The 'problem of the bridge' and that of understanding are resolved in theology, whose starting point is Scripture. But in accentuating this, is there not the risk that truth is reduced to the historical and cultural conditions wherein it appears? In this model, contemporary deconstructive thinking is unstoppable in its own logic. There is, however, more than one risk: a certain relativism which has led to the rediscovery of tradition, influenced by a contemporary hermeneutic, is a good thing.

Two inadequate responses to the problem of sign

The rediscovery of tradition and its limits

Hermeneutics does not actually stop at the semiological dualisms so far suggested. It knows the fecund interaction between the exterior and the interior, between the same and the other,[77] in intimate thought, moulded by language, directly communicable because expressed and fixed in the game of communication. All this has led to a rehabilitation of tradition. The big name is of course Hans-Georg Gadamer. In a voice more phenomenological and less metaphysical he has thus reconnected certain of St Thomas's profound noetical intuitions: not only the theme of necessary precognition, but also the very specific Thomist *cogito*, according to which it is only by an exterior detour that the human spirit is able to know itself.[78]

For Gadamer, the fundamental hermeneutical structure is that of question and answer, the dialectic of which always precludes an interpretative approach. Thomists would rejoice at this, accustomed, by the very poetics of the *Summa*, to by-passing the dialectical articulation of previous opinions, before proposing their own demonstration of truth. However, contemporary thought concerning tradition is not without ambiguities. Let us give two examples:

First, the hermeneutic of comparison between historical perspectives, elaborated since Gadamer,[79] allows hermeneutics to study sympathetically the cultural context of Thomas, by emphasizing the fecundity of temporal distance, to better discern the presuppositions pertaining to an age, and the prejudices formed in him by the Christian

---

77 See for example P. Ricoeur, *Soi-même comme un autre*, L'ordre philosophique (Paris: Seuil, 1990); or Julia Kristeva, *Étrangers à nous-mêmes* (Paris: Fayard, 1988 (new edn, Paris: Gallimard, 1991)). [ET: *Strangers to Ourselves*, trans. Leon S. Roudiez (New York: Columbia University Press, 1991).]

78 Cf. Chrétien, 'La connaissance angélique', p. 134.

79 See H. R. Jauss, *Pour une herméneutique littéraire*, trans. M. Jacob (Paris, 1978). [Originally published in German as *Ästhetische Erfahrung und literarische Hermeneutik* (Munich: Fink, 1977).]

culture within which he grew up, so that an internal coherence can be demonstrated. But it leads, as well, to the suggestion that it is impossible to attain absolute truth.[80] Between the impossible, uncontainable (a-temporal) situation and complete relativism, an equilibrium of relative interpretation, correct (right) if not true, is to be found. But as with all relativisms, is not this position contradictory, to the extent that it pretends to be true?

Second, Alasdair MacIntyre and others have explained the traditional, because narrate-able, nature of man.[81] The consideration of the linguistic conditioning of thought has thus led a number of theologians to define their discipline as a 'meta-narrative', a commentary on New Testament narration. But is there not here a danger of reducing the life of faith to an utterly voluntary support for a fiction? Those thinkers more attached to a narrative way of thinking have, in fact, developed the idea of the end of all 'meta-narration', and imagined that henceforth thought must content itself with playing the game of multiple 'small narratives'.[82] Is the Christian vision a vision among others, which is just as probable and just as refutable as any other? If it is faithful to the One who says 'I am the Truth', Christian thought can perhaps be somewhat more ambitious!

In reality, the identification of narration and understanding mixes up *occasion* and *cause*, as Aristotle would have said. Without the existence of small narratives, necessarily social, cause would not be the cause. Cause per se resides in the proper capacity of each man to pass from sound to meaning, a capacity precisely named *interpretatio* in the thirteenth century. Hermeneutics ought to be rendering an account of the everyday wonder at the combining together of meaning (something spiritual) and of sound or character (something material).

I return now to Saint Thomas: he contented himself with such a general solution that the historical gap kept alive a kind of 'fideistic semiotic' that was a clear departure from the gothic spirit. As the people of Romanesque times glimpsed an epiphany of the Creator in the cosmos, so the idea of nature, developing in the thirteenth century, emphasized the autonomy (more evident henceforth than the sym-

---

80 Cf. U. Eco, *Le Problème esthétique chez saint Thomas d'Aquin*, trans. into French by M. Javion, Formes sémiotiques (Paris: PUF, 1993). [Originally published as: *Il problema estetico in Tommaso d'Aquino* (Milano: Bompiani, 1970).]

81 A. MacIntyre, *Après la vertu, Étude de théorie morale*, trans. into French by L. Bury, Léviathan (Paris: PUF, 1997), p. 212. [Originally published as: *After Virtue: A Study in Moral Theory* (London: Duckworth, 1981).]

82 Cf. Gavin Hyman, *The Predicament of Postmodern Theology: Radical Orthodoxy or Nihilist Textualism?* (Louisville, KY, London and Leiden: Westminster John Knox Press, 2001), p. 66.

bolism) of creatures. As for language, one cannot be content with juxtaposing the ideal of transparency with a practical utilitarianism, which only a symbolic view of reality (understood as language) can harmonize. Saint Thomas was therefore led to meditate, in more detail, upon the articulation of being and meaning. He did this in his meditation on the *verbum interius*.

The theory of the interior word and St Thomas's teaching

A well-informed thomist might have been tempted to stop me above, when I was evoking 'aporias' in Thomist semiology, by maintaining that Thomas does not only suppose the solution: has not his invention of the mental word, as the pre-linguistic state of thought, allowed the dialectic of sign and meaning to be tackled? And this, by founding the primacy of thought on language and the subsequent essence of character on recourse to sign, not only in noetics, but also in metaphysics? In some research conducted at the Institut Saint Thomas-d'Aquin,[83] I have analysed what is at stake in thomism's actual rediscovery of the interior word – this mysterious speech that, upon contact with things, resonates without words within the spirit. It promises the pure intentionality of knowing and the realism of knowledge, against an exaggerated critique of representative thought.[84] A few remarks will suffice here.

The theory demonstrates that to know is, according to Yves Floucat, 'to say without words'! *To say*, because 'in anyone who knows and by the fact that he knows, something proceeds within him: to know, the concept of the thing known, proceeding from the knowledge of that thing'.[85] But 'without words', because 'if Aquinas teaches that *intelligere* intrinsically envelopes *dicere* . . . he will never advance the idea that *dicere* could be a properly productive speaking activity, a form of transitivity'.[86] Saint Thomas describes the *verbum interius* as purely relative, 'transparent' from the two 'sides' where it appears in being. From the side of spirit, if 'intentionality' is properly understood, the word is not the positive content of the intellect;[87] from the side of reality, it is as transparent as possible because to some degree, *things themselves* speak[88] the language of the *species*.

83 See our *Thomas d'Aquin, poète théologien*, Vol. 2. *La langue de l'ineffable, Vers une théologie du langage* (Genève: Ad Solem, 2004), pp. 243–472.

84 Yves Floucat, *L'Intime fécondité de l'intelligence, Le verbe mental saint Thomas d'Aquinas*, Croire et savoir, 35 (Paris: Téqui, 2001), p. 113.

85 Floucat, *L'Intime fécondité*, p. 93.

86 Floucat, *L'Intime fécondité*, p. 106.

87 Floucat, *L'Intime fécondité*, pp. 116–17.

88 Cf. E. Gilson, *Le Thomisme, Introduction à la philosophie de Saint*

In fact, the progressive development of word theory in the tradition of St Thomas Aquinas and the history of its reception within Thomism, situates the interior word at the junction of two intersecting foundations: first that of the divine Word and intellection, which is also that of theology and metaphysics – where the Word inspires a word. Second, that of expressed language and supposed thought without words – where the aforesaid word requires *verba*. This observation results finally in bringing the terms common to both foundations into relationship: the divine Word and human language. We will quickly examine these three points.

The theological dimension of the problem

The very motivation of the word 'theory' is theological. In effect, Holy Scripture offers an invitation to find in the created world a sufficiently opaque and sufficiently transparent *verbum* so that it can serve as the basis of analogy and can designate God as a person really distinct from the other two [members of the Trinity] though of the same substance as them.[89] What is striking then is the dialectical aspect of the invented word, inspired by biblical texts and Trinitarian dogma. In a first movement of thought, its existence, distinct from the noetical instances that have already registered philosophically, can be established. In a second movement, its ontological consistency must be minimized, until the point of pure relation, through essence, is attained. The spiritual immanence of knowledge and its realistic reference to the exterior world are to be simultaneously held in mind.

In this undertaking, Thomism runs two risks: on the one hand, admitting that the interior word appears as a sign, or, put differently, that there is 'something of the linguistic word (*mot*)' about the interior word (*verbe*); on the other, reducing an ontology of knowledge to ashes by denying any semiotic and representational dimension to the word (so as to conserve the realism of knowledge). By virtue of the fact they rest on an approximate dichotomy between formal sign and instrumental sign,[90] or on the identification of *species* as pure formal

---

Thomas (Paris: J. Vrin, 1972), p. 286. [ET: *Thomism: The Philosophy of Thomas Aquinas*, a translation of the 6th and final edn by Laurence K. Shook and Armand Maurer (Toronto: Pontifical Institute of Mediaeval Studies, 2002).]

89 Cf. O.-Th. Venard, *La Langue de l'ineffable, Essai sur le fondement théologique de la métaphysique*, Memoire de licence en théologie à l'Institut Saint-Thomas-d'Aquin de Toulouse, 2001, ch. 9. 'Une réponse thomiste: la métaphysique du verbe', pp. 344–81.

90 Cf. John of Saint Thomas, *Cursus theologicus*, Vol. IV, In Partem, Q. 27, disp. 32, art. 5 (Solesmes edn, 1953, p. 90, §77).

cause,[91] Thomist theories of language oscillate between an operative understanding of sign and concept, in the category of 'relation', and a resulting conception leaning towards the category of 'substance'. In the first case, verbality (the irreducible linguistic condition of thought) escapes from the philosophical field of a word which claims to be transparent to the real. In the second, verbality is more or less assimilated to the concept. Were this is not the case it would be easy to tell which one determined the other. This exposes a new dimension to the problem.

The irreducibility of language

A defence of the realism of knowledge which does not take into consideration the verbality of language, to the extent that it uses the exterior word, which is transitive, to demonstrate the pure relativity of the interior word, has not dealt properly with the problem. Certainly, the question posed by Thomas is less that of language and thought than that of language and truth. But his meditation on the mental word maps out clearly the two asymptotes between which all true thought about language must take place: on the one hand, it is necessary to postulate *a certain state* of thought before language (terminative thought never exhausted [*epuisée*] by uttered language); and on the other, the aforementioned thought, a concept which although a border-line epistemic entity is nevertheless indispensable, is unknown without language. The problem of the ontological validity of the human word cannot be resolved without being faithful to both observations.

One wonders whether, in the theory of the 'three' words, it is possible to see a rediscovery of the poetic character of quotidian activity which, thus understood and spoken, is more than an affirmation of a naive belief in the separation of words from thought. Numerous quotations from Saint Thomas, cited by H. G. Gadamer when he discusses Christian thinking on the incarnation[92] as that unique tradition in Western thought which, according to him, justifies the being of language, suggest this in every case.

Those thomists who are themselves interested in language are often very close to this interpretation when they emphasize, with Thomas, the creative character of thought.[93] In fact, what Marcel de Corte calls 'the

---

91 Cf. A. De Muralt, *L'Enjeu de la philosophie médiévale*, Études thomistes, scotistes, occamiennes et grégoriennes, Studien und Texte zur Geistesgeschichte des Mittelalters, 24 (Leiden: Brill, 1993), especially pp. 92–127 [94–5].

92 Gadamer, *Vérité et méthode*, p. 441.

93 *De Veritate*, Q. 1, art. 3

poematical source of the spirit'[94] comes to mind. Certainly St Thomas insists on the immanence of the intellectual process, to the extent that he often evokes an unmediated vision of reality, which is more than an abstract exercise.[95] However, language, exists before me in the same way as 'real' being. In the act of knowing I am engaged in a doing,[96] the production of a discourse (or might it be a 'definition'?) which is really and actually a something.[97] Acknowledgement of the word *follows on from* the articulation of word theory.

The relationship between the divine Word and language

As for its relationship with language, there is a similarity between the interior word and God: it can be suggested more easily than it can be named.[98] Because the mental word is never able to be thought other than in its expression through language, it will never be susceptible to exhaustive demonstration; it will never be grasped except through a logic of *suppositio*. It becomes necessary to move from mere verbal formulations to the deeper act, from which all verbalizations emanate.[99]

In a number of passages where St Thomas develops his theory of the word, thomists admire the divine perfection found to be inhering in human knowing.[100] For modern agnostics, the sublime experience of the metaphysician, expressing through analogy the proximity of the human word and the creative action of the Word, is something tragically ironic for human thought. He willingly accepts that creation is known as the (per) locutionary value of divine locution, and not as a result of transitive action, but will add that if the human word transpires thus to be 'marvellously' divine, this is perhaps because the divine word, from Genesis 1, was just a little bit too human! From a theological point of view, the book of Scripture is the first concrete manifestation of the

---

94 M. De Corte, 'Ontologie de la Poésie', *Revue Thomiste* 43 (1937), pp. 361–92 (p. 376); and *Revue Thomiste* 44 (1938), pp. 99–125.

95 See *ST* Ia, Q. 85, art. 1, ad 1.

96 Cf. Mary Carruthers, *The Book of Memory: A Study of Memory in Medieval Culture*, Cambridge Studies in Medieval Literature, 10 (Cambridge and New York: Cambridge University Press, 1990), p. 65; and *ST* Ia IIae, Q. 57, art. 3, ad 3.

97 Cf. J. De Finance, *Être et agir dans la philosophie de saint Thomas*, Bibliothèque des Archives de philosophie (Paris: Beauchesnes, 1945), p. 114, p. 114.

98 Cf. *De Veritate*, Q. 4 [*De verbo*], art. 1, ad 8.

99 Jean-Luc Marion, 'Saint Thomas d'Aquin et l'onto-théo-logie', *Revue Thomiste* 95 (1995), pp. 31–66 (p. 43, n. 26).

100 Cf. H. Paissac, *Théologie du Verbe, Saint Augustine and Saint Thomas* (Paris: Cerf, 1951), p. 201.

irreducibility of language, established on the reciprocal foundation of the Word and *verba*!

In the theory of the word, these two intersecting foundations suggest that the relationship between discourse (speech) and truth be more closely scrutinized. The invention of the single *verbum*, in its dialectic with the many *verba*, suggests that the word is neither the cause, nor the foundation of truth which it transcribes. As Joseph Rassam says, 'that by which a word is true is not another word, but an act'.[101] The invention of the single word, in its dialectic with the Word, allows us to grasp that 'every word presupposes a light which it could not create'.[102] This also means that every word presupposes an interior acknowledgement of this light; that the re-appropriation of realism in knowledge surpasses the discipline of just philosophy. To say this is not to naively eulogize again the ineffable, nor to assert that truth is external to speech. It is rather to discover that truth can only be grasped through an act interior to speech itself. J. Rassam continues:

> Truth, in its relationship to the word, is at once '*intus et foris*'. In the same way, according to Saint Thomas, the knowledge of principles, received by the senses, presupposes a light by which those same principles are received, just as '*fides ex auditu*' presupposes an '*habitus fidei infusus*'[103] ... [It is necessary to experience the fact] that beyond the sound which strikes the ear there is a secret voice which speaks interiorly, and that this spiritual and interior speech is the true predicate without which all that men say would be but useless noise ... Saint Augustin says of this fact: there is here, my brothers, a great secret, *sacramentum magnum ... Sonus verborum percutit, magister intus est.*[104]

Finally, along with language and the theology of the divine Word, the intersecting foundations in the theory of the interior word say nothing perhaps more than this: the word is neither transparent to truth in its plenitude – to believe this would lead to the deification of man – nor wholly indeterminate and in thrall to arbitrary passions – it would be better to say nothing if that were the case. The word is capable of truth to the furthest reach of the corporeal and the spiritual, of the relative

---

101 Cf. J. Rassam, *Le Silence comme introduction à la métaphysique* (Toulouse: Presses universitaires du Mirail, 2nd edn, 1988), p. 27.
102 Rassam, *Le Silence*, p. 27.
103 *In Boetium de Trinitae*, Q. 3, art. 1, ad 4, *in fine*.
104 Cf. J. Rassam, *Le Silence*, p. 29.

and the absolute, because it participates in divine language.[105] The question now is to understand how. This might be the hermeneutical task of actual Thomism.

The hermeneutical task of present-day Thomism

Recognizing the omission of reflection on expression

For many thomists to develop a reflection on expression would be to denature Thomism. When reading an author for whom 'the act of belief is not completed in the enunciation but in the reality',[106] a hermeneutical 'reflection' would lead to a general misinterpretation. Perhaps Etienne Gilson's assertion concerning modern principles of causality and the adequacy of reason, needs to be said of the Thomist problem of expression: 'Not only can Thomism be itself without explaining these principles, but, in doing so, it seriously compromises its purity.'[107] But the unique harmonics (aesthetic, moral and religious) of the term 'purity' which he employs, place the problem in an existential order much wider than mere conceptual rigour.[108]

Gilson, when recounting his 'A Philosopher's Childhood',[109] has himself insisted on the necessity of a religious context for the emergence of metaphysics. Yes, the laconic and chaste expression of being, characteristic of Thomas, requires a certain culture. I have shown that the well-known unspoken dialogue between Gilson and Maritain, about the intuition of Being, can be clarified by this.[110] The former vigorously defends the orthodoxy of Thomas's words, while the latter tries to suggest the content through the flamboyancy of metaphors. Maritain tries to suggest literally what Gilson states without words. If there needs to be a conclusion to this debate on the 'intuition of Being', we would say with Gilson that, in itself, such an experience is neither probable nor necessary; but, with Maritain, that for us, secular modern individuals, it is necessary. This is why there is an urgency today to embrace with enthusiasm the apologetics, the art of apologies (did I really say 'apologies'?), of Being.

---

105 See St Thomas, *In Ioan.*, cap. 1, lect. 5 (Marietti, 1952, numbers 127 and 129, p. 27).

106 *ST* IIa IIae, Q. 1, art. 2, ad 2.

107 E. Gilson, *Constantes philosophiques de l'être* (Paris: Vrin, 1983), p. 84.

108 See St Thomas Aquinas, *Commentary on Aristotle's Métaphysiques*, Book IV §576.

109 E. Gilson, 'Les enfances théologiques', in *Le Philosophe et la Théologie*, Le signe (Paris: Librairie Arthème Fayard, 1960), pp. 11–25.

110 Cf. Venard, *La Langue de l'ineffable*, pp. 20–53.

Thomism is still often haunted by the desire to find evidence for (to substantiate) reality. And certainly, for Thomas, 'we not only formulate statements so that through them we can have knowledge of things', all the time acknowledging that 'what goes for faith goes for science',[111] but 'it is by faith that we come to knowledge, and not the reverse'.[112] The 'evidence' in question unites faith, knowledge and science under the sign of articulated relation/reality. In 'science' the way of return back from statements to things is like that which exists in faith. It is open to question intentionally. It is like discovering something incredibly wonderful, as ancient as wisdom, that existed before beings and before letters. Certainly, we believe that we see the world as it really is, but as Maurice Merleau-Ponty explains, 'this faith has something strange about it which, if we try to articulate it in theses and expressions, if we ask ourselves what is this *we*, what is it *to see* and what is this *thing* or *world*, we enter into a maze of difficulties and contradictions'.[113] As for language, according to Fergus Kerr, 'the difficulty is to show that our understanding of meaning is normally a *perception* of meaning, and not the result of inferences starting from states of radical and intimate understanding of which words and gestures are but the consequence'.[114]

As soon as the clumsiness of language in representation and communication is really taken into consideration, the question asked of thomist thought by contemporary hermeneutics is ultimately that of the possibility of 'realistic' thought. The mingling of human with divine knowledge, discovered via abstract work with the pure perfections of knowable realities, is not sufficient to guarantee the validity of theological discourse *as* discourse. It is necessary to extend the idea (often expressed by St Thomas), of the mingling of the human word with the divine Word, to the verbal dimension of human language.

Rediscovering the presence of the absolute in language

We must here be more attentive to what J. Grondin proposes to call 'the ever-rhetorical incarnation of meaning'.[115] 'Finite beings like us

---

111 *ST* IIa IIae, Q. 1, art. 2, ad 2.

112 *ST* IIa Q. 32, art. 1, ad 2 : 'Per fidem venitur ad cognitionem et non e converse.'

113 M. Merleau-Ponty, *Le Visible et l'Invisible*, Bibliothèque des Idées (Paris: Nrf Gallimard, 1964), p. 17.

114 F. Kerr, *La Théologie après Wittgenstein, Une introduction à la lecture de Wittgenstein*, Cogitatio fidei, 162, trans. Alain Létourneau (Paris: Cerf, 1991), p. 191. [Originally published as: *Theology After Wittgenstein* (Oxford: Basil Blackwell, 1986).]

115 J. Grondin, L'universalité de l'herméneutique, p. 475 (see note 55 above).

only participate in the event of meaning through the many concrete forms of its manifestations and images . . . which do not in the first instance belong to sequential logic.'[116] The specifically Christian form of rationality is to be called 'rhetoric': at the heart of *sacra doctrina*, it 'is rooted in a meaning, already established and practiced, that addresses individuals not simply as rational beings'.[117] For a long time Thomism has been sterile, taking literally some of Thomas's anti-poetic, anti-rhetoric, anti-metaphoric and pro-scientific statements.[118] As with Aristotle, however, Thomas's practice in these areas turns out to be far more nuanced than the theory.

Language obsesses

The inseparable character of thought and representation is coupled with that of representation and expression, and implies that of *poesis* and *praxis*: man fabricates signs, and signs make man. The beginning of language is unthinkable, as the first words in the prologue of John suggest. 'Language is not formed through a mental act of reflection which, if *per impossibile* we were able to distinguish it as such, would have to happen before language, in the bosom of pure thought.'[119] As a consequence, the definition of man as a speaking being is prior to all others, notably those which define human being as historical being.[120] To avoid degenerating into a kind of linguistic monism, which is symmetrically derived from historicism, a theological ground is required.

Language dispossesses

The word is of itself open to transcendence. Comprehension, in its concrete exercise, is more a dis-appropriation (a letting-go-of) than an appropriation (a grasping-hold-of): is it not a rediscovery of the idea that intelligence is the capacity to be indefinitely 'other' in so far as it is possible to be other at all or that, in what is said, something is clarified without however being assured, judged, decided upon after full consideration? It is what happens everywhere when something encoun-

---

116 Grondin, L'universalité', p. 473.

117 Grondin, L'universalité', p. 476.

118 See Venard, *Littérature et théologie*, 'Pour une poétique théologique', pp. 140–5; ch. 6. 'Entre *necessitas et delectatio*, la métaphore', pp. 187–222; and 'Synthèse rhétorique et somme théologique', pp. 371–481.

119 Grondin, 'L'universalité', p. 479 (referring to H.-G. Gadamer, *Vérité et Méthode*, p. 449).

120 F. Martin, *Pour une théologie de la lettre: L'inspiration des Ecritures*, Cogitatio fidei 196 (Paris: Cerf, 1996), p. 322.

ters us from tradition. Immersion within a tradition is like an aesthetic experience which, through the sublimity of light, escapes all relativisms. The hermeneutical experience, as linguistic dialectic between meaning and event, recalls the ecstasy of *contemplatio* in the *lectio divina*.

Language precedes

The major presuppositions of any theory of meaning are not linguistic, but theological. The more lucid postmoderns appreciate this and seem to attempt to hide their discovery behind screens of abstraction such as, for example, the 'abstract messianism' inherent in the language used by one J. Derrida.[121] In fact, as Pierre Gardeil theorizes, even though we may have successfully made the Messiah of dogma disappear in a conjuring trick, we always feel 'an indescribable presence which reduces to ashes all inquiries purporting to be anterior'.[122] And, according to George Steiner, 'the semantic sign, when understood to be full of meaning, and divinity "has the same place and time of birth" (Derrida) . . . The age of the sign, says Derrida, is essentially theological.'[123] To look expectantly for a meaning at the basis of the hermeneutical stance, can be, after much discourse, to rediscover God, because God is at the origin of language. The existence or non-existence of this basis was already the problem which Renan and a part of modernism purported to resolve.[124] Today it is, once again, the postmodern problematic, which asks what comes first, 'revelatability' (*Offenbarkeit*: that which can be revealed) or revelation[125] (*Offenbarung*: that which is revealed).

The fact that there is no situation that exceeds language, means that every speaker is necessarily engaged in that which he speaks. Here is a fact of particular interest to the theologian influenced by Thomas's argument *de convenientia*: thought on language, because that which is known is always preceded by that which it tries to think, is necessarily sustained by a non-demonstrative rationality.

---

121 J. Derrida and G. Vattimo, 'Foi et savoir', in *La Religion* (Paris: Seuil, 1996), p. 28.

122 P. Gardeil, *Quinze regards sur le corps livré* (Genève: Ad Solem, 1997), pp. 25–6, n. 2.

123 G. Steiner, *Réelles présences, Les arts du sens*, trans. from the English by M. R. de Pauw, NRF essais (Paris: Gallimard, 1991), p. 149. [Originally published as *Real presences, Is there anything in what we say?*, London: Faber & Faber, 1989.]

124 See François Laplanche, 'Introduction' to Vol. 9 (*Les sciences religieuses. Le XIXe siècle (1800–1914)*) in *Dictionnaire du monde religieux dans la France contemporaine*, under the direction of Jean-Marie Mayeur and Yves-Marie Hilaire (Paris: Beauchesne, 1996), pp. v–xxv.

125 Cf. Derrida, *La Religion*, p. 26.

Reconstituting rationality on a theological foundation

Remarks on method and the history of thought: arguments to support the legitimacy of this movement

In recovering theology – let us emphasize this – the hermeneutical question rediscovers its 'natural place', lost since the Reformation. The problem of language posed by hermeneutical philosophies is not simply comparable to the problem of the 'hermeneutical leap', admirably assessed by G. Dahan in his lengthy meditation on the progression from literal to spiritual meaning in his exegesis of St Thomas; rather it participates in it. Many contemporary reading techniques are derived directly from the ancient disciplines of *lectio*. This buckle would have been the undoing of the history of hermeneutics . . . Certainly we might be tempted to see in this appreciation a mutation of St Bonaventure's old undertaking of *reductio artium ad theologiam*, or simply a return to balance of the ever-unstable equilibrium between philosophy and theology. But from a linguistic point of view, the dialectic between 'philosophy' and 'theology' is more than a sophism: it is the problem of language itself which puts thought *in medias res theologicas*. 'We never attain man reduced to himself'[126] is said, not by a gracious theologian, but by the linguist Emile Beneviste. This fact is not fully appreciated, it seems to me, by the postmodern critics of J. Milbank who reproach him for speaking with authority.[127]

Dogmatism is inherent to words themselves: they cannot exist without postulating being! Henri Hude says 'He who, not without disdain, rejects the alternative has already opted for one of its terms.'[128] Here then are *the facts*: the inveterate denigration of the divine origin of language in philosophies of language, then in linguistic works; the permanence of theology in deconstructive philosophies; the exigency of an ultimate logic up until the narratives recounting the end of narrative;[129] the major presence in contemporary hermeneutics of an ancient Christian theology, in a more or less secular form.

Even when the absolute 'compels' human understanding to conceptualize it as an 'idea', in the Kantian sense of the term, hermeneutics

---

126 E. Beneviste, *Problèmes de linguistique générale*, Vol. 1 (Paris: Gallimard, 1996), p. 259.

127 Refer in particular to Gavin Hyman, *The Predicament of Postmodern Theology* (see note 82 above).

128 H. Hude, *Prolégomènes*, Philosophie européenne (Paris: Editions universitaires, 1991), p. 8.

129 Cf. J. Milbank, 'Postmodern Critical Augustianism: A Short Summa in Forty Two Responses to Unasked Questions', in *Modern Theology* 7 (1991), pp. 225–37.

has replaced the *infinitum negativum* of a perfect God by the *infinitum privativum* of human words, endlessly inflating the fact of their imperfection, and in so doing implanting the principle of immanence into language.

Preserving a critical theological vigilance

The development of hermeneutics and its philosophical consequences can therefore lead to a rehabilitation of theological thought. But we are only on the threshold of theology, because there is still a question to ask: what is the 'that' which always precedes thought? Of course, it is towards an absolute and infinite sense that the concrete experience of the presence of meaning points, but an exigency of the absolute empowered by the human word is variably realized by actual culture. Could it be that God is no more an inevitable conclusion than the existence *of that which we name* God in terms of the 'five ways'? Moreover, it is not necessarily a Christian theology that matters. In proposing somewhat quickly that 'everything raised up converges', an optimistic and naive Catholic vision has for a long time neglected to pose this kind of question, as Tracey Rowland has recently demonstrated.[130]

Opening the way for a theology of language

Here then is the burning question to be asked in order to avoid the risk of presenting Christianity as just one way among others to salvation, if not as a somewhat complicated gnosis, with all its irrational dogmas. What conditions are needed, in our age, to identify the linguistic abstraction of a 'messianism' included in every word with the all-too-real Messiah, the Christ of Scripture and the Church? It serves to increase the profundity of, as E. Gilson says, 'the terrifying word of Saint Thomas, that language is an analogy of the incarnation of the Word'. Without a theology of the Word, being is reduced to language and language is mistaken for the *logos*. To counter Gnostic tendencies – but without however labouring under the illusion of having discovered the 'historical' origin of language – the advent of meaning in the word and the grace of God in the person of Jesus Christ and in the belonging to the Church, need to be articulated.

We are unable to *explain* this articulation, but we can clarify it, starting from a knowledge which, in being fully aware of its linguis-

---

130 T. Rowland, *Culture and the Thomist Tradition, After Vatican II*, 'Radical Orthodoxy series' (London and New York: Routledge, 2003), in particular ch. 1. 'The treatment of culture in *Gaudium et spes*'.

tic conditioning, has the audacity nevertheless to want to speak the source, in an auto-transcendent movement, which presupposes faith and enkindles it, characteristic of biblical revelation. On the one hand, one declares faith in a God who speaks (and in this sense reasoning is demonstrative only for the believer); but on the other, this knowing is completely open to the work of reason at least as the key to the integration of human phenomena in general (in this sense it is accessible to all men who are curious and have a desire to understand). We are in the realm of the hypothetical (or *convenient*) necessity.[131]

The thesis is as follows: the faculty of speaking, which constitutes the subject in society, receives its ultimate form from the incarnation. Only an explanation of this linguistic-*theological* doctrine can persuade our contemporaries about the representative nature of knowing, or can explain the immanence of thought open to that which is. Only such an explanation can elucidate the realistic intention of discourse and its potential to speak the truth, the foundation of its historical function. I have devoted two volumes to this, appearing in the next few years.[132] Let me open up just four lines of enquiry here.

1 *The genealogical* Since Heidegger, hermeneutics has surpassed its methodology and begun to search out the ontological foundations of all knowledge, understanding or science. This quest took place especially in the limited disciplines of biblical exegesis (Bultmann), the human sciences (Gadamer) and philosophy (Ricoeur). In observing that the formal object of the symbolic liaison is the mystery of God itself and that man is understood in symbols more than he understands them,[133] there is a reorientation of knowledge that returns each discipline to its theological foundation.

2 *The linguistic* This line of enquiry serves, *first*, to re-establish the speculative contact between language and the question of God in questioning the arbitrariness of sign (referring to the new tendencies in linguistics concerning the motivation of sign)[134] and in daring to pose once again the question of the origin of language.[135] *Second*, it

---

131 Cf. Gilbert Narcisse, *Les Raisons de Dieu, Argument de convenance et Esthétique théologique selon saint Thomas Aquin et Hans Urs von Balthasar*, Studia friburgensia, NS 83 (Editions universitaires de Fribourg, 1997).

132 Cf. the last two volumes of Venard, *Thomas d'Aquin poète-théologien*, Vol. 2. *La Langue de l'ineffable*, and Vol. 3. *Pagina Sacra*, De l'Ecriture sainte à l'écriture théologique (Genève: Ad Solem, 2005).

133 Trainar, *Transfigurer le temps*, p. 56.

134 Cf. M. Dat, *Matrices et étymons*, Thèse de doctorat Ecole Normale Supérieure Lettres et Sciences Humaines de Fontenay-Saint-Cloud a Lyon/ Section arabe et langues sémitiques, 2002, 2 volumes, First Part.

135 *Cf. Merrit Ruhlen, l'Origine des Langues, Sur les traces de la langue*

re-establishes contact between language and the mystery of Christ. It is well known that Augustine drew inspiration from the model of language to get closer to the mystery of the incarnation; it is less well known that Gadamer spent his last working years doing the opposite: taking his inspiration from the Christian model of the incarnation (and its developments in the form of the theory of the *verbum interius*) to rethink the character of language as both event and faith.[136] How can the functioning of language be brought into relationship with sacramentality and the ontology of language with the theology of grace?

3 *The exegetical* The exegetical line of enquiry restarts from holy Scripture to undertake once again the theological task and tries to respond very precisely to the following question: what is it in Scripture that escapes linguistic deconstruction and historical relativism? It evaluates a new and fresh historical articulation of the New Testament, taking into account an ontology appropriate for language and the Christological revelation of its Origin, neglected for so long by scientific exegesis.[137]

4 *The Christological* This line of enquiry tackles again the humanist project of a *philologia major* (G. Bude) hanging from the cross. It creates a 'hermeneutical apologetic' which, to use Pascal's terms, is centred around the key to reality and the Scriptures. It demonstrates that the Word made flesh is the 'concrete universal' (Balthasar) required by human modes of knowing and understanding.

To conclude, genealogies of knowledge, linguistics, exegesis and Christology, being veritable *arche*-ologies, in the Johannine sense of the word, are what matter. There is a need to elaborate a theology of language which comes to relieve philosophy's 'linguistic turn' of what it has that is true, so that the relativism inherent in the hermeneutical circle can be redirected to the absolute – given paradoxically in history – of Christian revelation.

---

mere (The origin of language, Tracing the Evolution of the Mother Tongue, New York, 1994), trans. into French by P. Bancel, Débats (Paris: Belin, 1997).

136 Cf. Marie-Andrée Ricard, 'Herméneutique contemporaine . . .', *Laval théologique et philosophique* 57 (2001); *Le discourse intérieur*, pp. 251–76.

137 Cf. Fredrick C. Bauershmidt, 'The Word made speculative? John Milbank's Christological poetics', *Modern Theology* 15 (1999), p. 417.

9. Phenomenology and Theology: The Contemporary Episode of a New Essay and of an 'Escape' from Metaphysics

VINCENT HOLZER

The theoretical conditions of the theological turn: Husserl's reception in France and the discovery of the notion of 'intentionality'

On the occasion of an assignment from the International Institute of Philosophy to review the state of French philosophy over the last 15 years, Dominique Janicaud identified a new phase in the reception of Husserl in France. This phase is characterized by what the author of this 'assessment' refers to as the 'theological turn' of French phenomenology. Whether you are a philosopher or a theologian, this very expression 'theological turn' that some have immediately taken to be a lampoon, can spontaneously cause two kinds of reaction. Does this work deal with a kind of theology that is derived from metaphysics and about to claim for itself a new 'knowledge' which endows it with the illusive status of science it would not give up? This new possibility would integrate phenomenology to the classic relation that theology elaborated to think and justify its dependence upon philosophy. This structure inherited from the golden age of the scholastic period would only perpetuate itself as a sign of a theology that is in a dilemma and in search of a rational justification for its expression of faith. The theologian is the one who can most certainly develop such a working hypothesis.

However, this does not seem to be Dominique Janicaud's conclusion. He does not blame the theologians and their uncontrollable need to annex knowledge but he criticizes three emblematic figures of contemporary French philosophy. Presumably, these figures are responsible for the 'turn' of phenomenology to theology which is problematic because it is unacknowledged in its explicit intentions. For Janicaud,

154

this 'turn' is far from being intrinsic to phenomenology since its method forbids any return to a causative transcendence and to a lesser extent, any immediate assimilation to ontology, considering phenomenology is defined as a method. This is exactly what is problematic. Phenomenology which is the concept of a method, becomes an ontology finally to be fulfilled in a theology. The theoretical conditions of a theological turn are somehow presented in Husserl's *reception* in France, and his first reception especially. Here, Janicaud refers to an emblematic text, written by Sartre in January 1939: 'Intentionality: a Fundamental Idea of Husserl's Phenomenology'.[1]

This was a founding text since, as Janicaud indicates, it acted as a manifesto for the new 'ontological phenomenology' in the 1940s-50s. Through the concept of intentionality, Husserl gave to Sartre and philosophy the means to go beyond the alternative that still opposed those in favour of idealism and realism, as if the truth in-between could still not be found today. In 1953 and 1967, Paul Ricoeur[2] made the same observation about Husserl's concept of intentionality, which was the only viable alternative both to honour and go beyond Kantian criticism. What exactly is this about and do Husserl's ideas represent a 'brutal change' in philosophy?

Husserl's discovery of intentionality is the concept of a method that allows us to go back, below ontological assertions about the nature of consciousness or of the *cogito*, which in its Cartesian version, was different from *res extensa,* the extended thing. For Husserl, subsequent to a process that would conclude in its necessary isolation,[3] the *cogito* is not separated from its relation to the thing that is both thought and perceived. To understand this idea we can refer to the

---

1 Jean-Paul Sartre, 'Une idée fondamentale de la phénoménologie de Husserl: l'intentionnalité', in *Situations* (Paris: Gallimard, 1947).

2 Paul Ricoeur, 'Husserl (1859–1938)', in E. Bréhier, *Histoire de la philosophie allemande* (Paris: Vrin, 2nd edn, 1967), pp. 183–96, text published in Paul Ricoeur, *A l'école de la phénoménologie* (Paris: Vrin, 1986); 'Sur la phénoménologie', *Esprit* 21 (1953), pp. 821–39.

3 We know that the rule of evidence is based on a first intuition, that of the *cogito*. This 'renewal' suppresses any possibility of establishing a knowledge of the existence of God in the field of sense perception: 'For Cartesians, what is given is the simple object of the intellectual intention and not the complex objects of sensation . . . To know reality, we have to close our eyes, plug our ears and refrain from touching; we have to turn to ourselves and, in our understanding, search for the ideas that are *clear for it*', Alexandre Koyré, *Entretiens sur Descartes* (Paris: Gallimard, 1962), pp. 217–18. For Husserl, the opposition between an inside world of representation and an outside world of transcendental things is an unbearable situation, cf. *Idées directrices pour une phénoménologie et une philosophie phénoménologique pures*, I., § 49, p. 163 [117 in the German edition of the *Husserliana*].

important changes brought by Husserl to the founding categories of Kantian epistemology. For Husserl, the world is an infinite regulative idea (*eine unendliche regulative Idee*), as a perspective for possible objects. However, by using the Kantian category of the Regulative idea, Husserl causes it to undergo a tremendous transformation. For Kant, the idea is not constituent, it results from understanding. On the contrary, for Husserl, the Idea does not consist in 'organizing' a world, that is ultimately making the connection or the synthesis of impressions, pretending the world had an order. It rather consists in discovering the idea of a completion of knowledge by listening to the world. The idea is never what consciousness gives itself to make the world thinkable, but what is given to the consciousness. What Husserl calls constitution consists in giving meaning to what is self-presented. The constituent consciousness, although it is absolute, does not produce an object in the world; it is the act through which an 'object meaning' takes shape with experience.

As Paul Ricoeur strongly pointed out in the programmatic text of 1967,

> Husserl first gives to the notion of intentionality its whole meaning: any consciousness is *consciousness of* . . . (consciousness here does not refer to the individual unity of a 'flow of real life' but to each different *cogitatio* turned towards a different *cogitatum*). Therefore there will be as many kinds of intentionalities and 'consciousness' as means for a cogito to turn towards something: reality, the unreal world, the past, what is wanted, what is loved, what is desired, what is judged, etc. From a strictly descriptive point of view, intentionality escapes from the alternative of realism and idealism . . .[4]

It is well-known that Hegel had already given to phenomenology the task of including the different components of the ethical, political,

---

4 P. Ricoeur, 'Husserl', p. 189. '[It clearly appears that] "constituting" is not building, and even less creating, but it actually is unfolding the designs of consciousness mixed up in the natural, thoughtless and naive capture of a thing' (p. 191). After all, that is the meaning of the eidetic renewal which aims at deepening the phenomenological reduction by preventing any dissipation of different types of constitution. The eidetic look gives access to the categories of the being. It is always a matter of unveiling the subjective operations that give rise to a world. That is all the meaning of *epoche*. The latter does not make the world disappear but reveals it in its being, relative to subjectivity, and therefore in its own being. In a certain way, one must force oneself out of the world to know it better, that is to say to go from the natural attitude to the idea of science and of its ideal unification task. *Epoche* is precisely conceived as a suspension of judgement where all transcendental objects exist. Only this operation can make the world appear as constituted.

religious and aesthetic experience by considering them as the phases or the signs of a unique development of the Mind. Husserl never studied phenomenology through this teleological perspective of metaphysical nature. As Paul Ricoeur underlines, Hegel deals with a certain form of phenomenology, from which theologians have learned a lot, not because of the long approach represented by the complexities of this great phenomenological description but because of its germinal assertion which bears a double characteristic. First, self-manifestation is essential for the Mind, and second, the evolution of this manifestation in the consciousness of men is homogeneous to temporality and historicality.

The phenomenological revolution consists in the commonplace assertion according to which the consciousness is first 'out of oneself' and it is so in several ways. Logical objectivity is just one of its forms whereas perception is its most fundamental form. It is to this original form that the phenomenological vocabulary of the donor institution which confers a primacy to perception belongs. Thus, logical objectivity, or the truth of science, builds itself on this first foundation of presence and existence, and that of the world lived in a perceptive way. The alternative to realism and idealism is then overtaken by the fact that the object transcends consciousness and that, correlatively, the object is *inside* the consciousness because it appears to this constituent consciousness. Outside of this correlation, nothing is known and nothing is given. The double and false exteriority of consciousness and of the object, give way to a philosophy of the being in the world. Its themes are also those of intersubjectivity, as in Husserl's last work in phenomenology.

This can be easily understood since the correlation between the subject and the world unveiled by intentionality, necessarily extends to a new relation, that of the link of consciousnesses, the only place where the objectivity of perceptions can be expressed and made explicit. That is why for Husserl, descriptive phenomenology is linked to transcendental phenomenology. Indeed, Husserl professes neither rude sensualism nor naive realism. For him, it is all about examining the meaning of intentionality. This can only be achieved through a 'deepening of the transcendental distantiation regarding experience', most certainly inherited from Kant, but by refusing to be trapped by the radicality of Kant's split between the phenomenon and the noumenon.[5] Husserl's transcendental 'I' does not give up the truth of idealism but gets rid of its Platonic and metaphysical correlate. There is no such thing as a realm

---

5 'Basically, phenomenology was born as soon as, setting aside – temporarily or permanently – the question of the being, we treated the way things appear as an autonomous problem', Ricoeur, 'Sur la phénoménologie', p. 821.

of essences that would tower above perceptible reality. The essence of intentionality must be found in phenomenal immanence which is the very meaning of this other fundamental expression: intentional transcendence.[6] Concerning knowledge, intentional transcendence is not reduced to an adequacy between the thought and the object. To understand what the phenomenological method is, representation has to be opposed to intentionality. Consciousness is not the pure presence to the self of an interiority capable of giving a representation of the world. The constituent consciousness is not constituted when a subject becomes aware of a pure activity producing thought. Of course, intentional consciousness provides meaning and the act of meaning contains the essence of intentionality. But here, the consciousness is a 'centre of enlightenment' and as it orientates its own clarity towards the world, it enables it to show itself and to appear as a phenomenon. In line with this, the consciousness comes out of itself to be next to the objects. Intentionality of knowing does not produce unity of the world through knowledge or an act of synthesis. The unity of the world is experienced as 'already done or already here' (*déjà faite ou déjà là*),[7] according to Merleau-Ponty.

---

6 D. Janicaud, *La phénoménologie éclatée* (Paris: Éditions de l'éclat, 1998), p. 33. [ET: *Phenomenology 'wide open'*, Charles N. Cabral, trans. (New York: Fordham University Press, 2005).] In phenomenology, the consciousness at first does not know through representation; it is always the aim of something, the intentional aim of an object. Husserlian phenomenology believes that any individual reality belongs to or pertains to an essence and that this essence is accessible by the mind, the ultimate aim of knowledge. But these essences are not existences themselves. They have to be defined as meaning (vision of essences, eidetics) or sense structures and the intelligible data of the experience has to be precisely described. The radical and initial question of phenomenology is as follows: from which layers of original meaning is the intentional meaning of nature, mind, thing and world created? How is the eidetic meaning formed, or the meaning of these eidetic objects that are nature, the thing, the world, the mind, the horizon, the figure, etc.? It is true that for Husserl, consciousness asserts itself as transcendental not because it appears to have the possibility of a priori knowledge, but because it is an absolute fact. Also, Husserl makes a distinction between the transcendental I and the consciousness, Husserl, *Méditations cartésiennes* (Paris: PUF, coll. Epiméthée, 1994), § 11, p. 69, trans. Marc de Launay. Brigitte McGuire clearly expresses this: 'Through the word transcendental, Husserl refers to the same subjectivity as Descartes, however it is not a *res cogitans*, a thing already constituted, but a subjectivity that simply constitutes transcendent things, as meaningful entities that have their own value, and that it can keep and fulfill freely. First monadically and then inter-monadically', 'L'origine monadique de la logique de Husserl', *Les Études philosophiques* (Paris: PUF, April–June 1998), p. 163.

7 M. Merleau-Ponty, *Phénoménologie de la perception* (Paris: Gallimard, 1945), p. XII [Preface].

How does this 'turn' happen?

According to Janicaud, the fundamental *dissociation* achieved by phenomenology allows this theological 'turn' to happen. In fact, the word 'dissociation' is a borrowed word from Paul Ricoeur's famous typology of phenomenology and refers to the dissociation between the being and the appearance. This fundamental dissociation is also the basis of the alternative between metaphysics and phenomenology. When we mention phenomena, what do we mean? It is a matter of identifying how things, values, people and any reality appear in relation with 'an eventual absolute reality'.[8] The shift to theology happens through an identification of this absolute reality thanks to the concepts of phenomenology rather than its methods. Yet, Husserl never completely identified this and consequently he never positively asserted that there was a transcendence of God that directly depended on the transcendence of meaning. Numerous contemporary philosophers, and important ones such as Lévinas, Marion and Henry, tend to change the original meaning of the Husserlian intentionality into an 'intention' of meaning or an 'intentionality of transcendence'. They insert transcendent into the immanent field of meanings to push it upwards. According to Dominique Janicaud, this operation is a 'jamming' (*brouillage*). 'In fact, phenomenology has been kidnapped by a theology that eclipses its name.'[9] This phenomenon is simple. It consists in the use of phenomenological concepts which are mixed with descriptions from the spiritual, religious experience and which are thematized as such. According to Lévinas, it is represented by the biblical book and its talmudic commentaries. According to Jean-Luc Marion, it is the *call-and-answer structure* which characterizes the religious experience in its dimensions of abandonment and expropriation. Its fundamental model is of Christ-like essence. In other words, Janicaud points out an attempt to expropriate the theological referents, which should be returned to their own absent origin which only the phenomenological principles could appropriately conceive. Consequently, we are confronted with two types of subversion: the first is of philosophy itself and the second of theology affected by philosophy. In a certain way, phenomenology would be the *tertium quid*.

We cannot analyse in detail the works criticized. This is not our purpose. What matters is to consider the confusion that affects philoso-

---

8 Ricoeur, 'Sur la phénoménologie', p. 822.

9 Dominique Janicaud, *Le tournant théologique de la phénoménologie française* (Combas: Éditions de l'éclat, 1981), p. 31. [ET: *Phenomenology and the 'theological turn'*, Bernard G. Prusak, trans. (New York: Fordham University Press, 2000).]

phers when they are faced with a literature that professes itself strictly philosophical although it tends to avoid, or at least not to respect the rules and limits of immanence. But only immanence allows phenomenology to consider itself as a 'strict science of foundation'. Dominique Janicaud's critical questions were the same as Jacques Derrida's about *Réduction et Donation* by Jean-Luc Marion. The latter conceives a phenomenon called 'pure donation', which is first linked to the phenomenological primacy of the appearance as we identified it before. But this phenomenon of 'pure donation' does not have a specific form. Marion thinks it should be understood as a 'pure form' of the 'donation' and the 'call'. This conception of what cannot be objectivized does not need the phenomenological methodology to be coherently expressed and thought. It can resort to the Christian tradition or revival of apophatism and even be initiated by it. If the sources of the phenomenological ideas of Michel Henry were updated, we would easily prove that its model comes from the mystical thought of Eckhart. And these references are admitted and explicitly treated in his impressive work, *L'Essence de la Manifestation*.

Consequently the fundamental question is still the same. It concerns the outcome of the phenomenologies of Lévinas, the 'Other' (*l'Autre*), of Marion, 'the pure donation' (*la donation pure*), of Michel Henri, 'the archi-revelation' (*l'archi-révélation*)[10] and, to a lesser extent, of the final work of Merleau-Ponty, 'the openness to the Invisible' (*l'ouverture à l'Invisible*). There clearly has been a shift in phenomenology in France over the last 30 years. Is there a feature which distinguishes it from the first reception of Husserl and Heidegger? Is this feature the break with immanent phenomenality?'[11]

The question disappears when it comes to understanding the sources or the unacknowledged intentions of Emmanuel Lévinas's ideas. Indeed, they would especially be exposed to the 'disaster and the catastrophe of an abandonment of the phenomena'[12] which would only lend itself to ingenuous language tricks or to *petitio principii*. The absolute precedence of the Other is asserted, but without any possible understanding, any determination of concrete objects. In a very harsh indictment, Janicaud asserts that 'the description is no longer heuristic. It just gently places its images into an edifying place whose conceptuality has been forever blocked on the Other . . . This "phenomenology" is reduced to the edifying, clear evocation of a disembodied caress and

---

10 What Michel Henry calls in *C'est moi la Vérité*, 'the phenomenological self-affection of the absolute Life' (Paris: Editions du Seuil, 1996). [ET: *I am the Truth*, Susan Emanuel, trans. (Stanford, CA: Stanford University Press, 2003).]

11 Janicaud, *Le tournant*, p. 8.

12 Janicaud, *Le tournant*, p. 18.

a cold eroticism.'[13] The sentence is harsh but must be taken seriously because it objectively detects a trend of corruption of the concepts. This trend is intra-philosophical since, as seen earlier, Janicaud does not accuse theologians but philosophers. Consequently, this means that theologians can and should take a stand concerning these evasive phenomena. The judgement given by Janicaud cannot be appealed against. 'Consequently, phenomenology has driven a return to the origin which is discovered as an extreme extenuation of any experience.' The methodological processes implemented result in a restoration of essentialism, although the latter comes on top of a negative theology. 'In the absolute unity of his radical immanence, the being affects and tests himself so that it feels everything in him, and every content which transcends his self-experience affects him.'[14] This assertion can link the ideas of Michel Henry to the Hegelian version of phenomenology, that is, 'the immanence of the absolute mind to its phenomenal manifestations'.[15] As Janicaud remarks, a great difference must be underlined. The divine immanence escapes to representation and to objectifying knowledge. In a surprising speculative move, Henry's 'religious' phenomenology thus links the development of Martin Heidegger's ontological difference to a 'phenomenology of the invisible'[16] and a phenomenology of 'Life' whose affectivity constitutes its essence. Indeed, affectivity is the essence of 'Life', it can be felt, you have to feel it and to let yourself

---

13 Janicaud, Le tournant, p. 30. The French philosopher from Nice alludes to the parts of Totalité et infini in which any relation to others is radically de-objectivized. It is the peak of an ethic of what cannot be objectivized. 'The decline of experience reaches astonishing proportions . . .', p. 30.

14 Michel Henry, L'essence de la manifestation (Paris: Presses Universitaires de France, 1963), p. 858. [ET: The Essence of Manifestation, Girard Etzkorn, trans. (The Hague: Nijhoff, 1973).] Do I have to remind the reader of the fact that for Henry, the self-affection of the absolute phenomenological life is opposed to the duality created when thought causes a split between essence and manifestation? From a phenomenological point of view, it is the opposition between philosophy of the world and philosophy of Life. The first conceives the truth in the exteriority of the world, through language, whereas the second conceives the truth as a self-revelation only supported by itself and therefore absent from the world conditions. Janicaud reveals a paradox. This Life is the place of an immanent experience. But self-affection continues to be 'the one of life, no historical, unfinished but forever and mysteriously linked to the self' (Le tournant théologique, p. 59). The vocabulary of essence is subjected to an impressive recurrence, the essence isolated in its radical independence and which is identified with Life. Life is synonym of plenitude and could not be reduced to the phenomenality of the world. The opposition between truth of the world and truth of Life disappears outside immanence. The problem is not to distinguish two orders of reality but only one which manifests itself in a unique truth.

15 Janicaud, Le tournant, p. 61.

16 The expression 'phenomenology of the invisible' was created by Heidegger in 1973 during the Zärhingen, cf. Questions IV (Paris: Gallimard, 1976).

be 'affected' by its passive radicality. The series of oppositions Henry draws between 'Life' and the world, affectivity and exteriority, immediacy and what is external seems to constitute a 'contradiction' which is part of the immanence of a self-phenomenalization of 'Life'. The conditions of the possible places for its development are always discredited as places of untruth. They are subjected to the illusory empire of exteriority and objectivization. Nature, language, history are all the negation of absolute 'Life' and they are never conceived as the possible place for its eternal development. Can we say again that the phenomenology of the invisible is no more than a philosophical version of negative theology?

Dominique Janicaud, the theologians' best friend

In *Ideen*, published in 1913, Husserl wrote that the world constitution, in its unity and its rationality and 'in' the pure consciousness, leads the transcendental subjectivity to the idea of a transcendent foundation. Once again, Husserl differentiated himself from Kant on a decisive question of teleology and receptivity to knowledge which is not determined by our finitude. The argument according to which the finitude of human knowledge lies in its receptivity [sensibility] is not a proof of its in-absoluteness because the absolute being is precisely 'the being which constitutes the world [West-konstituierende]'.[17] Consequently, the idea of God is required because of the 'immanent teleology'[18] associated with facts and not because of the facts of the world's being. 'It is not the fact in itself (*Faktum*), but the fact as a source of possibilities and realities whose values are set according to an increasing order to infinity, which forces us to ask the question of foundation (*Grund*) and which gives "rational reasons" (*Vernunftgründe*) to think that there is a "divine being" external to the world . . .'[19]

In his impressive study dedicated to the Husserlian theme of teleology, Arion L. Kelkel refers to texts about theological questioning. He emphasizes that the *Nachwort* to *Ideen*, published in 1930 as a preface to *Ideen I*, confirms the 'metaphysical ambition' of phenomenology. It could be thought that it is no part of the field of phenomenological description since Husserl contemplates a philosophy of history. The 'great *factum* of the absolute being' is history, the field where ultimate

---

17 Arion L. Kelkel, *Le legs de la phénoménologie* (Paris: Kimé, 2002), p. 92.

18 Kelkel, *Le legs*, p. 94.

19 *Ideen zu einer reinen Phänomenologie und phänomenologischen Philosophie*, Erstes Buch in *Husserliana*, III, § 58, p. 139, fr. tr., p. 191, quoted by Kelkel, *Le legs*, p. 94.

questions 'which form a unity with the questions about the absolute direction of history'[20] are thought and shaped. The programme conceived by Husserl is at the crossroad of phenomenology and metaphysical teleology, and therefore at its possible articulation. 'Making the latent reason evolve into the understanding of one's possibilities, and thus discovering the possibility of metaphysics as a real possibility, is the only way to begin the great work of metaphysics, that is of a universal philosophy.'[21]

Essentially, Husserl's phenomenology can obviously be understood as a transcendental idealism, since the infinite universe of meaning is opened from the consciousness that determines the being of the phenomena. This has major consequences for the philosophy of knowledge. Truth can no longer be defined as an adequacy of the thought and the object, nor as a pure relation of the thought with itself.

Are Husserl's ultimate findings in philosophy 'available' for the effort of the theological thought, or should we give up a too easy 'assumption' [Aufhebung] of the phenomenological categories in theology? Moreover, in the context of French philosophy a clear shift from classic Husserlian phenomenology (descriptive phenomenology of intentional objects) to a 'phenomenology of the unapparent' from Martin Heidegger can be observed, however this conception is exposed to the 'disaster and the catastrophe of an abandonment of the phenomena'.[22] This assumption concerning the phenomenon is not brought about by theologians but by philosophers who come to theology. Because of them, theology also undergoes fundamental changes, that some could consider illegitimate on the grounds of a tradition of faith and of theological epistemologies that have proved themselves. Thus, Michel Henry, in his book *C'est moi la Vérité*, launches a harsh confrontation with a way of thinking whose whole tradition consists in an acknowledgement of the indomitable transcendence of a free and creative God. This book tries to bring back this so-called transcendence and even the peculiarity of the dogmas supporting it, to the immanent structure of Life, as self-affection and pure presence to the self. We clearly see that we are discussing more than a theology that eclipses its name. The questions discussed remain philosophical. They especially deal with the possibility of phenomenology to substitute itself for metaphysics by going beyond it through its capacity to open itself to transcendence, the absolute and the original. Are these theological questions of the highest importance? We have our doubts, just as we doubt the relevance of Jean-Luc Marion's invitation

---

20 *Husserliana*, VIII, p. 506, quoted by Kelkel, *Le legs*, p. 97.
21 Kelkel, *Le legs*, p. 13.
22 Janicaud, *Le tournant*, p. 18.

to today's theologians. Obviously, there is a 'conflict' between epistemologies.

Conclusion and perspectives: the danger of a new theological 'positivism'

We have achieved our purpose through the deliberate deployment of a provocative and enigmatic title: 'Dominique Janicaud, the best theologian of all'. Far from denying theology a proper epistemology, Janicaud is concerned about 'cross-overs' or conceptual assimilations which may give the impression that methods and disciplines have been fused together. This warning is not without foundation and, in the particular case of theology's use of phenomenology, it cannot be totally heeded. To understand our own reservations, it is apposite to return to the heart of the debate which counterposes Jean Luc Marion against contemporary rational theology.

Having absented God from being, Jean-Luc Marion recently attacked the ascendancy of hermeneutics within the discipline of theology. By no means am I calling into question the legitimacy of a phenomenological reading of the events of revelation found in Scripture. This activity reveals an intra-philosophical perspective from which the theologian can most certainly benefit. However, I shall attempt to respond to a question that Marion consistently addresses to the theologian. At the end of this, we must briefly recall the controversial data which sets Janicaud in opposition to those who, surreptitiously, would allow theological themes and, in addition, theological thoughts, to be subordinated to phenomenology. A good number of contemporary philosophers, not least Lévinas, Marion and Henry, would transform the original meaning of Husserlian intentionality into an 'intention' of meaning or an 'intentionality of transcendence'. It would be a question of injecting transcendence into the immanent region of meaning, in the hope that it would burst forth. Janicaud considered this exercise an exercise in 'obfuscation': 'In fact, phenomenology has been taken hostage by a theology that does not want to say its name.'[23] The phenomenon appears to be simple. It is characterized by the use of phenomenological concepts combined with descriptions that are already part of spiritual and religious experience, and thematized as such.

Let us begin with the distinction established by Marion in a text that appeared in 1996, entitled 'Phenomenology of giving and the first

---

23 Janicaud, *Le tournant*, p. 31.

philosophy'.[24] 'Recall,' affirms Marion 'that it is necessary to distinguish clearly between two theologies . . . metaphysical theology . . . and revealed theology . . . the latter, by virtue of the fact it is grounded on given facts which are positively revealed as figures, appearings and manifestations (even apparitions, miracles and revelations, etc.) enters the natural realm of phenomenology and belongs to a phenomenological capability.'

Marion, however, brings about an important clarification, which to my mind, only worsens the theologian's malaise: 'phenomenology cannot decide whether a revelation ever should or ought to give itself, but it (and it alone) can establish whether in that case, such a phenomenon of revelation ought to become the paradox of paradoxes',[25] wherein the superiority of intuition over intention surpasses all phenomena. This reintroduction of a transcendental perspective is astonishing. He even speaks in a Christological way about Rahnerian inspiration. If such an influence were confirmed, it would make phenomenological argumentation inconsistent. It is a question, says Marion, 'of bringing the visible Christ into conversation with its potential conceptual representation, to establish it eventually as a paradigm'.

Given all of this, we will formulate a simple though decisive question, because it determines the legitimacy of the phenomenological enterprise translated into theological terms. What does the expression 'theological revelation' mean exactly? Is not this expression, in the context we have described, similar to the Hegelian version of *offenbare Religion*? In addition, is not Jean-Luc Marion guilty of a questionable reductionism, of theology to Scripture, not theology construed as biblical commentary homologous to the *sacra pagina*, but identified as Scripture that is supposed to deliver and translate an original experience? The radical question Marion addresses to the theologian is, without any ambiguity, the following: 'Why do theologians privilege ontical, historical and semiotic hermeneutics over more entrepreneurial and phenomenological readings of the events of revelation found in Scripture, in particular the New Testament?'[26] I am tempted to answer in a lapidary way: because they are unable to do so. To understand why this is so, we must revisit the usage of the expression 'theological revelation'.

What is the origin of this terminology? Is it common among theologians? And can it claim to be part of a Thomist conception of *doctrina*

---

24 Marion, *De surcroit* (Paris: PUF, 2000), p. 33.

25 Jean-Luc Marion, *Étant donné: Essai d'une phénoménologie de la donation* (Paris: PUF, 1997), p. 327. [ET: *Being Given: Toward a Phenomenology of Givenness*, Jeffrey L. Kosky, trans. (Stanford, CA: Stanford University Press, 2002).]

26 Marion, *De surcroit*, p. 34.

VINCENT HOLZER

sacra? Jean-Luc Marion appears perhaps to have perverted its meaning.[27] Certainly the expression *sacra scriptura seu doctrina* [*ST* Q. 1, art. 2, ad 2] is found in Thomas's works. This means that Scripture is at the forefront of Thomas's mind when he deploys the expression *sacra doctrina*. But *doctrina sacra* encompasses to some degree all the commentaries, the glosses and theological elaborations that readings of sacred Scripture have spawned over the centuries. This process goes for all biblical texts. In effect, when the biblical word is put into writing it has already undergone a long process, more or less, of oral genesis. In addition I am suggesting that the development of *sacra pagina* of the ecclesiastical schools to the *doctrina sacra* of the *studia*, is the development of biblical commentary on the *quaestio* and the *disputatio* of Lombard's *Sentences*. It is for this reason that even the articulation of revealed theology, understood in the restricted and too narrow sense as the assimilation of revelatory events found in Scripture, is not legitimate and cannot be entertained without theological clarification. Not even these clarifications though can rescue a discredited hermeneutical perspective.

For the Christian theologian, the 'given' offers itself in the form of a paradosis the exemplary matrix of which can be found in the pre-Pauline kerygma, 1 Corinthians 15.3-4. This kerygma reveals an originary Christianity: it is never a 'pure' point of origin but an already stratified and an already complex time. It is in this, and only this, that theologians receive the 'given' of which Jean-Luc Marion speaks. Revelation is, in an inseparable way, event and commentary. The conflict between Marion and theologians first treats of the description and the conception of the 'given' which, in Christianity, is to some degree 'sediment' in the form of 'active tradition'.

---

27 '[*Sacra doctrina*] covers the whole field of Christian teaching from its equation with sacred scripture to theological speculation ... *Sacra doctrina* is teaching that emanates from revelation: with all its resources and all the treatments the human spirit can devise derived from reading the Bible to theological deduction.' M. D. Chenu, *La théologie comme science au 12ème siècle* (Paris: Vrin, 1943), p. 85.

10. The Ethics of Doing Theology: Towards the Recovery of a Withering Practice

BERND WANNENWETSCH

The title indicates a perspective on theology that is rarely adopted in our days. If we ever take the luxury of stepping back from what we do to reflect upon theology in this vein, we are usually concerned with questions of epistemology, the relation between metaphysics and faith and the like. The papal encyclical letter *Fides et ratio* (1998) is a case in point. Notwithstanding the passing reminiscence to the Second Vatican Council's call for theology's 'renewing its specific methods' (§92), *Fides et ratio* as a whole shows little interest in the question as to how theology is to be *practised* and the role that the mode of its practising plays for the understanding of theological truth claims. John Paul II's concern remains focused on the traditional question of the relation between theology and philosophy and marks the latter's role as one providing the conceptual framework for the development of the theological articulation of the *intellectus fidei* (§65; §98). The encyclical seems to absorb the practical dimension of theology, the shaping 'in the truth' of those who inquire into the divine truth, into the distinction of catechesis from theology that comes into view 'in addition to theology' (§99). It is only this second type of teaching the Christian truth that is clearly conceived as a practice. 'The teaching imparted in catechesis helps to form the person.' What is attributed to catechesis, the 'unique bond between teaching and living that is otherwise unattainable' (§99), is obviously not expected from the doing of theology as such which apparently remains the purely intellectual quest for understanding, though certainly 'at the service of the proclamation of the faith and of catechesis' (§99).

When it comes to ethics, we are happy to note that in most theology syllabuses nowadays, it is firmly established as one of the theological disciplines. While we are thus familiar with ethics *within* theology, the ethics *of* theology, the inquiry into the moral dimension of the practising of theology itself, yet remains a different and still fairly distant question.

Why this question? Celebratory theology and ethics

Let me first address a legitimate concern that we may have here. Considering this festival's[1] motto of 'festive theology' – would a shifting of the focus to the ethics of theology not spoil the celebratory mood by introducing a sour moralist perspective? It is indeed worth reminding ourselves that, throughout the Christian tradition, the joy of theology has been understood as an essential feature of the very discipline. When the term 'theology' was first adopted into Christianity in the third century (under the influence of Origen, in particular), it was precisely in the sense of what the poets and hymn-singers of the ancient Greek cults were known for: to sing the praises of the gods and to tell their stories in celebratory mode.[2] This Gentile background of the term *theologein* had, understandably, caused Christians an initial hesitation to use it at all.[3] When it was finally adopted, it was christologically modified, but retained its proclamatory flavour. *Theologein* was still used conterminously with *hymnein*, and the activity of a theologian was a kind of doxological expounding of the Christian truth, with a strong emphasis of the 'naming God of Christ' as a way of evoking the presence of the Lord in his name. Little surprise therefore that theology was first thought to be particularly at home in the liturgy. In the Eastern Orthodox tradition, the term 'theology', understood from the chanting of the heavenly hosts, is still in use as a name for the *trishagion* in the Eucharist, and the intellectual endeavour of theologizing is, in most cases, still firmly rooted in the liturgy and directed towards a deeper understanding of it.[4]

---

1 The paper was originally delivered as an address to the two theology faculties at Kampen, Netherlands, on the occasion of their 150th anniversary in April 2004. Only light revisions such as the addition of footnotes were made, in order to retain the character of a talk.

2 On the musical dimension of theology, historically, practically and hermeneutically, see my 'Singen und Sagen. Zur musisch-musikalischen Dimension der Theologie', *Neue Zeitschrift für Systematische Theologie und Religionsphilosophie* 46 (2004), pp. 330–47. Cf. also, though from a different perspective, Jeremy S. Begbie, *Theology, Music and Time* (Cambridge: Cambridge University Press, 2000).

3 On the history of the notion and practice of theology, see Gerhard Ebeling, *Theologie I. Begriffsgeschichtlich, Religion in Geschichte und Gegenwart*[3] IV, pp. 756ff.

4 The distinction of *theologia prima* and *theologia secunda* reflects this

In the Christian West, however, theology's development took a very different route. Here, the earliest poetico-musical incarnation of theology would eventually give way to an alternative pattern. With the rise of universities in the high Middle Ages and the establishing of various faculties, it was the notion of theology as (another) science that was to determine the shape the discipline subsequently took. This academic and 'scientific' mode of theology has become the Western heritage – to the point of near oblivion for the other, earlier type. In the West, sapiential theology and its characteristic mode of *meditatio* have been almost completely overshadowed by scholastic theology and its paradigm of *disputatio*.[5] Though the former type of theology survived to some degree within monastic contexts, most people today would not even recognize it as a form of theology but would put different labels on it, such as 'reflective spirituality'.

The one-sidedness of our Western heritage is as rarely recognized today as it is deplorable. It is deplorable in that it robs those who are used to its reign of the healthy challenging that the other type of theology could provide. The triumph of scientific theology in the West has, in effect, not merely defeated the earlier type; but it has also weakened the enterprise of theology as a whole, including the scientific form itself. As I have argued elsewhere: even the truth claims of individual theological sentences – the proud domain of scientific theology – can only be properly assessed if their analysis does not stop on the propositional level, but takes them into consideration as audible phenomena, which is to understand them as utterances, not just sentences.[6]

Given this appeal for a recovery of the doxological, celebratory dimension of theology, let us take up the question again: what has ethics got to do with it? Another look into the history of our discipline has another surprise to offer: it can be shown that it was precisely the hymnological nature of the early type that was perceived as possessing an innate moral quality. While scholastic theology can very well present

liturgical focus. While the former is basically identical with the effect that the liturgy – with its complex interaction of reading, singing, praying, keeping silence, and so forth – has on the congregation in terms of their understanding and embodying of God's salvific story, the latter is, as the activity of 're-flecting' on the former in a methodologically transparent mode, conceived as an auxiliary device to aid and deepen the liturgical theology in its primary form. See Aidan Kavanagh, *On Liturgical Theology* (Collegeville, MN: The Liturgical Press, 1984).

5 On the difference between monastic and scholastic theology, *meditatio* and *disputatio*, see Oswald Bayer, *Theologie. Handbuch Systematischer Theologie I* (Gütersloh: Gütersloher Verlagshaus, 1994), pp. 27–31.

6 See my 'Singen und Sagen', pp. 342–6. Cf. also George Lindbeck, *The Nature of Doctrine: Religion and Theology in a Postliberal Age* (Philadelphia, PA: Westminster Press, 1984), p. 64 *passim*.

a proper account, say, of what the divine law demands of human beings, it must still leave it to the individual will to act or not to act in accordance with what is perceived as an external moral code. Monastic or doxological theology, on the other hand, *in its very process* actually prepares the soul to love the law and follow it from within. In this vein, Psalm I speaks of the one who 'murmurs over the torah night and day' as being planted – or as the Hebrew actually suggests, trans-located – to the banks of a river that affords an abundance of good fruits in his life.

Martin Luther elaborated this connection in a fascinating account of the moral shaping power of the Psalter. In his commentary on the Psalms he calls the Psalter – that is, the book of Psalms as it is actually sung in the community of monks and thus perceived as a phenomenon of sound – a 'training ground' or even 'wrestling ground' for the affections: *psalterium affectuum palaestra.*[7] What happens, according to Luther's analysis of the psalmody, is that in the course of this activity the chaos-waters of human affections are defeated by the divine affections of the Psalter that are instilled in those who sing and meditate the Psalter on a regular basis. It is precisely from the re-ordering of our affections and desire – the 'heart' – that the Reformer expects good works to flow. The good works that we can elicit from the power of our will, Luther maintains over against main currents in high medieval theology, are not really good works since they are always tainted by selfish interest. Only a renewed heart (another name for the directedness of the affections) will enable us to act according to God's will;[8] and the kind of theology the sung Psalter represents is a preparation for

---

7 At the end of his exposition of Psalm I in his *Operationes in Psalmos*, Luther puts it like this:

> At the end of this psalm I wish to exhort us, as many of the fathers like Athanasius and Augustine did, not simply to sing along or read the psalms as though they had no business with us; rather we are to read and sing them in such a way that we thereby be bettered, our faith be strengthened and our conscience be consoled in all sorts of trouble. After all, the Psalter is but a schooling and exercise of our heart and our affections, as to how these are and are to be minded and inclined. (My translation)

On the historical details and wider contexts, see the splendid study by Günter Bader, *Psalterium affectuum palaestra. Prolegomena zu einer Theologie des Psalter* (Tübingen: Mohr, 1996).

8 See my, 'Caritas Fide Formata. "Herz und Affekte" als Schlüssel zu "Glaube und Liebe"', in *Kerygma und Dogma* 45 (2000), pp. 205–24; an English version of this is forthcoming in *International Journal of Systematic Theology*. Cf. also my 'Affekt und Gebot. Zur ethischen Bedeutung der Leidenschaften im Licht der Theologie Luthers und Melanchthons', in Anselm Steiger (ed.), *Passion, Affekt und Leidenschaft in der Frühen Neuzeit*, vol. I (Wiesbaden: Harrassowitz Verlag, 2005), pp. 203–15.

this renewal. It does so because it provides the apt form of exposure to God's living word – that is, as sounding voice, not just text.[9]

In Luther's theology of the Psalter we find not only strong repercussions of his monastic life but also of Augustine's emphasis upon what we may call a *moral epistemology*.[10] Every mode of understanding must imply the adopting of a certain posture which reflects the particularity of the respective object under inquiry. Just as we must form our hands in a specific way if we want to, say, grasp sand, water, or feel the texture of a cloth, so it is with the understanding of immaterial objects. What could it mean to shape our organs of perception in a way that is suitable in regards to God? It certainly means to adopt a certain posture of our mind – one that does acknowledge that we can never encompass God, but embrace him only insofar as he makes himself known to us. Yet, since God is the all-encompassing one, we cannot mean to grasp his reality through the activity of our mind alone. Rather, to understand God also necessitates a certain shaping of our emotions, of our will, and indeed of our actual ways of life – hence Augustine's famous claim of the Decalogue as an epistemological prerequisite for our understanding God truly. Only the one who is willing to live according to God's revealed will as it is known through Scripture can hope to come to know this will more fully; and if he wants to understand Holy Scripture, he must live by it, because knowing is loving and only loving is truly knowing.[11] When in his autobiography Augustine looks back to the many years of being a searching, not-quite-yet Christian, he makes the telling confession about the problem which the young and aspiring rhetorician had with the Bible. Compared to his beloved *Hortentius*, the Latin Bible seemed such a plain, simple book. His problem was actually not of an intellectual nature, but of a moral one: it was a matter of pride.[12] In his pride, he was simply not yet prepared to 'bend his neck' in order to find the truth where God has put it. Hence his intellectual conversion, in which he finally learned to rejoice in the inexhaustible

9 See Martin Luther, *Vox est anima verbi*, in *Werke*, Kritische Gesamtausgabe V (Weimarer Ausgabe) (Weimar: Hermann Böhlau, 1883–), p. 379, lines 5ff.

10 See Alasdair McIntyre's characterization of Augustine's mode of moral reasoning in his *Three Rival Versions of Moral Inquiry: Encyclopaedia, Genealogy, and Tradition* (Notre Dame, IN: University of Notre Dame Press, 1990), pp. 82–104.

11 On Augustine and Luther as exemplary readers of the Psalter see Brian Brock, *Ethics in Scripture: Singing the Psalter with Augustine and Luther* (Grand Rapids, MI: Eerdmans, 2007).

12 *Confessions* III/5; Library of the Nicene and Post-Nicene Fathers of the Christian Church, vol. 1: *The Confessions and Letters of St. Augustine* (Edinburgh and Grand Rapids, MI: T&T Clark and Eerdmans, reprint 1994), pp. 62.

riches and depth of God's word, was preceded by his moral conversion, which, in turn, would be deepened by what he then came to understand intellectually.

On the basis of these historical reminders of the inherent ethical dimension within celebratory theology, if we now turn to an analysis of the ethical hot-spots in our current situation, it should be clear that, in addressing a number of critical issues as regards our mainstream patterns of doing theology today, we are not set up to spoil the celebration of theology but rather to aid it by unmasking the real *spoilsports* of the joy of theology.

Can we identify the ideas, attitudes and structures that act as potential or actual joy-killers in our doing theology? A first point can be made in recognizing what we presuppose when we speak of theology as a practice. Aristotle famously defined *praxis* as a mode of activity which has its *telos*, its purpose, within itself; as such, *praxis* is opposed to *poiesis* or production, which aims at a purpose external to the activity, as a mere result of it. In speaking of theology as celebration, an intrinsically joyous activity, we are, of course, already conceiving of it as a practice. Understood this way, ethical considerations will be a genuine feature of the doing of theology, as any deliberative human action is susceptible to moral judgement. Alas, there is an uncomfortable conclusion involved in this. Why is it that when theologians are reflecting on their discipline, ethical questions are almost never raised? What else could this fact indicate if not the loss of understanding of theology as a practice, and indeed, the withering away of theology as a coherent practice in many of our established institutions of higher learning?

Will it be useful? Instrumental reasoning and the skill-driven paradigm of professional schools

Everyone who begins studying or teaching in theology will soon be confronted with questions like this: 'Before I enrol in this seminar, tell me: will it be relevant to the exam?' 'As I am going to become a pastor, I don't see the point in struggling through Kant's three critiques. Can we not rather concentrate on what will be really useful, useful that is: for our future professional life?' Of course, professors don't approve of such an attitude. But even in their disapproving, they may well underestimate the degree to which such an attitude does less reflect student laziness than a dominant cultural pattern – a pattern that subjects everything, education and intellectual endeavours included, to the dire imperative of efficiency and cost-benefit calculus. The professor may dislike the attitude when she encounters it in the form of a student who does not seem to be overly interested in the small-type stuff that she loves to teach; but at the same time, the professor may not be wholly un-inclined to, say, only slightly rework this same old article of hers in order to publish it for the second time but under a different title. There is no reason to assume that professors are less immune to the reign of instrumental reasoning than their students. As the managerialist pressure in universities that puts everything and everyone under rigid quality assessment schemes is stepping up, academics must now busy themselves in demonstrating how productive they are, which means producing more and more paperwork that fewer and fewer people have time to read.

Some moral implications are obvious which relate to us all: what is my attitude towards labour? How does my conscience respond to the imperative of self-marketing and out-performing others? Other aspects touch upon political questions: are we content as an institution, say as a faculty of theology, to march to the drums of the managerialist ideology, or are we courageous enough to resist and suffer the marginalization of dissenters? If we expect theology faculties to be particularly sensitive to these questions, or even to spearhead movements of resistance within their universities, we are likely to be disappointed. As there is no reason to think of theologians as a species that is particularly lacking in courage, can we think of another explanation for the apparent quietism – an explanation that goes beyond the general human tendency to float downstream rather than swimming against the stream? A historical reflection seems in place here.

Many theological institutions, at least within the Protestant world, have been heavily influenced by F. D. E. Schleiermacher's definition of theology as a 'practical science' that is essentially geared at church leadership.[13] In the beginning of the nineteenth century, this was a clever strategic move by which Schleiermacher succeeded in safeguarding the place of theology in the modern university after it had been challenged in the 'battle of the faculties'. Theology, so Schleiermacher's point, is really like medicine or law. Just as a society needs well educated physicians and lawyers, it must take an interest in educated clergy – educated, that is, according to the highest standards of excellence as

---

13 Friedrich Daniel Ernst Schleiermacher, *Brief Outline of the Study of Theology* (Edinburgh: T&T Clark, 1850). On the history of theology as a (modern) academic discipline see: Edward Farley, *Theologia: The Fragmentation and Unity of Theological Education* (Philadelphia, PA: Fortress Press, 1983); cf. also by the same author, *The Fragility of Knowledge: Theological Education in the Church and the University* (Philadelphia, PA: Fortress Press, 1988).

guaranteed in the state faculties of his day. This pattern paved the way for an understanding of theology as being essentially (the theoretical part of) professional education. While such an understanding may have been less a problem in Schleiermacher's day or in his own teaching – which was of the most impressive scope and width of horizon – it has certainly become a problem today, at least in those educational contexts in which theology is taught as a professional degree, that is in church seminaries or state faculties. Here, the temptation is for *Ausbildung* to absorb the wider notion of *Bildung* into a rather narrow concept of the provision of a list of useful professional skills. 'Will I really need this in my later life as pastor?' Of course, the acquisition of skills is a good thing. But the problem with the skills-model is its profound belief in control. It readily assumes that the requested individual skills can be induced in a way that is ascertainable by methodology, and believes that when the required range of skills is engendered, the result will be a theologian.

We can easily understand why persons, say, in charge of churches' personnel planning may relate to this idea. Yet, as with any genuine practice, the more you try to control it, the less of it you will get. The more theology is being subjected to instrumental reasoning and the strict paradigm of a professional school, the more it will be a mere semblance of theology. The problem is that we are usually prone to believe more in *poiesis* than in *praxis*. Thus we do not trust in the doing of theology proper and its capacity to freely bring about good practitioners who will be good at what they do, be it as pastors or whatever other professional contexts they find themselves in.

'This is not my field.' From the discipline of theology to theological disciplines

Apart from the focus on goods internal to it, there is another necessary requirement for an activity to amount to a practice. As Alasdair McIntyre's famous definition of 'practice' puts it:

> By a practice, I am going to mean any coherent and complex form of socially established cooperative human activity through which goods internal to that form of activity are realised in the course of trying to achieve those standards of excellence which are appropriate to, and partially definitive of, that form of activity . . .[14]

---

14 Alasdair MacIntyre, *After Virtue* (Notre Dame, IN: University of Notre Dame Press, 1984), 2nd edn, p. 187.

If we put our current state of affairs in theology to this test, what can we say about the coherence and co-operative character of our discipline? The traditional four patterns, ecclesiastical history, biblical exegesis, systematic theology and practical theology, are increasingly understood as disciplines in their own right – matters of specialist knowledge, each following different methodologies that are not necessarily mutually commensurable. Under the sway of this logic, what is done in individual disciplines is theological only insofar as it *contributes* to theology, but not as it actually *practises* theology. In other words, theology is seen as a kind of sum of its individual disciplines, a whole that is assumed to be coming into being in a mysterious way, once these disciplines are all done under the same roof. As a result, for lack of a commonly accepted idea of that in which a genuine theological judgement consists, the notion of 'theology' becomes increasingly individualized. It practically becomes a name for the synthesis which the individual student or teacher of theology makes up for herself: highly subjective, if not bluntly idiosyncratic.

I still harbour the image of a former professor of mine, a New Testament scholar, who would use up his lecture time with purely historical or linguistic observations; yet right into the ringing of the bell at the end he would ostentatiously step aside from his lecture stand and 'say something theological'. This was usually pretty interesting and the students, who were waiting for this moment, would listen closely to what he had to say. But the manoeuvring made it entirely clear that for him, his business as New Testament professor was one thing – detached, objective, scientific – and theology was an altogether different matter, his thoughtful private opinion as a Christian. Though this professor did not help us students to answer the question of what we were doing when studying theology, we clearly preferred his approach to the one of another representative of the exegetical disciplines who when asked for a theological judgement would simply snort at us: 'That's not my field.'

It is interesting to see that Thomas Aquinas, who decisively shaped the notion of theology as a science in the thirteenth century, was concerned with this question at the outset: 'whether sacred doctrine' – his word for theology – 'is (not) one science'.[15] This was to be even then a critical question, since theology's unusually wide scope, encompassing 'creator and creation', did not seem compatible with the philosophical definition of a science as 'one which treats only of one class of

---

15 St Thomas Aquinas, *Summa Theologiae* I, Q. 1, art. 3. Quoted after the translation by Fathers of the English Dominican Province, *Great Books of the Western World*, Vol. 19 (Chicago, IL: Encyclopaedia Britannica, 1952), p. 4.

subjects'. Certainly, God and humans could not belong to the same class. The answer that Aquinas provides pertains very much to our situation today. 'I answer that sacred doctrine is one science. The unity of a power and habit [that is science, in this case] is to be gauged by its object, not indeed, in its material aspect, but as regards the formal aspect under which it is an object.'[16]

In other words, the diverse material fields that a science covers do not constitute a problem to its unity as long as they are treated under the same 'formal aspect'. In theology's case, Aquinas identifies the unifying formal aspect as divine revelation. The unity of the theological fields of inquiry is (to be) rooted in the consistency of a perspective that engages a variety of subjects under the same aspect of their 'bearing the stamp of divine knowledge' and activity.

The Reformers of the sixteenth century would put the matter similarly. For Luther, the subject of theology is twofold: *deus iustificans et homo peccator*.[17] The unity, and indeed, the wit of this particular discipline lie in its persistent refusal to have its twofold subject absorbed into a single one. Theology would cease to be theology if, on the one hand, it were content with metaphysical speculations about the divine, which could only reach as far as to the *deus absconditus*. On the other hand, theology's abstraction from the *deus revelatus* and the existential interest that he demonstrates *pro me* would equally disqualify it as Christian theology. And by the same token, theology would cease to be its proper self if it meant to inquire into the created world, as abstracted from God's calling for it and his active engagement with it. Even the study of the Christian religion or the Christian faith would not be theology, unless it reckoned with God as an active player in the field rather than as merely an object positioned therein.

Against the backdrop of these classical definitions, we can see how the present trend towards a segregationalist expert culture threatens the essence of theology. The specialization of individual disciplines in theology is precisely and factually achieved at the expense of the unity of the 'formal aspect' (in Aquinas's terms), and at the expense of the double-object-ness (in Luther's terms) of the discipline. The notorious autonomy or *Eigengesetzlichkeit* of the individual disciplines is a function of the giving up on the critical check that the double-object required and afforded. As a result, the individual sub-disciplines in theology look increasingly similar to their respective secular satellite

---

16 Aquinas, *ST* I, Q. 1, art. 3, p. 5.
17 '*Subiectum Theologiae homo reus et perditus et deus iustificans vel salvator.*' Exposition of Psalm 51, WA 40 II, 328, 1f. On Luther's understanding of theology, see Bayer, *Theologie*, pp. 35–126.

disciplines.[18] For example, for the German divine, Friedrich August Tholuck, one of the last universal scholars of the eighteenth century, ecclesiastical history was basically the art of retelling God's economy of salvation throughout the centuries. But in our days, it has precisely lost this focus on God making history and instead rather models itself after the principles of secular historical studies. The only echo of theology that is left – that this branch of historical studies deals with Christianity – is, ironically, what Aquinas called the 'material aspect' – the one which he deemed *not* decisive for the integrity of a science. In this shift, we see ecclesiastical history trading away the claim for theological unity and accordingly its unity with other theological disciplines for another unity: the unity with its secular satellite discipline with which it now shares the decisive 'formal aspect' in terms of methodology, epistemology and so forth.

Not that ecclesiastical history is at all special in this respect. Similar stories could be told of any other of our theological disciplines. Just as ecclesiastical history becomes history of the Christian religion, so biblical exegesis becomes 'Old Testament studies' or 'New Testament studies', differing from other 'oriental studies' only in the choice of their body of texts, while the exact same canon of historical critical methods is applied. In the same vein, dogmatic theology becomes systematics, and moral theology becomes ethics – both undertaken in a fashion very similar to parallel philosophical modes of inquiry. And last, not least, 'practical theology' often comes across today like a mixture of psychology, sociology, aesthetics or whatever other trend-discipline is in sight.

To resume our focal point of interest again: What are the ethical problems associated with this tendency? Should we be morally concerned to sell something under a label which is no longer validated through the content? There are still numerous 'faculties of theology' in Europe, but given the withering of the actual practice that deserves this name, would it not be a matter of honesty and transparency to follow the Anglo-Saxon trend and rearrange these faculties as 'departments of religious studies'? One does not have to be in favour of such a move to recognize the question as a serious one.

When, as is the case in most institutions of higher education, the whole burden of making sense of the various bits and bytes that are taught under the rubric of 'theology' is effectively left to the individual student, how could we fail to perceive this as an ethical problem? If the theological curriculum is organized as a patchwork of unconnected fields of knowledge and professors of theology are thereby invited to hide behind their walls of expertise, is there not a question of moral

---

18 Farley, *Theologia*, p. 145 *passim*.

cowardice involved – cowardice that is, as it were, sanctioned and fostered by the system as we maintain it? Can it ever be fair to expect students to compensate individually for what the theological establishment is unwilling or incapable of delivering? What is hell for the student, the experience of an atomized course system, is heaven for the educated specialists.

Farley is referring to the way in which the Humboldtian ideal of the autonomy of the researcher is practically shaping and colonizing the teaching experience as well. But there is another moral point in this. If the research ideal sets the agenda, the splendid isolation in which most researchers in theology work on their projects becomes formative for the *patterns of teaching* as well.[19] The segregation of theology into a number of satellite disciplines is a moral problem inasmuch as it feeds off and nourishes the tendency to shut ourselves off from others who are different or have a different knowledge or language. Not only does this result in an unhealthy peer-group mentality, it is also a way to satisfy the lust for power. The narrower a field of expertise and the more shut off it is from other fields of expertise through firewalls of methodological incompatibility, the more can I excel in mine, and the less will others be able to compete or challenge my stronghold in it. The system as it stands rewards those who play it safe, those who trade the promise of non-interference for their own security. In spite of the fashionable lip-service to interdisciplinary endeavours, the actual mechanisms rather punish than reward those who dare to cross their disciplines' boundaries and 'poach' in the homeland of other experts: *Noli me tangere*!

As with any such development, this trend is not philosophically blind. It does not simply 'happen'. Rather, it is the embodiment of a particular ideology which is itself subject to theological judgement. The giving in to the process of specialization and disintegration of the mother discipline actually reflects the very same belief that has come to supply the metaphysical basis for our capitalist economy. By allowing the disintegration to happen the way we do and still call it by its unifying name 'theology', we implicitly buy once again into capitalism's central myth that is colonizing every sphere of life: the idea that if we leave the pursuit of self-interest undisturbed by moral or political intervention – if we leave, in other words, individuals and individual systems to their own systemic egoism – the outcome will be beneficial to the whole, guided towards this end by the mysterious power of an 'invisible hand'. It seems ironic that while theology (theology of liberation in particular) has contributed a good deal to the historical unmasking of

---

19 Farley, *Theologia*, pp. 141–9.

this ideology which is based on the redefinition of individual vices as communal virtues, systemically, it finds itself busily organizing its own discipline according to the very logic of the capitalist myth.[20]

We are by no means the first to lament the tendency towards ever greater disintegration of academic theology as a threat that is more dangerous to its existence than any calling it into question from outside. The unease about the atomization of *scientia divina* has engendered a number of suggestions to deal creatively with the problem. One idea that comes to mind quickly is the addition of a special teaching provision to the syllabus – say, a lecture series of theological encyclopaedics in which questions such as the unity of the discipline, and the relations to it of individual sub-disciplines, can be addressed. Though certainly a sensible suggestion, such a solution would still retain the air of driving out the devil with Beelzebub, when the system of sub-differentiation which causes the problem responds to it by intensifying its own pattern: that is, by creating another sub-folder to address the problem. Even the most excellent encyclopaedic account of theology will remain a mere *theory* of integration or unity, unless the individual sub-folders begin mutually to open up to the others.

Will interdisciplinary classes and seminars then do the job? Again, there is much to be said in favour of such attempts. Joint classes and seminars that cross the boundaries of theological disciplines are, in fact, the most imperative endeavours if we wish for a counterweight to the atomized expert culture. Yet, as many an experiment of this kind has brought to our sober recognition: interdisciplinary seminars, where they are ventured at all, will not so much function as problem solvers, but primarily as problem revealers. They are good at teaching us a lesson about the long and troublesome route that is ahead of us, if we are to relearn a common theological language and shared modes of judgement. From a moral point of view, we would have to say that however modest their actual success in reintegrating the theological disciplines, they are still worth the trouble, if only as a token of fairness to the students. In facing up to the actual difficulties of making joint seminars work, and to the many ways in which they can fail, theology teachers at least demonstrate their willingness to suffer the lack of theological unity alongside their students, instead of simply abandoning them to it.

---

20 On the interrelatedness of the capitalist myth and contemporary sociological paradigms, see my *Political Worship: Ethics for Christian Citizens* (Oxford: Oxford University Press, 2004), pp. 207–34.

What would you do if you caught me in bed with another woman? Expert and master

The quote is from Stanley Hauerwas with whom I taught a graduate seminar at Duke many years ago. I remember the instance well. On one occasion, out of the blue, Hauerwas confronted his students with this question, and one of them replied in a similar upfront way: 'I would surely kill you.' Yet, why should she? Are we not all prone to temptation, weak human beings after all? Why should a professor of theology be any different, just because he happens to teach ethics? Yet, I take it that the point of this disturbing piece of conversation was really less about sexual ethics than it was about the ethics of doing theology – the ethics of *teaching* theology in particular. While both professor and student were obviously of the opinion that extramarital affairs are not to be recommended as a matter of principle, the proclaimed readiness of the student to kill her teacher, when catching him in the act, reflects a particular understanding of the student–professor relation as highly morally qualified. That is to say: if she were to point her gun at her teacher, she would do so as one who has been betrayed – not sexually but intellectually and morally. Granted, such a strong feeling would not automatically arise just because a teacher fails to live up to what he teaches. After all, would we really want to make theological truth dependant on a sort of proof by the moral achievement of the individual?

Yet, considering the way in which Hauerwas is known to conceive of the task of doing theology and is known to practise it with his students, it is actually quite straightforward to understand both the student's point and also that the teacher was rather more satisfied than put off by her tough response. In his writings, Hauerwas has often likened the learning of theology to the learning of a craft. Just as the learning of a craft needs a master craftsman to introduce the apprentice into the appropriate language, tradition, tools, and handlings, so it is with theology.[21] It is taught best in a personal vein that allows a mutual engagement between the personalities of student and teacher. The teacher's aim in the teaching process is actually to invite his students to participate in his own theologizing, assuming that they will be drawn to the truth of it by the force that they perceive to be at work in his own practice: as someone who is actually 'possessed' with the truth of

---

21 'The Politics of Church: How We Lay Bricks and Make Disciples', in Stanley Hauerwas, *After Christendom? How the Church is to Behave, if Freedom, Justice, and a Christian Nation are Bad Ideas* (Nashville, TN: Abingdon Press, 1991), pp. 93–111; also Stanley Hauerwas, *Sanctify Them in the Truth: Holiness Exemplified* (Nashville, TN: Abingdon Press, 1999), p. 9.

Christian theology. This is, of course, worlds apart from the idea of *possessing* the truth as an entitlement to impose it on to others. Instead, the other is invited into the whirl of the teacher's own explorations as a journeying towards the truth. The doing and teaching of theology is the risky business of radical self-exposure to the truth – in a communal way. If you practise theology like this, you may well run the risk of getting shot. You would not be the first, either.

This example invites another useful conceptual distinction. The difference between a 'master-type' and an 'expert-type' is, I suggest, significant for the ethics of doing theology. While the expert is genuinely interested in keeping the distance from those whom she addresses, so as to preserve her surplus in expertise over them, the master is precisely interested in eventually diminishing this distance by initiating the student into her own practice, and she rejoices in the developing mastery of the apprentice. While the expert is – again for distance's sake – keen on maintaining the boundaries of ideally rather narrow fields of expertise, the master assumes that the student will learn more when watching the master as she deals with daring questions and unknown territory or experiments with new thoughts. The master, as it were, invites the student to work with her at her theological work-bench, and instead of simply showing off a rounded and well finished product, she will rather let the student participate in her trials, failures and reworking. Accordingly, for the student of a master, the master will not become smaller through his exposure to failure, as status difference is not itself an issue. Essentially, the difference from the expert-type is the joy of practising theology as a joint enterprise.

Of course, this is far from being a novel paradigm: it is just how the first Christian theologians conceived of their teaching, in keeping with some pedagogical ideals that they adopted from the philosophical schools of the classical Greek period. A striking example comes from the first Christian academy, the Schools of Catechumens in Alexandria in the third century: a moving eulogy that a famous student, Gregory (later to be called 'Thaumaturgus'), made about his teacher Origen on the occasion of the completion of his study – a degree ceremony speech, we might say today.[22] As one would expect, the student praises Origen as a great teacher. Yet he gives a very interesting account of what this greatness consisted in: Origen, he says, converted him to the intellectual life precisely by offering no less than his friendship. It was precisely through the teacher's *philia* (friendship-love), through Origen

---

22 To be found in Gregory's *Panegyric*. See on the wider contexts: Robert L. Wilken, 'Alexandra: A School of Training in Virtue', in Patrick Henry (ed.), *Schools of Thought in the Christian Tradition* (Philadelphia, PA: Fortress Press, 1984), pp. 15–30.

as 'the friend and interpreter' of the Word that Gregory learned to love the Word 'whose beauty attracts irresistibly'.[23] Thus the teacher dug, fertilized and dug again the soil of Gregory's personality until it was ready for the seed of theology. What moved Gregory apparently at first was not the beauty and excitement of theology as such, but the beauty and excitement that he came to know as the force which moved Origin's own theologizing. The *philia*[24] of his teacher – received and returned – was crucial for the love of theology to eventually emerge in Gregory.

There is, of course, a circularity involved in any such happy instance of successful teaching and learning. The teacher's love for the student would not have led the student to loving theology, had it not been for the palpability of the teacher's love for theology that provided, as it were, the 'material' side for the personal relationship between the two. Purely 'formal' love, deprived of any such materiality, would have created an idolizing of the teacher as a sort of guru (in the flat, 'Western' sense of the term) instead of eliciting the student's love of theology. The key to Origen's success with Gregory was the inviting character of the teacher's love that initiated the students into the teacher's love of theology by offering to participate in its practice.

In such vein, we can trust that joint intellectual engagement with Scripture and the theological tradition of the Church actually fosters a community among those who are engaged in this as practitioners of theology. But to have this trust, we may need actively to counter attitudes or structural patterns that have built up and now act as obstacles on the road to such a fertile community. We have identified the prevailing models of 'experts' and 'professionals' as precisely such patterns and attitudes. Splendid isolation cannot be the paradigm here, since theologians do not have to be afraid of the fragmented character of their work. Isolated working patterns may well reveal a basic and essentially pagan anxiety that does not allow one to expose one's work to others before it is considered rounded, watertight and perfected. The moral point at stake here is not merely that we should not be guided by anxiety, fear and pride, but is again a relational one. Perfected or at least intentionally perfected work excludes others by putting one's own safety before the well-being of the theological enterprise. The ethics of doing theology in a way that is genuine to its very object, would rather suggest that we prepare our work in such a way as to invite others to write it forth, to elaborate what we have left undeveloped, to correct

---

23 Gregory, *Panegyric*, §6.84.

24 Friendship is, as Gregory notes, 'not something one can easily resist, it is piercing and penetrating, an affable and affectionate disposition which is shown in the [teacher's] words and his association with us'. *Panegyric*, §6.81.

what we have put inaccurately, or simply to steal from us what we have put well.[25]

Conclusion

We have established that a theologian is someone who is at home *practising* theology as an integrated discipline; for it is not the theologian who makes theology, but theology that makes the theologian. Yet this insight has a most disturbing implication in regards to our institutions of higher learning today, because it tells us that we cannot be sure of producing theologians in our theological faculties. Degrees won't really tell. How could they, if even doctors and professors of theology, by their own self-understanding and practising of it, do not have to be theologians these days? In such a situation, the request to keep the drifting disciplines together in one integrated theological practice sounds overly ambitious; and it really is demanding on a variety of levels, structurally and politically. But the greatest challenge is perhaps a moral one: in order to practise theology as an integral whole, we need the courage to be amateurs again – in the original sense of the word as lovers of a certain activity, but also according to the modern slant the word has acquired as juxtaposed to 'professional'.[26] We need the courage to let go of the comfortable and comforting 'expert' security if we are to cross intra-theological boundaries and stray into unfamiliar territory. Of course, this can be said for any genuine intellectual endeavour, but it still remains particularly adequate for theologians: if the Christian life as a whole is but a journeying across and towards unchartered territory, based on hope and promise, how could the doing of theology be anything less?

---

25 Cf. the statement by Stanley Hauerwas: 'I do not try to write "the last word" about anything. This is partly because I do not believe in the last word about anything, but also because I find the politics of such scholarship offensive. "Perfection" kills community'. Stanley Hauerwas, *In Good Company: The Church as Polis* (Notre Dame, IN and London: University of Notre Dame Press, 1995), p. 13.

26 See my 'Der Profi – Mensch ohne Eigenschaften. Oder: Warum die Kirche Amateure braucht', in *Alles ist Nichts. Evangelium Hören II., Arbeitskreis Kirche in der Marktgesellschaft*, Nürnberg 2001, pp. 45–55, or online at http://www.evangelium-hoeren.de.

11. On Valuing Truth in Practice: Rome's Postmodern Challenge[1]

PAUL D. MURRAY

Introduction

This essay represents something of a bridge between two research projects. The first, issuing in various essays en route and culminating in a monograph publication in 2004, explored the style of rationality that should most appropriately characterize Christian theology given the pluralist, postfoundationalist, postmodern context in which this task is now situated.[2] Specifically, this question was pursued through close engagement with varying contemporary articulations of the American pragmatist tradition characterized, for all their differences, by a common disavowal of the aspiration for epistemic neutrality and a view of rationality as encompassing both the practical and the cognitive. The dual concern was to identify the lines of a viable postfoundationalist understanding of human rationality and to explore the possibility of

---

1 Earlier versions of this essay were presented to the Heythrop College Research Seminar, February 2005 and the joint meeting of the Society for the Study of Theology and the Irish Theological Association, Dublin, April 2005. I am grateful to the respective conveners and those who participated in the ensuing discussions for their helpful questions and comments. In addition, I am particularly grateful to Dr Gerald Loughlin of Durham University and Dr Gerard Mannion of Liverpool Hope University for reading and commenting upon an earlier draft.

2 See Paul D. Murray, *Reason, Truth and Theology in Pragmatist Perspective* (Leuven: Peeters, 2004); also 'Theology After the Demise of Foundationalism', *The Way*, 38 (1998), pp. 160–9; 'Truth and Reason in Science and Theology: Points of Tension, Correlation and Compatibility', in C. Southgate (ed.), *God, Humanity and the Cosmos: A Textbook in Science and Religion* (Edinburgh: T & T Clark, 1999), pp. 49–92; 'A Liberal Helping of Postliberalism Please', in Mark D. Chapman (ed.), *The Future of Christian Theology* (Aldershot: Ashgate, 2002), pp. 208–18; 'Epistemology', in J. Wentzel van Huyssteen (ed.), *The International Encyclopedia of Science and Religion*, Vol. 1 (New York: Macmillan Reference, 2002), pp. 266–8; 'Fallibilism, Faith and Theology: Putting Rescher's Philosophy to Theological Work', *Modern Theology* 20 (2004), pp. 339–62.

pursuing an integral theological appropriation of such ways of thinking – with 'integral' here understood to mean a theological appropriation that could be seen to cohere with and to expand key commitments and instincts already recognized as being authentic to the practice of Christian or, more specifically, Catholic theology.

In the main, the explicitly theological aspect of this work focused on fundamental issues such as the relationship between faith and reason; the dynamic character of Christian life, tradition and identity; the relationship between integrity and openness in Christian theology; the character of certitude and its compatibility with a recognition of the fragility of theological understanding. In the course of exploring these issues, however, various other matters of a more directly ecclesiological character were also inevitably raised pertaining to the appropriate processes for the discerning of contemporary Christian understanding. That is, pursuing the initiating question concerning the appropriate character of theological rationality in the contemporary context in turn prompted a further question as to what it means for the Church – both the Church collectively and for Christians personally – to be called to discern together the living truth of God's ways with the world.[3] Alternatively stated, what does it mean for the Church to be called to be a learning community or, in Nicholas Lash's terms, a school for the purification of desire, a place of growth in understanding and know-how in what it means to live before and in relation to the mystery of God in Christ and the Spirit?[4] And what does this mean in practice and not simply in principle? What does it mean for the structures and shape of the Church and for the governance and procedures of the Church?

It is such concerns, raised but not explored in the previous work, that are the driving force behind the second project alluded to earlier which might, in some respects at least, be described as an exercise in

---

3 For the phrase 'God's Ways with the World', see Daniel W. Hardy, *God's Ways with the World: Thinking and Practising Christian Faith* (Edinburgh: T & T Clark, 1996).

4 For Lash on the religious traditions as '*schools* whose pedagogy has, albeit differently in each case, the common twofold purpose of weaning us from our idolatry and purifying our desire', see *The Beginning and the End of 'Religion'* (Cambridge: Cambridge University Press, 1996), p. x; also pp. 21, 27, 37, 50 and 60; also *Easter in Ordinary: Reflections on Human Experience and the Knowledge of God* (London: SCM Press, 1988), pp. 241, 248, 258–9. Lash acknowledges a debt here to Friedrich von Hügel in formulating this idea, see *Easter in Ordinary*, p. 167, citing von Hügel, *Essays and Addresses on the Philosophy of Religion: Second Series* (London: J. M. Dent, 1926), pp. 143 and 144; also *Easter in Ordinary*, pp. 148–9, 162. Perhaps also significant here is St Benedict's understanding of the monastery as a 'school of the Lord's service', see 'Prologue', *The Rule of Saint Benedict*, trans. David Parry (London: Darton, Longman & Todd, 1984), p. 4.

ecumenical ecclesiology. The working title for this subsequent project is 'Catholicism Transfigured: Explorations in Ecclesial Learning' and lest this somewhat portentous, even pretentious sounding phrase suggest otherwise, it is worth stating from the outset that the connotations of life, light, hope, passion and transformation that are evoked by the language of transfiguration are intended to convey that this project cannot with integrity reduce to an exercise in self-righteous denunciation and bitter whining about contemporary Catholicism's various perceived faults. Rather, it must unfold as an exercise in theology as ministry – by which is meant healing service – within and for the ecclesial Body of Christ, concerned to identify, diagnose and tend to the Body's stresses and strains so as in turn to aid its service of and witness to the Kingdom. Again, it seeks for the *transfiguration* of Catholicism, not its *re-formation*. It neither indulges in futile hankering after an illusory past golden age, nor seeks for the discontinuous refounding of Catholicism on a fundamentally different basis. It seeks rather Catholicism's integral growth; its becoming more fully, fluently and creatively what it already, though imperfectly, is; its expansion not its reduction, so that the transfiguring light of God's truth, goodness and beauty might shine more clearly in the world, focused and reflected in the glass of the Church.[5]

Situated against this background, then, this essay represents a linking piece between the projects here outlined. It draws upon aspects of the earlier work – particularly the analysis and counter-critique of Richard Rorty's hugely influential revisionist account of truth-talk that was conducted there – but seeks to put this to the task of ecclesiological reflection in a considerably more direct and extended manner than previously. The essay is structured around the question as to whether there can be any real and fruitful dialogue – by which I mean one where there is the possibility of genuine mutual learning – between Roman Catholic self-understanding in relation to truth and postmodern questioning of the value of all such truth-talk, at least as traditionally conceived. The exploration moves through four phases.

First, there are some initial reflections on the place of truth in Catholic self-understanding and the significant shaping force this exerts on

---

5 Initial publications so far issuing from this project include 'The Lasting Significance of Karl Rahner for Contemporary Catholic Theology', in Eamonn Conway (ed.), *The Courage to Risk Everything . . . Essays Marking the Centenary of Karl Rahner's Birth, Louvain Studies* 29 (2004), pp. 8–27; 'Roman Catholic Theology After Vatican II', in David F. Ford and Rachel Muers (eds), *The Modern Theologians: An Introduction to Christian Theology Since 1918* (Oxford: Blackwell, 2005), pp. 265–86; 'Varieties of Roman Catholic Ecclesiology', in Gerard Mannion and Lewis Mudge (eds), *The Routledge Companion to the Christian Church* (London and New York: Routledge, 2006).

Catholic structure and practice. Particular attention is paid here to the vigorous espousal of the need for objective truth to be found in the encyclical writings of John Paul II. Second, attention shifts to asking after the motivating factors behind Rorty's trenchant disavowal of 'objectivity' in favour of 'solidarity', or localized agreement, as the only viable basis for interpreting and acting within the world. Having noted the challenges that Rorty's concerns pose to Catholic self-understanding, attention turns in the third part to review the counter-case that can be made for the lasting significance of a revised aspiration for truth as the articulation of reality. The final section further probes the challenge that this position – deriving from *charitably thinking through* Rorty's concerns rather than simply *arguing against them* – in turn holds for the concern that Catholicism give appealing, inspiring, convincing and, in this sense, authoritative witness to the task of discerning together the truth in love.

Catholicism and truth

In as much as the Catholic Church is understood as the divinely instituted and authorized witness to, even continuation of, the incarnate presence of God the Word in Jesus of Nazareth, who is in his person 'the way, and the truth, and the life' (John 14.6), an unbreakable and reciprocally reinforcing bond is forged in the Catholic psyche between Catholicism and truth.[6] This mutual relationship is explored at length

---

6 The closer the presumed link between the incarnate, risen and ascended Lord and the Church, or Body of Christ, as the continuation of the incarnation, then the more absolute also is the presumed identity between Catholicism and truth to the point of becoming incapable of conceptualizing error, failure and sin in the Church – with the latter regarded as a 'perfect society' – as anything other than the error, failure and sin of its members considered individually. Vital here is the recognition that the Church is constituted as the Body of Christ by the Spirit who enlivens the Church without herself being contained by the Church. In other words, the Church's being the Body of Christ is a dependent reality. It depends upon the Church remaining open to and inspired by the Spirit in such a fashion as allows both for the confidence that, on account of the Spirit's guidance, this will never utterly fail even in this pilgrim state and the realism that, on account of human frailty, nor will it ever be realized finally and perfectly in this order. For an illuminating discussion of the significant practical importance of a pneumatocentric rather than exclusively Christocentric orientation in ecclesiology, see L. Boff, *Church, Charism and Power: Liberation Theology and the Institutional Church*, trans. John W. Diercksmeier (London: SCM Press, 1985); also Nicholas M. Healy, '"By the Working of the Holy Spirit" – The Crisis of Authority in the Christian Churches' (The Richardson Lecture 2005), *Anglican Theological Review* (2006). On the 'sin of the Church' as not simply the accumulation of the sins of its individual members, see Karl

in John Paul II's 1998 encyclical letter *Fides et ratio*. On the one hand, the world's confused search for truth is thought of as requiring Catholic understanding for its sure guidance and salvific fulfilment.[7] On the other hand, this ecclesial self-understanding itself presupposes that such a search for truth is indeed innate in human life.[8]

The first assumption – that Catholicism is the answer to the world's question – is in evidence in traditional modes of apologetical argumentation from the second century onwards and, as noted in *Fides et ratio* §24, perhaps most classically of all in St Paul's speech before the Council of the Areopagus.[9] In an analogous way, transposed into a form of historically orientated apologetics, it figures in the characteristic Counter-Reformation assertion of Catholicism as the one, true Church, the

---

Rahner, 'The Church of Sinners' (1947), *Theological Investigations, Vol. VI*, trans. Karl-H. and Boniface Kruger (London: Darton, Longman & Todd, 1969), pp. 253–69; 'The Sinful Church in the Decrees of Vatican II' (1965), *Theological Investigations, Vol. VI*, pp. 270–94.

7 See John Paul II, '*Fides et ratio*. Encyclical Letter on the Relationship Between Faith and Reason' (henceforth *FR*), in Laurence Paul Hemming and Susan Frank Parsons (eds), *Restoring Faith in Reason: A New Translation of the Encyclical Letter* Faith and Reason *of Pope John Paul II Together with a Commentary and Discussion* (London: SCM Press, 2002), §6 (p. 13), §15 (p. 29), §33–34 (pp. 55–7), §38 (p. 63), §99 (p. 161); also Congregation for the Doctrine of the Faith (henceforth CDF), *Donum Veritatis*. Instruction on the Ecclesial Vocation of the Theologian (Vatican City and Slough: Libreria Editrice Vaticana and St Paul Publications, 1990), §1 (p. 3), §7 (p. 10) & §13 (p. 15) citing, in the last instance, '*Dei Verbum*. Dogmatic Constitution on Divine Revelation', §10, in Austin Flannery OP (ed.), *Vatican Council II: The Conciliar and Post Conciliar Documents* (Leominster: Fowler Wright, 1980), pp. 750–65 (pp. 755–6).

8 See *FR* Preface (p. 3), §3 (p. 7), §33 (p. 55), §82 (p. 133), §92 (p. 151); also 'The splendour of truth shines forth in all the works of the Creator and, in a special way, in man, created in the image and likeness of God (cf. Gen 1.26). Truth enlightens man's intelligence and shapes his freedom, leading him to know and love the Lord.' John Paul II, *Veritatis Splendor*. Encyclical Letter Regarding Certain Fundamental Questions of the Church's Moral Teaching (London: Catholic Truth Society, 1993), Preface (p. 3), henceforth *VS*. In turn, developing this in the context of a long and moving reflection on the gospel narrative of the rich young man, we find 'the *question* is not so much about the rules to be followed, but *about the full meaning of life*. This is in fact the aspiration at the heart of every human decision and action, the quiet searching and interior prompting which sets freedom in motion' §7 (p. 13). Again, drawing upon §16 of Vatican II's '*Lumen Gentium*. The Dogmatic Constitution on the Church' and reflecting upon 'those who, through no fault of their own have not yet attained to the express recognition of God, yet who strive . . . to lead an upright life', we find 'whatever goodness and truth is found in them is considered by the Church as a preparation for the Gospel and bestowed by him who enlightens everyone that they may in the end have life' *VS*, §3 (p. 7); also CDF, *Donum Veritatis*, §1 (p. 3), §7 (p. 10).

9 See *FR*, §24 (p. 43), referring to Acts 17.23–34.

power of which irrevocably to move lives is testified to not least in the writings of John Henry Newman.[10] In turn, the assumption that the search for truth is innate to the human condition is most clearly evident in the long-held claim, subsequently defined as an article of faith by the First Vatican Council, that it is possible, in principle at least, to demonstrate the reasonableness of belief in God[11] and, likewise, in the positive regard more generally accorded to reason in Catholic theology.

Taken together and doubtlessly admixed with various other factors worthy of anthropological, psychological and sociological analysis, the belief that the Church is the sole authentic interpreter of a more pervasive, life-and-death search for truth that is otherwise bound to be frustrated promotes within Catholicism a distinctively heightened sense of its own authority and a corresponding sense of responsibility for the defence and proclamation of truth that is one of Catholicism's defining characteristics, if not its core characteristic. As *Fides et ratio* expresses it, 'Among the various duties which she (*the Church*) is bound to offer to humanity, there is one in particular that is understood as clearly her own, the *diakonia of truth*.'[12] We touch here on the very heart of the Catholic psyche, in its official manifestation at least.

The most notable expression of this is, of course, the First Vatican Council's formal declaration of papal infallibility amidst the political and intellectual tumult of mid-nineteenth century Europe. In line with

---

10 See Newman, *Apologia Pro Vita Sua* (New York: Doubleday, 1989 [1864]).

11 See Vatican I, '*Dei Filius*. Dogmatic Constitution on the Catholic Faith', ch. 2, in N. P. Tanner (ed.), *Decrees of the Ecumenical Councils. Vol. II: Trent to Vatican II* (London: Sheed & Ward, 1990), p. 806; compare *FR*, §§52–3 (pp. 85–9) and §67 (pp. 107–9). For an insightful discussion of quite what is being maintained in this regard in *Dei Filius*, see Karen Kilby, *Karl Rahner: Theology and Philosophy* (London and New York: Routledge, 2004), pp. 101–2.

12 *FR*, §2 (p. 5); also §6 (pp. 13–15). Again, 'For the Catholic Church is by the will of Christ the teacher of truth. Her charge is to announce and teach authentically that truth which is Christ, and at the same time with her authority to declare and confirm the principles of the moral order which derive from human nature itself.' Vatican II, '*Dignitatis Humanae*. Declaration on Religious Liberty', in Flannery (ed.), *Vatican Council II*, §14 (pp. 810–12), cited in *VS*, §64 (p. 97); 'I address myself to you, Venerable Brothers in the Episcopate, who share with me the responsibility of safeguarding "sound teaching" (2 Tim 4:3), with the intention of *clearly setting forth certain aspects of doctrine which are of crucial importance in facing what is certainly a genuine crisis*, since the difficulties which it engenders have most serious implications for the moral life of the faithful and for communion in the Church, as well as for a just and fraternal social life.' *VS*, §5 (p. 10); also §30 (pp. 49–51), §64 (p. 97) and §29 (p. 49) with the latter citing and referencing respectively Vatican II, '*Dei Verbum*. Dogmatic Constitution on Divine Revelation', §10, in Flannery (ed.), *Vatican Council II*, pp. 755–6 and Vatican I, '*Dei Filius*', ch. 4, in Tanner (ed.), *Decrees. Vol. II*, pp. 808–9.

the prior conviction that the Church as the authoritative witness to God's truth in Christ will be preserved from fundamental error (that it is *indefectible*), this dogma maintains that when the Roman Pontiff is declared to be speaking solemnly, *ex cathedra*, as the head of the Church on earth he is to be regarded by Catholics as making infallibly binding pronouncements not subject to the subsequent consent of the Church for their authentication.[13] The logic at work here is that such a statement represents not a stage in the discerning of the Church's mind but its terminus. As such, it is simply nonsensical to think of such *final* pronouncements as requiring *subsequent* ratification either by the college of bishops or the body of the Church more broadly. Perhaps less well recognized, however, is that it is equally nonsensical to then extract from this the quite distinct claim that the *prior* consent and adherence of the broader body of the Church is likewise irrelevant to the process whereby the Church in her hierarchical dimension might appropriately arrive at an absolutely irreformable judgement on an issue.[14] On the

---

13 Vatican I, '*Pastor Aeternus*. Dogmatic Constitution on the Church', ch. 4, in Tanner (ed.), *Decrees. Vol. II*, pp. 811–6 (p. 816); also Vatican II, '*Lumen Gentium*. Dogmatic Constitution on the Church', §25, in Flannery (ed.), *Vatican Council II*, pp. 350–423 (p. 380). For the prior belief in the indefectibility of the Church as a whole and, with this, the infallibility of the 'sense of the faith (*sensus fidei*) of the whole people', see Vatican II, *Lumen Gentium*, §12, in Flannery (ed.), *Vatican Council II*, p. 363; also CDF, *Donum Veritatis*, §4, p. 7. It is significant to note that Vatican II extended the teaching of Vatican I on infallibility by explicitly including within its reach the teaching of the dispersed college of bishops when 'they are in agreement that a particular judgment is to be held definitively.' '*Lumen Gentium*', §25, p. 379; also CDF, *Donum Veritatis*, §23, pp. 23–4; John Paul II, '*Ad Tuendam Fidem*. Apostolic Letter Motu Proprio' (18 May 1998). For comment on this and the claim that it represents, in part at least, the logical implication of Vatican I's claim that what the 'ordinary and universal magisterium' holds to be 'divinely revealed' is 'to be believed with divine and Catholic faith' (*Dei Filius*), see Francis A. Sullivan, *Creative Fidelity: Weighing and Interpreting the Documents of the Magisterium* (Dublin: Gill & Macmillan, 1996), pp. 101–8. As Sullivan notes, however, the difference between Vatican I's emphasis on the status of the ordinary Magisterium's teaching in relation to revealed truth and Vatican II's looser reference to teaching that is 'to be held definitively' is significant for subsequent discussion given that what it means for something to be definitively taught is itself patient of different interpretations. He explores this particularly in relation to John Paul II's clear teaching – the precise status of which, he claims, is ambiguous – against the possibility of women's ordination; see *Creative Fidelity*, pp. 22–3 and 181–4.

14 'What is excluded is his [the pope's] dependence on subsequent approval, not his need of previous consultation. The reason why the subsequent consent of the Church is excluded as a condition is that it is understood to be unnecessary; the guarantee of infallibility entails that nothing will be solemnly defined which is not the faith of the Church. Yet the terms of reference of the doctrine of infallibility, as we have received them, seem to me to entail that *recognition* by the Church at large comes in somewhere.' Robert Murray, 'Who or What is Infal-

contrary, as even Pius IX's own, albeit somewhat minimalist, practice prior to the dogmatic definition of the Immaculate Conception in 1854 suggests, such *prior* consent and adherence is a logically and pragmatically necessary prerequisite for bringing a process of deliberation and discernment to absolutely definitive closure as distinct from mere enforced punctuation.[15] These are significant issues to which attention will return.

More immediately relevant is the way in which Catholicism's distinctive sense of authority and responsibility in relation to truth is routinely expressed in terms of the high value placed on loyal adherence to Church teaching in the name of ensuring the consistency and credibility of the Church's witness to the world. It is against this pervasive concern that we should understand the uncompromising words in *Veritatis Splendor* apparently condemning all criticism of Church teaching equally, regardless of its precise status, as an act of damaging dissent that diminishes the quality of the theological service that is 'of the utmost importance, not only for the Church's life and mission, but

---

lible?', in A. M. Farrer (ed.), *Infallibility in the Church: An Anglican-Catholic Dialogue* (London: Darton, Longman & Todd, 1968), p. 39, cited in Bernard Hoose, 'Introducing the Main Issues', in Bernard Hoose (ed.), *Authority in the Roman Catholic Church: Theory and Practice* (Aldershot: Ashgate, 2002), pp. 1–16 (p. 7); again 'I do believe that the Church has the charism of truth in its faith and witness, so that it can indeed be said to have received from Christ a share in his divine infallibility. But this charism is received in human minds and must work its way through them, and in the whole Church. To assert that the charism has produced an exhaustively satisfying statement before many in the Church (bishops, theologians, lay people) have engaged in fair and sincere dialogue and borne their witness, is dangerous and may be an expression of human impatience and longing for over-simple answers rather than of living faith.' R. Murray, 'Who or What is Infallible', p. 44, in Hoose, 'Introduction', pp. 7–8. The point of Sullivan's perceptive reflections on the lack of definition surrounding what it means, since Vatican II, for something to be definitively taught and held (see n. 12 above) is that it opens the door to this due process of discernment and judgement being short-circuited through an elision of the difference between the ordinary (i.e. reformable) though firm teaching of the Magisterium and its genuinely irreformable teaching pertaining to the revealed deposit of faith in such a fashion as claims the fact of the former as meeting the conditions of the latter, see Richard R. Gaillardetz, 'The Ordinary Universal Magisterium: Unresolved Questions', *Theological Studies* 63 (2002), pp. 447–71.

15 See Francis A. Sullivan, 'The Sense of Faith: The Sense/Consensus of the Faithful', in Hoose (ed.), *Authority*, pp. 85–93 (pp. 89–90); James L. Heft, 'Accountability and Governance in the Church: Theological Considerations', in Francis Oakley and Bruce Russett (eds), *Governance, Accountability and the Future of the Catholic Church* (New York: Continuum, 2004), pp. 121–35 (pp. 126–7); also John Henry Newman, *On Consulting the Faithful on Matters of Doctrine* (1859), ed. John Coulson (Kansas City: Sheed & Ward, 1961), p. 13.

also for human society and culture'.[16] More generally, within official Catholic thinking under John Paul II such dissent tended to be viewed as representing the infiltration into the Church of the very disregard for objective truth that is held to be the central ill of the contemporary world.[17] Where, in the nineteenth century, the Church had to defend its own claim to be dealing in truth against the contrary forces of rationalism and fideism, now it is the more general claim for objective truth itself that is under threat. It is vital, in John Paul II's opinion, that as the world teeters on the brink of the void, far from colluding, the Church must trenchantly resist by clearly witnessing to the human orientation to absolute truth. For the late great philosopher pope, this was key to proclaiming the gospel in the postmodern world.

As this suggests, however, and as perhaps befits the form of an encyclical, the tone in *Veritatis Splendor* and elsewhere is more one of assertion and exhortation than it is of close argumentation. Lacking either definition or ascription, a host of terms such as individualism, subjectivism, relativism, vague pluralism, historicism, utilitarianism, pragmatism, agnosticism, atheistic humanism, scepticism and nihilism are variously employed simply as labels by which to refer to a general disregard for there being an objective order of truth and goodness in accordance with which humans should aspire to be conformed.[18] While, then, we are presented here with a vigorous challenge to the contemporary *Zeitgeist*, it is one requiring to be extended and refined through closer attention to specifics if it is to find a hearing beyond those who already share the anxieties John Paul II expressed. Nor is this to do just with the rhetorical effectiveness of the encyclical. More substantively,

---

16 VS, §111 (p. 166); also §4–5 (pp. 7–11), §29 (p. 49), §110–13 (pp. 164–9).

17 See CDF, *Donum Veritatis*, §32–41 (pp. 28–40), particularly §32 (pp. 28–30); also John Paul II, *FR*, §6 (p. 15). This picture needs qualifying a little. As noted above (n. 12), official Catholic teaching since Vatican II distinguishes between the revealed deposit of faith, 'definitive' teaching 'intimately connected with Revelation' and non-definitive teaching intended 'to aid a better understanding of Revelation.' *Donum Veritatis*, §23 (pp. 23–4). It is here envisaged that a theologian may, with good faith, find him/herself at odds with a particular aspect of non-definitive ordinary teaching but with particular conditions applying such as a complete lack of any general hostility to the Magisterium, a sincere desire to conform and a willingness to 'refrain from . . . untimely public expression', see *Donum Veritatis*, §25, 27 and 31 (pp. 26 and 28). It remains the case, however, that anything outside of these parameters is viewed as a damaging and debased stance without any apparent thought being given to the correlative desirable institutional virtues for the workings of the Magisterium with the consequence that all the power and initiative is reserved to the Magisterium without any checks and balances being put in place.

18 See *VS*, §32 (p. 53); §84 (p. 129); §106 (p. 158) and §112 (p. 167); also *FR*, §5 (p. 11), §46 (p. 77), §87 (p. 143) and §98 (p. 159).

as John Paul II commended Pius XII for recognizing, it is about seeking after the significant if distorted truth in the positions with which one disagrees and from which, to extend this point, Catholicism may itself have something to learn.[19]

It is interesting, in this light, to draw Rorty into the conversation given that his hugely influential neo-pragmatism bears striking resemblance to the brief sketches John Paul II gave of the position against which he wrote.[20] At the heart of Rorty's programme is a thoroughgoing disavowal of objective truth and correlative advocacy of a considerably looser, purely commendatory view of truth as *what is deemed good and helpful in these parts*.[21] Further, for all Rorty's self-described dilettantism, Richard Bernstein argues that a serious moral intent motivates his espousal of solidarity over objectivity.[22] It is in asking what this moral intent is and probing whether Rorty can ultimately secure his own constructive intentions that the possibility of a genuinely reciprocal dialogue between Rorty and Catholicism can unfold.

The force of Rorty's disavowal of objective truth

In rejecting 'objective truth', Rorty's target is the seductive allure of the hope for reality in the raw; reality devoid of the supposedly dis-

---

19 See *FR*, §54 (p. 89) citing Pius XII's 1950 encyclical, '*Humani Generis*', §9.

20 For example, see *FR*, §56 (p. 95).

21 See, for example, Richard Rorty, *Philosophy and the Mirror of Nature* (Princeton, NJ: Princeton University Press, 1979), pp. 10, 157, 170, 176, 179; also *Consequences of Pragmatism (Essays: 1972–1980)* (New York and London: Harvester Press, 1982), pp. xiii, xvi-xvii, xxxvii; *Objectivity, Relativism, and Truth: Philosophical Papers, Volume 1* (Cambridge: Cambridge University Press, 1991), pp. 21–2, 30; compare John Paul II, *FR*, §5 (pp. 11–13), §56 (p. 95) and §87 (p. 143).

22 See Bernstein, *Beyond Objectivism and Relativism: Science, Hermeneutics and Practice* (Oxford: Basil Blackwell, 1983), p. 204; also p. 255 n. 38. Suffice here to note that the charge frequently made against Rorty (e.g. by Alvin Plantinga) that his dismissal of foundationalism and pure objectivism is parasitic upon an underlying presupposition that the concern for truth, reason and knowledge must necessarily be conceived in these terms, does not strike home in any straightforward fashion. Sure, in practice he might end up being locked into a binary opposition between foundationalist objectivism and non-foundationalist relativism and collapsing things down on the sceptical, relativistic side of the divide, but his contrary intention, at least, is to overcome this entire problematic and to articulate an understanding of truth, reason and knowledge better fitted to the contingencies of human discourse. See Plantinga, *Warrant: The Current Debate* (New York and Oxford: Oxford University Press, 1993), p. 85; compare Murray, *Reason, Truth and Theology*, pp. 28–9.

torting slant of language, perspective and context.[23] It equates to what Nagel, with somewhat more positive intent, describes as the 'view from nowhere',[24] or to what Rorty, along with others, refers with the theologically unfortunate notion of a 'God's-eye view of things'[25] – unfortunate because it suggests a removed, perspectiveless form of 'knowing' on God's behalf that stands in tension with the intimate, committed, searching presence attested to in the Judaeo-Christian scriptures.[26] Rorty's reasons for seeking to break with objective truth so construed are threefold.

First, he views it as an unattainable illusion – the illusion, that is, of guaranteed, incontrovertible immediacy to the reality of things. Drawing, in turn, upon Wilfrid Sellars' critique of the notion of there being any epistemically significant pre-linguistic experience, Willard Van Orman Quine's critique of the analytic-synthetic distinction and Donald Davidson's critique of there being such things as fundamentally incompatible conceptual schemes, Rorty concludes that there is no meaningful sense in which it is possible to think in terms of a pre-linguistic given underlying our language use and to which, when 'true', our language is to be thought of as accurately referring.[27] We are always situated within language. We cannot escape from it, nor get behind it in order to check its fit with 'objective reality'. As such, the aspiration for objective truth is an illusory waste of time.

Second and more importantly, however, it is an illusion that serves to devalue the only sort of knowledge of which we are in fact capable – that is, contingent, rooted, linguistically shaped knowledge – by comparing it with a supposedly ideal, 'objective', form of knowledge that is utterly unattainable by us. In more traditional terms, rather than securing our knowledge claims, as intended, against sceptical concern, the

23 See *Consequences of Pragmatism*, p. xx; also *Philosophy and the Mirror of Nature*, pp. 3, 8 and 333–5; *Objectivity, Relativism and Truth*, pp. 21–2.

24 See Thomas Nagel, *The View from Nowhere* (Oxford: Oxford University Press, 1986).

25 See *Objectivity, Relativism and Truth*, pp. 24, 27, 202; also *Essays on Heidegger and Others: Philosophical Papers, Volume 2* (Cambridge: Cambridge University Press, 1991), pp. 131 and 144 n.3; *Contingency, Irony and Solidarity* (Cambridge: Cambridge University Press, 1989), pp. xiii and 5.

26 See Rowan Williams, 'Trinity and Ontology', in *On Christian Theology* (Oxford: Blackwell, 2000), pp. 148–66 (pp. 155–6). For God's 'knowing' rather being an intimate scrutinizing of *all* perspectives, see Ps. 139; also Williams, *Open to Judgement: Sermons and Addresses* (London: Darton, Longman & Todd, 1994), pp. 13–18.

27 See *Philosophy and the Mirror of Nature*, pp. xi, 7–8, 10, 95–6, 101–2, 169–209, 259–66, 299–305, 309–11 and 317; also *Consequences of Pragmatism*, p. xviii; *Objectivity, Relativism and Truth*, p. 1. For a detailed critical reading, see Murray, *Reason, Truth and Theology*, pp. 27–49.

aspiration for extra-linguistic objective truth intensifies such concerns by subjecting ordinary conversation to an impossibly high standard.[28]

Third and more importantly still given the high value he accords to liberal democratic norms, Rorty views the aspiration for objective truth as complicit also in the promotion of elite castes that arrogate to themselves the unique ability to know reality truly in such a fashion as leads to the institutionalized anti-democratic privileging of their voices over ordinary conversation.[29] When situated socially, that is, the objectivist aspiration promotes a closed, hierarchical authoritarianism that systematically excludes other voices even from a place at the negotiating table. Notably for Rorty, the classic examples are priests in premodern Europe and scientists in the contemporary West.[30]

The way in which Rorty proceeds with his case develops along an interesting course at this point. Far from seeking, incoherently, *to prove* objectivism wrong on its own terms, he seeks to expose what he takes to be the historically particular and, hence, non-necessary status of the entire objectivist aspiration.[31] By so doing he seeks to show the possibility of simply replacing it with what he takes to be the less problematic view of truth as localized consensus.[32] Before turning to ask whether the kinds of concerns John Paul II expressed about this position are justified, however, it will be fruitful to pause to reflect on the implications of Rorty's critique for the strong adherence to objective truth earlier noted as intrinsic to Catholicism.

Looked at in one way it might be maintained that Rorty's critique of the aspiration for objective truth in the epistemological tradition is of questionable relevance to theological understanding. On the one hand, the former is framed by the Cartesian concern for absolute certainty and the Kantian distinction between phenomenal and noumenal reality in such a fashion as embeds anxiety about a subject–object divide in its

---

28 See *Philosophy and the Mirror of Nature*, pp. xi and 114; compare Murray, *Reason, Truth and Theology*, pp. 49–52.

29 See *Essays on Heidegger and Others*, pp. 132–3; also *Objectivity, Relativism and Truth*, pp. 1 and 13; compare Murray, *Reason, Truth and Theology*, pp. 53–6.

30 See *Objectivity, Relativism and Truth*, pp. 35–6; also *Contingency, Irony and Solidarity*, pp. 3, 21 and 52.

31 See *Philosophy and the Mirror of Nature*, pp. 10–11 and 33.

32 Compare 'I shall try to back up the claim . . . that to think of knowledge which presents a "problem," and about which we ought to have a "theory," is a product of viewing knowledge as an assemblage of representations – a view of knowledge which . . . was a product of the seventeenth century. The moral to be drawn is that if this way of thinking of knowledge is optional, then so is epistemology, and so is philosophy as it has understood itself since the middle of the last century.' *Philosophy and the Mirror of Nature*, p. 136; also pp. 114 and 390–1.

very foundations. On the other hand, the latter – within Catholic tradition at least – is framed by the quite different assumption that all that exists has being in and through the Word and so analogically reflects – albeit always in a way elusive of strict determination – something of the abundance of God in ways to which, in turn, our intellects resonate. This is partially at least, on account of their being likewise formed in analogical accordance with that same Word.[33]

In this way of thinking, the question is not *whether* our words can truly speak a world otherwise devoid of words but *how* or *in what manner* our words give frail but real voice to the Word in which the world has life and, likewise, to the world whose life is this Word? Accordingly, here the tendency should not be to see our situated, linguistically shaped knowing as an intrinsic barrier that must be escaped from if objective truth is to be attained. Rather, it should be to value our situated, contingent knowledge for what it is – a true but partial knowing of the total intensity and complexity of things – and to aspire for its enrichment. As we find in *Fides et ratio* §2, 'this community is constrained to the duty of proclaiming the certainties which she knows, while conscious herself that every truth arrived at is just one stopping-place on the way to that fullness of truth which will be shown forth in the final revelation of God'.[34] Even in the case of solemn dogmatic definitions John Paul II explicitly acknowledged that their binding truth neither exhausts all that can be said on a given matter, nor proscribes against the truth they articulate needing to be reformulated in order to be preserved as contexts change.[35] All of which, it might be noted, is to suggest a primarily regulative or grammatical rather than purely propositional view of doctrine.[36]

In these regards, then, far from Catholic understanding of the human orientation to truth necessarily falling foul of the significant problems that Rorty identifies in the epistemological tradition, it would seem to represent a richer account of things which may even hold the potential, in some respects at least, for the latter's redemption.

But this, of course, is not the whole story. Rorty's strictures against absolutist aspirations that serve only to denigrate and dismiss, rather than support and enrich, our contingent ways of knowing begin

---

33 See Thomas Aquinas, *Summa Theologiae. Vol. 3 (1a.12–13): Knowing and Naming God*, Herbert McCabe OP (ed.) (London: Eyre & Spottiswoode, 1964), Ia, Q. 12, art. 2, Q. 13, arts. 1–3 and Q. 13, arts. 5–6, pp. 7–11, 47–59 and 61–71.

34 *FR*, §2 (p. 5); also §11 (p. 21) and §14 (p. 27).

35 See *FR*, §92 (p. 149) and §96 (pp. 155–7).

36 See George A. Lindbeck, *The Nature of Doctrine: Religion and Theology in a Postliberal Age* (London: SPCK, 1984), particularly pp. 73–90 and 98–104.

to hit closer to home when we turn attention to natural law theory. Repeatedly in *Veritatis Splendor*, for example, the shift is elided from maintaining 'The affirmation of moral *principles* is not within the competence of formal empirical methods' (§112 p. 167, my emphasis) to maintaining that moral teaching can in no way depend upon empirical process or lived experience (§113, p. 168). It is odd, to say the least, to espouse a natural law theory while ruling out all appeal to the methods and processes of investigating the reality of things that are authentic to modern, as distinct from Aristotelian, natural science.

There seems to be something of a confusion here between epistemological and procedural issues that potentially relates to Catholicism's aforementioned heightened sense of authority and responsibility in a way that is relevant to Rorty's critique of the objectivist aspiration as promoting an authoritarian elitism. In this regard, it is worth noting that whatever qualifications and safeguards may be hedged around the formal performance of papal infallibility, its definition in the context of a dominant theology of papal absolutism and Roman centralism unqualified by an appropriate theology of the episcopacy, the local church and the laity promoted within modern Catholicism a pervasive ethos of unidirectional hierarchical authoritarianism that was, in turn, reflected at each and every level of Catholic life and structure and from which contemporary Catholicism has still yet fully to emerge. This ethos encourages a view in which all official, in particular papal, teaching tends to be treated as though it is on the same level, a seamless robe as it were, whereby to tease away at any part is taken as indicative of a dissent that threatens to unravel the good of the entire Church. Alternatively stated, while papal infallibility itself has only been rarely and exceptionally invoked since its promulgation and on each occasion with public formality, there has been a more widespread tendency to view all papal teaching alike as equally binding and so closed to criticism, rather than as significant punctuation marks within broader processes of deliberation which will properly continue until they be capable of being brought to genuine closure, as distinct from being declared closed prematurely. Catholicism currently lacks both the habitual ethos and the necessary structures to address this point.

In short, Catholic understanding of truth in varying ways both outstrips and falls down under the terms of Rorty's criticism. But what of the sharp concerns that John Paul II, as with so many others, would in turn raise against Rorty? For all Rorty's stated intention to affirm the value of our situated, contingent ways of knowing, freed from corrosive sceptical doubt and in a way that ensures the appropriate access of all to participation in conversation, does he in fact serve to compound the very sceptical doubts he seeks to quash and, likewise, to give conversation over to being dominated by the voices of the most powerful without possible check or restraint? The next section briefly reviews the case in support of such charges and, with this, the claim that Rorty likewise undermines the necessary basis for transformative action in the world. In the course of so doing, a constructive case will be outlined in support of the retention of the aspiration for truth as the articulation of reality, albeit in significantly revised form to that against which Rorty sets his face.

The need for truth in practice

In prosecuting his critique of the aspiration for objective truth as a striving after untainted immediacy, Rorty abandons not only this particular version of objectivity but with it any concern whatsoever to know a reality construed as being always greater than any particular conversation can articulate. This wholesale, undiscriminating abandonment of all concern for truth as the articulation of reality serves to undermine his intentions in three ways.

First, while Rorty seeks to return us to the contingencies of ordinary human life and conversation, unencumbered by insatiable anxieties as to their correspondence to reality in the raw, his relinquishing of all concern for truth as the articulation of reality jars with the actual force with which such ordinary conversations are actually pursued. In ordinary conversation people ordinarily assume themselves to be speaking true, or at least partially true, things about reality. Rorty's ignoring of this gives the impression that, far from uprooting sceptical concern, he has collapsed things down on the sceptical side of the divide. If Rorty genuinely wishes to dissolve the epistemological-sceptical problematic then, rather than sidelining the notion of truth as the articulation of reality, he would be better advised to follow the likes of Wittgenstein, Davidson and McDowell in exploring the ways in which language can properly be viewed as enabling rather than hindering access to something of the richness of reality that necessarily exceeds what can be told in any one telling.[37]

Second, common throughout the pragmatist tradition is the concern to give full heed to the fact that human engagement with reality is both cognitive and practical in character in such a fashion as should have significant implications for the way in which truth is conceptualized. Rorty shares this concern fully as does also, it might be noted, John Paul II.[38] The problem for Rorty, however, is that our ability to act

---

37 See Murray, *Reason, Truth and Theology*, pp. 32–4, 39–49 and 70–4.
38 See FR, §25 (p. 45) and §99 (p. 161); also §3 (p. 7) and VS, *passim*.

purposefully in the world presupposes our ability to know something at least of the contours of reality and that is just what he refuses to engage in. He draws the conclusion, 'The final victory of poetry in its ancient quarrel with philosophy – the final victory of metaphors of self-creation over metaphors of discovery – would consist in our becoming reconciled to the thought that this is the only sort of power over the world that we can hope to have.'[39] In contrast, if we are genuinely to heal the breach between, 'contemplation and action, between representing the world and coping with it', it again seems necessary to take more seriously than Rorty does the aspiration for truth as the articulation of reality.[40]

Third, key to Rorty's concern to break with the aspiration for objective truth is the way in which he believes it to play into the hands of powerful elites claiming for themselves privileged access to reality at the expense of other less powerful voices. Now this might follow when objectivity is construed in terms of the escape from normal modes of knowing to a mode of knowing the like of which us lesser mortals are incapable of sharing. It does not, however, necessarily follow if objective truth is understood as something with which we are all already in touch even though the richness of it permanently exceeds exhaustive understanding. In this way of thinking, it is *always* in one's self-interest, broadly conceived, to take other perspectives seriously; even when they contradict what one otherwise immediately assumes to be in one's self-interest, narrowly conceived, as there may be vital insight to be gained by so doing.[41] Indeed, without some such notion it is difficult to imagine what basis there might be for seeking to move any of us to extend our range of conversation beyond a narrowly self-interested protectionism.[42]

In short, if Rorty's constructive intentions in calling for the abandonment of the futile objectivist pursuit for the bare 'in-itself' of things are genuinely to be supported, it is necessary for him to retain a much richer sense of truth than he does. More specifically, it is necessary for him to retain a sense of truth not as an attempted escape from language but as the aspiration for the articulation of reality in language cognizant, moreover, that the diverse, polyvalent richness of reality will permanently elude full and adequate articulation in any one discourse and from any one perspective and so requires patient, hospitable attendance

---

39 *Contingency, Irony and Solidarity*, p. 40.

40 *Philosophy and the Mirror of Nature*, p. 11. Again, for further here see Murray, *Reason, Truth and Theology*, pp. 75–9.

41 It should, perhaps, be clarified that such serious minded attention to other perspectives does not require their uncritical adoption as necessarily superior to one's own.

42 See Murray, *Reason, Truth and Theology*, pp. 79–87.

to the other voices and perspectives operative. But if there is here a truth for Rorty to learn by attending seriously to the kinds of concerns expressed by John Paul II, it is equally the case that the revised understanding of truth that emerges into view holds significant challenges, as we have already begun to explore, for the practice, ethos, polity and performance of Catholicism; challenges, moreover, that press towards an enriched and expanded rather than diminished and distorted ethic of Catholicity.

Discerning together the truth in charity – Rome's postmodern challenge

The ideas I wish to begin to explore here come, in turn, under three interrelated subheadings: 'Democracy redeemed', 'Expanding Catholicity' and 'Receptive Ecumenism'.

Democracy redeemed

In all contexts there are words that can and must be said and words that cannot and should not be said: words that evoke warm fellow feeling and that require no explanation because all are assumed to agree on their reference, meaning and importance; words that provoke equally instinctive, unreasoned reaction as to their inappropriateness. Within Catholicism, in its official manifestations at least, 'democracy' is clearly of the latter sort. Compare, for example, the way in which the familiar adage 'The Church is not a democracy' is frequently intoned as though it is simply an absolute, unqualified, self-evident truth requiring no further explanation and about which there can be no discussion.[43] When, however, we do begin to tease out what might be meant here, things become somewhat stranger.

If by 'The Church is not a democracy' we mean that the Church should not be a site of agonistic power-play and narrowly self-interested assertion and counter-assertion such as passes for the service of the common good in the English parliamentary system or the American House of Representatives, then there would seem to be something unarguably true about this. Democracy thus viewed is itself in need of redemption rather than capable of providing an unambiguous model. I say this without wanting either to idealize the Church as itself devoid of all fallen power-play or to neglect the extent to which lobbying,

---

43 See John Paul II, VS, §113 (pp. 168–9); also CDF, *Donum Veritatis*, §35 (p. 33).

negotiation, voting and the like are, in fact, real and proper features of Catholic life, not least at Vatican II.

Likewise, if by 'The Church is not a democracy' is meant that decisions regarding God's truth in Christ and the Spirit and how the Church should live within this cannot be decided on the basis of whim, unformed, unchecked desire and prejudice and superficial inclination there, again, seems to be something unarguably true about this.

So also, if by 'The Church is not a democracy' we mean that the Church has not got a horizontal structure of authority; that from the circle around Jesus onwards there have been levels of leadership, responsibility and authority understood as part of the divine institution of the Church such that 'One person, one vote' simply cannot apply without contravening the authentic executive function of the episcopate in Roman Catholic understanding there is, again, something unarguably true here.

But is this all that democracy can be? Saying that 'The Church is not a democracy' does not necessarily mean and should not be taken as implying that the practice of the Church should be anything less than the performance of democracy with all its faults. On the contrary, surely the sense in which the Church is not a democracy is in terms of it being something more not less; something that learns from the strengths of democracy while avoiding its limitations and pathologies by resituating and reconfiguring them within the body of the Church?[44]

Nor need this be viewed as alien terrain for the Church. There exist numerous elements of democratic process within the history of the Church, not least within the religious orders and perhaps most notably

---

44 This project has some affinity with the recent argument of Jeffrey Stout in *Democracy and Tradition* (Princeton: Princeton University Press, 2004). However, whereas Stout's core concern – with which I have a great deal of sympathy – is to encourage religious traditions to engage with rather than withdraw from the practices of secular democracy with a view to its potential renewal, my correlative core concern is to explore how the practice and polity of the Church can itself be authentically and integrally renewed through, in part, attending appropriately to what might be learned from democratic thought and practice. Taking seriously the notion that an authentic Christian political theology should equate with the theology and practice of the Church, the concern here is to ask after what it might mean for the Church to be sacramental of *democracy redeemed* in its practices and procedures of discerning together the truth of God in Christ and the Spirit. As such, it might best be construed as a performance of ecclesiology as a political theology of the Church. Compare Stanley Hauerwas, *The Peaceable Kingdom: A Primer in Christian Ethics* (London: SCM Press, 1983), p. 99; also Hauerwas, *A Community of Character: Toward a Constructive Christian Social Ethic* (Notre Dame, IN: University of Notre Dame Press, 1981); John Milbank, 'The Other City: Theology as a Social Science', in Milbank, *Theology and Social Theory: Beyond Secular Reason* (Oxford: Blackwell, 1990), pp. 380–438.

within the Dominicans.[45] Indeed, there is an important claim to be
made that far from being some alien, post-Reformation, enlightenment invention, modern democracy is, in part at least, a child of the
Church.[46] As such, the challenge is to explore how the child democracy
might be brought home and brought to maturity in Christ so that it can
help with the ecclesial task of discerning together the truth in love.

Expanding Catholicity

If democracy is a word laden with negative connotations within certain
Catholic circles, Catholicity understandably sounds a more positive
note. It variously evokes images of integrity, authenticity, universality, tradition, communion, unity, diversity and richness. It means all
these things, but in meaning all of them so also it qualifies all of them
and means none of them in isolation. It refers not to the rigid, narrow
uniformity of a sect but to the differentiated unity of a communion that
stretches to encompass all of creation in all of its diverse particularity.
Equally, it refers not to the diversity of assertive autonomy and absolute individuality but to a diversity in which all are brought to coherent
configuration in their immensely diverse particularity within the provi-
dential plan of God. In this way Catholicity well construed bespeaks a
vision of *all* as being gathered in intensely differentiated yet configured
communion so that something of the infinite richness of God might
be seen in kaleidoscopic vision or heard in concert. The writings of
Johann Adam Möhler and Henri de Lubac are each worthy of careful
consideration in these regards.[47]

This is an understanding of Catholicism as a project to be lived and
lived into rather than just a bald given to be preserved. In different
terms we might say that it is an understanding of Catholicism as a
practice requiring certain communicative ethics or virtues both of indi-

45 See Timothy Radcliffe OP, 'Freedom and Responsibility: Towards a
Spirituality of Government' and 'Dialogue and Communion', in Radcliffe, *Sing
a New Song: The Christian Vocation* (Dublin: Dominican Publications, 1999),
pp. 82–120 and pp. 248–50; also James Sweeney, 'The Experience of Religious
Orders', in Hoose (ed.), *Authority*, pp. 171–80; Philip Endean, 'The Draught-
horse's Bloodlines: Discerning Together in the Ignatian Constitutions', *The Way
Supplement*, 85(1996), 73–83.
46 See Brian Tierney, 'Church Law and Alternative Structures: A Medieval
Perspective', in Oakley and Russett (eds), pp. 49–61.
47 See Johann Adam Möhler, *Unity in the Church or the Principle of
Catholicism: Presented in the Spirit of the Church Fathers of the First Three
Centuries* (1825), trans. Peter C. Erb (Washington, DC: Catholic University of
America Press, 1995) and Henri de Lubac, *Catholicism: Christ and the Common
Destiny of Man*, trans. Lancelot C. Sheppard from the 4th French edn of 1947
(San Francisco: Ignatius Press, 1988 [1950]).

vidual Catholics and of Catholicism institutionally if Catholicity is to be more fully realized. At the level of the individual such virtues might take the form of being committed always to seeking what is true in the other's position and asking oneself what can be learned from it; of being open to and patient of the testing of one's own position and, with this, of being desirous of greater conversion to the truth and of being patient with the body of the Church when it is elsewhere than one would have it be.[48]

Correlatively, at the level of the institution or assembled Church such communicative virtues in service of expanding and intensifying Catholicity might take the form of a commitment to hold the field of deliberation open for discernment to happen; of ensuring that all relevant voices are represented and taken seriously; of not moving to closure or definition (which is also always an opening and a fresh departure as well as a defined closure)[49] until the time is right; of allowing even firm, for example encyclical, guidance short of absolutely and bindingly defined proclamation, to be returned to for further deliberation and, finally, of transparency in and accountability for decision making.

The inculcation of virtues such as these, both personal and communal/institutional is, I suggest, essential to the nurturing, deepening and sustaining in vitality of a rich Catholicity genuinely capable of showing forth the value of truth in its practice.

Receptive ecumenism

The ethic of Catholicity just outlined lends an appropriately centrifugal dynamic to Catholic life such that receptive learning, dynamism and growth can be held to be properly intrinsic to the people who are Catholic.[50] In relation to the issue of structural and institutional transfor-

---

48 For an outstanding articulation of such a theological ethic that would make good reading for any starting out or re-focusing on the vocation of theology, see Gareth Moore OP, *A Question of Truth: Christianity and Homosexuality* (London: Continuum, 2003), pp. 2–5 and 16–37.

49 Rahner spoke in this regard, for example, of the Chalcedonian definition as both an ending and a beginning of theological reflection, see 'Current Problems in Christology' (1954), *Theological Investigations, Vol. I*; trans. Cornelius Ernst OP (London: Darton, Longman & Todd, 1965), pp. 149–200 (p. 149–50)); also Timothy Radcliffe, 'Reform', in Radcliffe, *I Call You Friends* (London: Continuum, 2001), pp. 71–8 (p. 77).

50 Balancing this, there is of course also an appropriately centripetal dynamic to the life of the Church – having first been gathered in communion, the Church moves out to then gather again in enriched communion in order, in turn, to be further energized for mission and outreach. Further, the centre of both centripetal and centrifugal movements is not the Church itself but the Triune life of

mation within Catholicism it is significant to draw out the implications of this within the ecumenical context. Here, alongside the fine-detailed work of the patient clarification, increased understanding and creative negotiation of past knots of disagreement that has borne such fruit in the various bilateral processes of recent decades, there is a further need. That is, the need for an ethic of constant receptivity to what Catholicism can learn with integrity – concerning how its own Catholicity might be enriched – by receiving imaginatively yet appropriately from aspects of Catholicity in other traditions that may be being performed there considerably more clearly than within Catholicism itself.[51]

Such a practice of receptive ecumenism has some affinity with the attitude of 'spiritual ecumenism' encouraged by Cardinal Walter Kasper and Archbishop Rowan Williams.[52] Whereas, however, 'spiritual ecumenism' focuses in the main upon the individual's potential learning and receptivity in the context of deepened affective communion, the practice of 'receptive ecumenism' here espoused transposes this to the institutional level and seeks to ask how the practice and understanding of the Church might receive with integrity from other traditions.

God within the dynamics of which the Church exists; see Radcliffe, 'Consecrate Them in Truth (John 17:17)', in Radcliffe, *I Call You Friends*, pp. 113–17.

51 This is to extend the recognition found both in *Lumen Gentium* and Vatican II's, '*Unitatis Redintegratio*. Decree on Ecumenism' that while the Roman Catholic Church lacks none of the essential marks of the Church of Christ, this does not equate with claiming that they are either perfectly or exclusively to be found there (with the exception in the latter regard of the mark of unity which is viewed in Catholic thinking as being inextricably tied up with full sacramental communion with the Bishop of Rome); see *Lumen Gentium*, §8, and *Unitatis Redintegratio*, §3, in Flannery (ed.), *Vatican Council II*, pp. 452–70 (pp. 455–6) and pp. 357–8. Indeed, we already find in these documents clear statements that the Roman Catholic Church is both 'always in need of purification, follow[ing] constantly the path of penance and renewal' (*Lumen Gentium*, §8, p. 358) and capable not only of offering riches to others but also receiving and so being brought to 'a more perfect realization of the very mystery of Christ and the Church' (*Unitatis Redintegratio*, §4, p. 458). This joint principle has, perhaps, received its clearest and most remarkable near recent expression in the request John Paul II made in his 1995 encyclical, *Ut Unum Sint*, to Church leaders and theologians in other Christian traditions to help re-imagine the papacy in the light of their criticisms of it so that it might once again be the focus of unity rather than the continuing cause of division that it currently is; see '*Ut Unum Sint*. Encyclical Letter on Commitment to Ecumenism' (London: Catholic Truth Society, 1995), §95 and 96 (pp. 105–7); also §13–14 (pp. 17–19) and §16 (pp. 20–1).

52 See Walter Kasper, 'The Current Situation in Ecumenical Theology', and 'Spiritual Ecumenism', in Kaspar, *That They May All Be One: The Call to Unity Today* (London: Continuum, 2004), p. 17 and pp. 155–72; Williams, '"May They All Be One" . . . But How?', unpublished paper delivered to the St Albans Ecumenical Conference, 17 May 2003; also *Unitatis Redintegratio*, §7 (p. 460); *Ut Unum Sint*, §15 (pp. 19–20).

Two specific examples, or potential case-studies, are Anglican syn-odical structures and Methodist connexionalism. Leaving aside the vexed question of what, from a Catholic perspective, appears as the lack of sufficiently robust international structures of communion, it is notable that the executive role of the episcopate is preserved within local and national Anglican synodical arrangements while allowing laity and clergy a genuine voice and role in decision-making in such a fashion as might be fruitful for Catholicism seriously to ponder. Again, perhaps even more so than is the case with Anglican synodical structures and procedures, it is notable that 'connexionalism' within Methodism – the practice of making decisions in relation to the whole – operates as a pervasive governing ethos and not simply as a structure of governance. If Catholicism's default instinct is one of hierarchical authoritarianism, Methodism's is one of co-responsibility which should, when lived well, act as a spiritual discipline, an *ascesis*, for the entirety of ecclesial life. What might it mean for Catholicism to grow into such a wholesale, second-nature ethos of connexional Catholicism? It is perhaps signifi-cant in this regard that John Wesley once went wooing the Catholics of Dublin with a sermon/essay under the title of 'In Search of the Catholic Spirit'.[53]

Conclusion

In conclusion, what I have sought to indicate in this paper is that, while allowing for John Paul II's understandable and well-founded anxieties about recent postmodern questioning of the value of truth-talk, a chari-table thinking through of Rorty's position from the inside can reveal not only where the fault-lines in his work truly lie but also what it is that Catholicism might have to learn from the constructive, if some-what confused, aspects of the case he presents.

It emerges that if the Roman Catholic Church is genuinely to be the authoritative, convincing witness to the truth of God's ways with the world that it claims to be, then it must grow beyond its default instinct of absolutist authoritarianism to develop the procedures, structures and all-pervading ethos of a mature and vibrant Catholicity. It should be noted that if this is *aggiornamento*, it is not about a distorting adapta-tion to the ways of the world but about the enrichment of the authentic

---

53 John Wesley, 'Catholic Spirit. Sermon 39', in A. C. Outler (ed.) and F. Baker (Editor in Chief), *The Works of John Wesley, Vol. II* (Nashville, TN: Abingdon, 1985), pp. 79–99; also David M. Chapman, *In Search of the Catholic Spirit: Methodists and Roman Catholics in Dialogue* (Peterborough: Epworth Press, 2004).

identity of the Church so that the splendour of truth might shine more visibly through her in service of the redemption of the world. Indeed, far from such conceiving of change in the Church serving to compromise the integrity and credibility of the Church's witness, as is sometimes maintained, it would itself bear eloquent and powerful testament to the way of continual conversion to greater truth and fullness of life that *is* the message that the Church is charged to proclaim in word and deed. This *is* in practice surely what it means for the Church genuinely to value and live in accordance with the truth of God in Christ and the Holy Spirit.